BE
THE
LION

HOW TO OVERCOME
BIG CHALLENGES AND
MAKE IT HAPPEN

TIM CASTLE

This book is for anyone who is facing a challenge and wants to pull together to overcome it.

To Levi, my Lion in the making.

You are my inspiration, a joy to be around and you light up my soul.

I am proud of you always.

Love Dad

CONTENTS

PART 2: CONDITIONING (MIND AND BODY)

PART 3: CERTAINTY (SELF-BELIEF STRATEGIES)

INTRODUCTION – HOW I LEARNT TO MAKE IT HAPPEN

WHILST WRITING MY first book *The Art of Negotiation,* I had plenty going on. I was managing multiple projects, as well as planning our destination wedding on the sunny beaches of Koh Tao, Thailand, enjoying our 6-month-old baby boy whose energy and determination knew no bounds, completing an MBA and working full time as a sales director. Oh, and in the midst of it all, we moved countries and continents from Australia to Singapore.

It's fair to say that a lot of big life-changing events were happening, but through it all, a phrase that kept presenting itself in my head, repeatedly, was: "MAKE IT HAPPEN!"

While going through this chaotic period, I was desperate for any strategies that would help me "make it happen". I learned a number of valuable techniques from the likes of Tony Robbins, Jen Sincero, Gabrielle Bernstein, and Napoleon Hill. As I listened to their words repeatedly via audiobooks and podcasts, my faith grew. The more I consumed their powerful content and engulfed myself in their proven strategies and mantras, the more I strengthened my own mindset that it all indeed *would* and *could* happen.

In order to overcome the variety of new and diverse challenges that presented themselves with each of the balls that I was juggling, I needed to be totally immersed in successful ways of thinking. I had to design effective processes to organise my time to make each day as focused and successful as possible. Obviously, I had a lot to change, but taking the time to learn, create and implement consentient habits rather than just fudging my way through it forced me to move up a level. It was through this process of creating success habits that I gained a fundamental understanding of what I am really capable of.

Every small win brought me one step closer to making it happen. This sense of daily progress through the unknown gave me the courage, grit and belief to push through. As I am sure you're aware, facing the unknown can be scary. Moving my family from Australia, which had been our home and our life for 5 years to a new job, in a totally new part of the world, with a toddler was massively overwhelming, and unnerving at times.

I am happy to tell you that it did all work out, and I am writing this book from the comfort of our wonderful apartment overlooking the city of Singapore. We have a happy and healthy baby boy, exciting jobs and our own businesses that give us fulfilment. Life really could not be better.

I am so grateful to be in this position, it is a far cry from the 5 years we spent cooped up in a studio apartment in Manly, spending every waking hour focused on building our businesses and not knowing how we would make rent from one month to the next. The road has certainly not been easy, but with the help of the simple but effective strategies and habits that I am going to share with you in this guide, I have found that by consistently showing up every day it is possible to create the life you envision.

In this book, I share everything I learned about 'Making It Happen'. I offer processes, strategies and optimisations to turbocharge your life when you are taking on mighty challenges. In my case, over the course of the last 2 years, I was attempting multiple life-altering changes all at once, so it's fair to say this philosophy has been stress-tested in the real world.

As an individual, I am constantly impressed by and drawn to those who are willing to take big calculated risks to see their dreams and vision come true and make the most of this awesome opportunity we call life.

So, if you have a challenge you're currently wrestling with, or have been thinking about making a big change to the way you live your life for a while, this book will help to coach you through it.

No matter how impossible your goal might seem. I will show you how to turn towards your fears and find joy and happiness in the journey of moving forward towards your goals. I'm not promising that it will be easy, or that it won't take a massive input and commitment on your part. There will be ups and downs, but overall you will make progress and you will find habits and patterns of behaviour that support who you want to become so that you can start living it today!

If you're wondering what all this has to do with being a lion, that would be a good question so let me explain. The analogy of being the lion as a concept relates deeply to the characteristics of a lion. A lion is a symbol of courage, and whether you have found this book because you need to overcome destructive habits that are keeping you trapped in a damaging cycle of regret or you simply want to elevate your life because you know you are capable of more, ultimately it requires you to be courageous.

When we take a look back in history, lions have always been a symbol of strength and courage, both of which are two core tenants that you will need when faced with overcoming big obstacles in your life. Therefore, I want to dig a bit deeper into what we can learn from the mighty lion below so that you really understand what it means to be the lion.

- Lion's face challenges head-on. They do not wing it. Lions have certainty that they will succeed, and they engage in specific behaviours to maximise the chances of successful outcomes. You can see this in the way that female lions hunt together in order to catch larger prey.

- Lions have the grit to dig in and the determination to keep trying. Lion's don't give up when the going gets tough, they may change the strategy, but never the goal. You don't get to be king of the jungle without knowing how to adapt to your surroundings and overcome all manner of obstacles. The lions reign supreme because of their ability to leverage their strengths and take advantage of their surroundings.

- Lions exemplify the balance that supports their lifestyle. A lion knows when to take action and when to conserve their energy. For example, by resting during the day and hunting at night when it is cooler; lions have discipline.

- Lions work smarter not harder. Lions understand their strengths and use their innate abilities to their distinct advantage, like opting to hunt in the darkness so that they can leverage their razor-sharp eyesight for all its worth and take their prey by surprise. (A lion's eyesight is 6x more sensitive to light than humans.)

- Lions are brave. Being the lion is fundamentally about having the courage to continue down your right path, even though it's scary and unknown; being brave enough to go against the grain of society, and to do what it takes to see your vision come to life. You are worth it, so being a lion is about changing your mentality to understand that not everything everyone else does is well thought-out or in line with your vision. **A lion is brave enough to stand strong and walk in the other direction if needed.**

- Lions are creatures of habit. Lions are able to perform consistently because they have dedication to the areas of their life that matter and they spend time and energy maintaining these habits.

From now onwards, whenever you are facing a challenge or an unknown obstacle, I want you to visualise an image of a lion in your mind. Really feel yourself become consumed with the passion, courage and strength of a lion and believe that you have what it takes to figure out whatever life throws your way.

There's plenty we can learn from the lion. Being the lion is a state where you push your boundaries, you face challenges, you do it anyway even though it is different and scary. You have a plan, you stick to your habits and you trust that there is more for you to bring to the world.

Throughout this book, and as you go about your daily life, I want you to notice the area's where you shy away from stepping out of your comfort zone, I want you to look out for areas where you could add more value to other people's lives and how you can adopt the lion mindset. Where are you holding back? When and where do you experience doubts? Where does the lion mindset need to be applied most rigorously?

In reading through this book, I want you to get in touch with your inner self. This book is about doing the inner work so that you can transform your outer world, and in doing so you will challenge yourself to bring more to your life. Be the lion is a way of living, achieved by carefully and purposefully aligning your daily habits to help you overcome big challenges head-on and move courageously in the direction that was intended for you.

Be The Lion is your handbook for living large and in charge, a guide for connecting with your purpose and achieving outstanding outcomes.

It is about you becoming the *you* that you were meant to be. The you that you already are but may not have found yet or only seen rare glimpses of. If this resonates with you, then you're in the right place. Feel the words as you read them and know that you have changed even by just engaging with the content and material.

Above all, be the lion will help you to restructure your daily habits so that you can be the very best version of yourself and enable you to live the life you dream of.

To summarise, if you haven't got the picture yet, this book is for anyone who wants more out of life and is hell-bent on achieving big, outlandish, supersized, colossal levels of success in any area of their life that they chose.

Ready to kick some ass?

Ready to Be The Lion?

Remember to join the be the lion community by sharing your journey and showing your support to others by using the hashtags #bethelion #iamready. Sharing your story with others on social media, in your blog posts or in person is a great way to feel connected and feel the love as you progress on your journey to changing your life and becoming your best self.

CHAPTER 1

MY THEORY FOR OVERCOMING BIG CHALLENGES

"Go confidently in the direction of your dreams. Live the life you imagined."

Henry David Thoreau

THE BOOK CALLS upon the lessons and frameworks for creating habits of success, based on the best bits that I have learnt from my extensive study of the best gurus and motivational leaders in the world, either by spending time with them in person, through their courses or by complete immersion in their teachings. I will also provide my own models for you to use. These are based on my own real-life experiences and what I have found to really works for me.

Throughout the book, I will share relevant real-life examples with you in the hope that it allows you to identify areas in your own life where these strategies could be effectively applied. Giving you real-life examples will be more useful than just plain old theory and will motivate you to shift the needle on your journey to living a life of fulfilment and joy.

The examples I will use are as real as it gets, and I will share them in an authentic and genuine way as if I was talking with a friend, with no BS or sugar coating. I won't hold back, and I hope you won't either on your quest to implement new habits and change the destructive patterns that are holding you back.

I truly understand that you may have picked up this book because you are facing a gigantic challenge or obstacle in your life right now, one that you can't seem to overcome. If this is you then fear not, you have come to the right place. Together we will go on a journey of transformation.

However, I must warn you, if you are looking for a quick fix then this is more of a journey and takes real commitment. If you hope that this book holds the secret (which it does), then bear in mind that it may not be the one you expect.

However, I need to make it abundantly clear before you dive right in and commit at least a few hours of your life to digesting this delightful manifesto – there is no one quick fix answer which will solve it all, or give you a short cut to achieving success when you're overcoming big challenges. Almost all of us go through a crisis or face big challenges at some point in our lives, but those who successfully overcome them do so by consistently applying certain techniques and strategies on a daily basis; in essence, they do the work no matter what.

In doing countless hours of research over the years and submerging myself in the content of the most applauded and respected inspirational leaders of the past hundred years, I have designed my own framework which I have named the 4Cs.

Through the consistent application of the 4Cs framework shared in this book and the adoption of the principles laid out by the leaders that I reference, we will make solid progress in the direction you would like your life to go. My hope is that this guide will give you the tools to change the destructive patterns of behaviour that are no longer serving you (we all have some) and lead you to overcome anything that life throws your way in the future.

These methods have worked for me, my friends and many of the inspirational leaders shared in this book.

My goal is to help you to overcome any challenge or difficulty that might be holding you back from achieving your full potential. As we go forward together on this journey of discovery, I will provide you with tools and techniques that you can pick up and use right away. Yes, the learning in this book should be applied right away.

Don't wait until you finish it to start making changes to your daily habits. If you have an insight or a penny drop moment, make a note of it and apply it. The time to get started is NOW.

Try not to get hung up on the past or mistakes that you have made, release the need to compare yourself to other people's successes and focus on your own journey. This is about you becoming the best version of yourself that you can be. If there are moments of doubt, or times you feel you are stepping into the unknown, know that this is the right path, you are on the right track and it is completely normal to feel a bit freaked out from time to time or even all the time. Some of the things I cover in this book may seem to be a little strange at first if you are not used to the lion mindset. The most important thing is that you don't let the fear stop you. If you find yourself doubting that you can take action or if you really need to apply this process, then stop, take a deep breath, and calmly remind yourself that this is a journey.

Missteps and going off course are all part of the ride, what matters is that you find the resilience and courage within yourself, much like the lion, so that you can keep trying something new and unfamiliar.

Introduction to the 4Cs framework

To make this manual easier to digest, I have divided the book up into four compact sections for overcoming big challenges and changing your life for the better. These are **Creation**, **Conditioning**, **Certainty** and **Connection**. These 4Cs relate to areas of focus for your life. These are Action, Mind and Body, Self-Belief Strategies and Spiritual respectively.

As you go through the book, we will take a look at each focus area of your life in turn and take stock of how successful you are in each of these specific areas.

Part	C	Life Area
1	Creation	Action
2	Conditioning	Mind & Body
3	Certainty	Self-Belief Strategies
4	Connection	Spiritual

Together, these are the four building blocks of my 4Cs framework and are required in equal measure to ensure success. No one building block should be prioritised over another. Each component supports the other and contributes in equal measure to the success of the whole. I would argue that the application of balance in this framework is more important than the individual components themselves. **The power of being the lion comes from the combined building blocks working together in unison.**

When I first left home at the age of 19 and began making decisions for myself, balance across the 4Cs was not something I adhered to, and as a result, I suffered the consequences for years, struggling in my own life. I had a deep preference for one of the 4Cs over all the rest; in fact, I pretty much ignored the others completely. I was significantly unbalanced. It wasn't until I found out (the hard way) that being balanced across the 4Cs and 'doing the work' consistently every day was the only way to start moving towards the vision I had for my life, did it began to fall into place and change rapidly.

I was your classic taking action junkie. My mindset was heavily biased towards taking action and for years, I thought that if I just took action, I was achieving success. In this area of my life, I was focused only on what I could do and was very busy doing, doing, doing, but it was to the detriment to the rest of the 4Cs. In fact, when I reflect on it, I was only producing a small amount in proportion to my potential and I don't want you to make the same mistakes.

To describe it using a different analogy, it was much like I was going to the gym but only working out my biceps and skipping leg day completely, every time. I was thinking I was fit, and this represented a healthy lifestyle. But, in truth, strength comes from working all areas of your body, even the bits that are boring, painful or just downright hard.

Having a lifestyle that will support you through all manner of obstacles is just like maintaining a fit and healthy body that will support you long into old age and allow you the flexibility to do anything you desire. It takes dedication and discipline, and of course, a holistic approach to all areas. Everything needs to be exercised in balance or you will end up with a very strange body shape. In my experience of overcoming big challenges, the more alignment and balance I have in my life with respect to the 4Cs framework, the less daunting the road ahead and the more achievable the outcome.

Each of the four parts should be seen as a mini-experiment that will challenge your own beliefs about the world around also and what is possible. It is my hope that by applying this framework, you will be able to transform what your life looks like currently into one of endless possibility and fulfilment.

Imagine we're taking a bus and at each stop, we are going to get off and go to a boot camp where we'll learn the skills and drills to prepare us for the ultimate life experience.

There are no shortcuts, no easy hacks, and you must be 100% committed to doing the work in all of the four life areas to achieve in a big way. As you work your way through the book, I want you to pay close attention to which of the four areas you favour and which you have been avoiding more. By identifying your preferences, you'll generate an increased awareness around this bias. With awareness comes change and you will be able to consciously direct your focus to the life areas that need the most attention, nurturing and development without overcompensating on others. As hard as it is, this the work that needs to be done.

The 4Cs in detail.

No, I'm not talking about grading diamonds here (anyone who's brought an engagement ring will know that the 4Cs are a rite of passage when learning to evaluate diamonds). My **4Cs** are the foundation of my process of overcoming big challenges and making it happen. Let's break these 4Cs down further.

Part 1: Creation: Life area of focus = Action

This part is about getting into **creation** mode. Here I will guide you through the steps to take to get you up off the sofa and out into the world to see your wants, desires and plans gain traction. They say Rome wasn't built in a day but it did get built, and consistently taking action each day towards your goals is a large part of what makes the successful, successful. Without transferring our grand ideas into **action** nothing would get done, meaning no mountains would be scaled, no shifts in mindset would take place, no legacies would prevail and, certainly, no obstacles would be conquered. Therefore, action is a fundamental life area. The lion needs to learn how to eat, it is vital to its survival, so it gets out into the wilderness of the savanna to test out strategies for catching its prey. I chose to start the book with action because I am setting you up for success, by asking you to take action first, you will be thrust into a place of testing out new strategies, learning and interpreting the feedback and then calibrating for optimal performance. This will instantly allow you to uncover new ways of working and approaching problems.

Part 2: Conditioning: Life area of focus = Mind and body

Like everything in life, whether it's your car, bike or air conditioning unit, it all needs maintenance.

Without fine-tuning your **mind and body** and **conditioning** your inner and outer world, you won't reach a state of peak performance. A lion is meticulous in the preservation of its cleanliness, hygiene and athletic ability. A lion knows that its mind and body is its vehicle to success and that it is vital to be in tip-top condition if it wants to retain its status as the leader of the pack.

Part 3: Certainty: Life area of focus = Self-belief strategies

It goes without saying that most of us have struggled with **self-belief** issues at some point or another in our lives. A lion, however, conquers its fear to reign supreme at the top of the food chain as king of the jungle. A lion is proud of its accomplishments and remains humble to the cycles of life and the importance of balance. A lion seeks out new strategies to better itself and is not afraid to implement new processes so that it can go after bigger rewards. The thing I love about lions is they're **certain**. They don't doubt themselves, unlike us humans, who get super confused, start questioning our existence and feel guilty about nearly everything we do by continually comparing ourselves to others. Lions are the boss! Be the Lion! It will help you to enhance the level of certainty and self-belief that you have on an ongoing basis.

Part 4: Connection: Life area of focus = Spiritual

The final part of the book will be spent developing your **connection** to the Universe and helping you to become more **spiritual**.

Quite frankly, this is an area that often gets missed but is absolutely vital to supporting the other three areas of your life. I can't stress enough the rivers of gold that can be found by tapping into the spiritual aspects of life and the healthy formation of habits.

I myself used to deny the value of spiritual oneness in my own life, thinking it was a 'nice to have' but not really a necessary element for success. I was wrong. If you look at the way a lion operates, they are connected to the earth and all that is around them. I'm not sure if you've ever come face to face with a lion before, but there is a presence and a knowing that is so evident it cannot be mistaken for anything else but the energy of power, strength and deep understanding. Acknowledgement of the spiritual aspects of your growth will open new doorways to the transformation of your destructive patterns and give life to each of the other areas. Spiritual oneness and connection with a deeper self are what all inspirational leaders, coaches and self-help professionals in the field point to. It is a destination and understanding that you reach when you allow the greatness of your gifts to be shared with the world; you focus on ways to give rather than on what you can get.

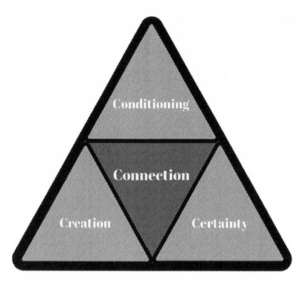

The 4Cs Framework of Making It Happen

I will now go into what each C means in the context of its core field of success. Before I go any further, I want to make sure that you understand the importance of balance. In order to have momentum when faced with big challenges, it's vital to have a balanced approach to each one of these areas. If one area is relied upon too heavily then there will be an imbalance; for example, if you are creating enough action but don't have the appropriate mission-driven mindset (**Conditioning**) and self-belief (**Certainty**) you will only get so far down the road before becoming stuck. Taking action for action's sake is not the aim, it must be purpose driven and prioritised. To be a strong and successful lion, you must have balance. Notice in the diagram above, the elements of **Creation**, **Conditioning** and **Certainty** touch **Connection** equally.

Creation (Action) is the creativity needed to inspire the start of any action that needs to be carried out. It refers to the ability to create opportunities for yourself and how you manifest these through taking action. In the **Creation** section, I will show you what 99% of people get wrong. As a result, you will become a master of prioritising tasks and taking massive action so that you can focus on the top 20% of tasks that generate exponential results.

By understanding what to ignore and what to focus on, you remain consistent, uninhibited by fear, and look only to maximise the ROI of your most valuable resource, your time.

Conditioning (Mind & Body) is about operating in a peak state, both mentally and physically. In the **Conditioning** section of the book, I will share the habits you can adopt to build the life you want, as well as how to ensure you have the right strategies in place for dealing with any event. Here, I will show you how to optimise your lifestyle for high performance and avoid the pitfalls of analysis paralysis, procrastination and poor time management. This section will help you to build a lifestyle that is more resilient, resourceful and fined tuned for success.

Certainty (Self-Belief Strategies) is a deep grounding in self-belief and the strategies and rituals you can develop to manifest this at your core. In the **Certainty** section of this book, I will show you how to multiply both your self-belief and your confidence in abundance so that you can achieve outstanding results. This puts you in control of your life's direction and empowers you to tackle all manner of situations. Think of **certainty** like the rudder of a superyacht. It cuts through the water pointing the boat firmly in the direction of the destination; no matter how rough the seas, it never wavers.

Connection (Spiritual) refers to your higher power and putting your faith in the belief that life is working *for* you and not *against* you. It's something that I myself have often missed, only to realise that I was doing all the heavy lifting myself. It was only when I let go of trying to rely on my own strength alone that I actually got closer to achieving my greatest good and adding more value to the world. After all, that is what success is really about, finding ways to add more value to others and greater ways to serve. Enhancing your connection will help you to get closer to your fullest potential and give you faith in the bigger picture of your life. When all of the day-to-day **creation**, **conditioning**, and **certainty** is taking place, **connection** is what allows you to relax into a deep knowledge that you are supported by something larger than yourself and it is all meant to be.

Below you will see what my model looks like with each of the life areas, followed by the relevant C, and a suggested behaviour to live through. Using this framework, we will cover the why, the how and the result. This is how I want you to imagine each section of the book as you are reading it, as zones that can transition you through to find your why, your how and produce the intended result that will support you so that you can not only achieve but also continue to achieve for the long term.

The 4Cs Framework With Respective Life Areas

For anyone who's up against it, going through the struggle and wants to learn some tried and tested strategies, practices and habits that have been designed by the very best world-class leaders in the field, I encourage you to keep on reading. Do NOT give up now, keep reading!

Your road may be paved with rocks right now, and the storm may be raging, but it will eventually lead you to your true purpose. Keep on going and commit to practising one thing from this book that piques your interest.

To those who have chosen this book because they are hungry and want to up their game, to those who are totally focused on consistent self-improvement, who dream of adding more value to the world and are in pursuit of taking all dimensions of their life to the next level, welcome…

PART 1

CREATION (ACTION)

INTRODUCTION TO PART 1: ACTION

"Expansion. Always. In all ways."

Ryan Serhant,
American Real Estate Broker

IN THIS BEGINNING section, I wanted to start with the most hard-hitting and game-changing topic of taking action because I believe that it is the element that people struggle with most. It is only those who genuinely believe something is possible who are truly motivated to take the action needed to achieve it.

I also believe that it is the success step that is most misunderstood.

Action for action's sake is not necessarily a good thing, but the ability to strategically apply consistent action in focused areas of your life, directing towards a goal is a key differentiator.

Deciding when and how to take action, what steps to take next and how to approach obstacles without getting defeated or feeling like a failure is no mean feat.

This section should be read and reread whenever you face your next struggle or have a tough time deciding on which direction to go, or what you should prioritise next in order to reach maximum potential. Remember it doesn't matter if you're Warren Buffet or Mark Zuckerberg, even the most highly motivated struggle with this stuff at times. That's why those that can afford it have teams of advisors around them to help navigate this terrain time and time again.

In it, you will discover sage advice and a variety of practical tools to help you identify, create and stick to habits that will set you up for success. So, shake off that fear you might have and take action anyway. Throw yourself into the strategies and optimise your time to get the most out of every single day, this is the fast-track express highway to smashing your goals and living the life you desire.

Time to get into action mode.

CHAPTER 2

GETTING MENTALLY PREPARED FOR ACTION

"When we close our mind to what is possible to us or is possible for humanity, it closes off to the genius that resides in each of us."

Dr Wayne Dyer

Nothing is impossible

Before we start, I want to be clear on one thing. In life, I have learnt that much of what we achieve is dependent on the actions we take and those moments of inspiration and brainwave ideas that pop into our heads very randomly at 2am in the morning.

It might sound obvious, but the ability to maximise opportunities and take the required amount of directed action to open new doors is not always straightforward, but it is the key to going from good to great to outstanding.

Why then do so few people go on to do the things they love? Or settle for less than they deserve? Or fail to play to their strengths? Or have all the right tools but do not apply them?

The answer to these questions, I believe, lies in the underlying belief that something is impossible or simply unachievable. This often causes people to stop trying right before their big breakthrough. Deep down, this subtle and hidden doubt causes us to limit the action we take, and more specifically the massive action required to create an opportunity for success.

> When people don't fully 100% believe that something is achievable, they are not committed to making it a success in the same way as someone who believes in it completely.

My philosophy is to champion the notion that anything is possible. This, I believe, is the fundamental path of people who push the boundaries of their own limitations and actually achieve greatness. They discover that impossibility is merely just a cover-up for the improbable.

And if this road is walked long enough by an individual in the course of their lifetime, they will begin to see ways of achieving the improbable. This causes a permanent perception shift as the notions of impossibility and doubt change to become just potential obstacles to overcome and challenges

People who condition their minds in this way go on to achieve more audacious and outlandish goals which fuel greater success. They have learnt and practised the formula for success mastery. I do not mean to simplify the science and art of success or imply that the mechanics can be learned by a shift in mindset alone, but I do believe there is something to be said for going after big goals. If you look to those who repeatedly take on the impossible and win, like Elon Musk, Jack Ma, Jeff Bezos, they all achieve time and time again.

The optimist's mindset

> "For, when you work with a definite objective, in other words, when you work with a Definite Chief Aim, when you know exactly what it is that you want to achieve, your mind can produce unlimited force and energy which will propel you in that direction more rapidly than you could possibly imagine."
>
> The Law of Success, Napoleon Hill

Your mind is your most powerful tool; therefore, you must pay attention to your thoughts. If you are telling yourself that it *can't* or *won't* happen, or you don't act on golden opportunities when they present themselves for fear of failure or embarrassment, then you are missing out on being the very best you that you can be.

What I mean by this is playing safe and not grabbing the opportunity when the ideal job pops up. If you send out a message to the world that admits defeat, then that's exactly what the world will give you.

> "Whether you think you can, or you think you can't – you're right."
>
> Henry Ford

When you catch yourself saying something self-limiting, even in your head, like, 'I am not able', 'I never', 'I can't', 'I doubt' then you need to take a moment and course correct. To do this, replace the negative with its opposite thought. Recognise the negative thought and laugh at it, then move in the other direction by using phrases like, ''I am able', 'I always', 'I can', 'I know', and watch what happens.

I am aware that what I am asking is no walk in the park. It takes huge amounts of directed conscious effort and hard work to challenge our natural tendencies and mental habits. They are deeply ingrained in our psyche. But do this for three weeks and watch how your world changes, literally before your eyes.

This shift means changing the conversation we have with ourselves and how we respond to the world. This requires constant checking in with the brain and carefully rerouting the thought each time back to alignment with the life that we want to experience.

Carrie Green, Founder of the Female Entrepreneur Association, says you must have absolute certainty that it will happen in your mind for it to happen. Carrie is one of those genuine people who sweeps you away with her authenticity, so you can't help but relate to her.

In her talk at TEDx Manchester[1] on programming your mind for success, Carrie unpacks how our mind can hold us back from exciting, lucrative or beneficial opportunities by making bad decisions that originate from poorly constructed thought patterns. At the beginning of the talk, Carrie demonstrates this with the

---

[1] Tedx Manchester (2014). https://www.youtube.com/watch?v=MmfikLimeQ8

audience by asking for a volunteer to come up on stage. However, as you might have predicted, it takes a while for her to coax a volunteer from the audience even though there are over a thousand people in the room. Finally, she gets one and they come up on stage. In return, Carrie gives them twenty pounds and instructs them to go back to their seat. The point is clearly made, we miss out on opportunities (in this case 20 pounds for walking on stage) because we let fear, doubt and worries take control of our mind. In this case, the lack of volunteers could be attributed to the expectation of potential embarrassment, fear of stepping into the unknown (on stage) or a diffusion of responsibility by the collective audience rationalising that someone else from the large crowd would do it. Either way, it's clear to see how our minds can play a trick on us, holding us back from the rewards, even though the outcome is a made-up story in our heads.

Carrie has a gift for wording things how they are and she explains in this talk how you have a need to move from negative thoughts into a mindset of abundance, and explained the process she went through to reprogram her mind and replace the disempowering thoughts with positive, uplifting and inspirational words. When she first noticed this pattern of negative self-talk and the mismatch between how she was living her life and how she wanted to be living, Carrie said, *'I'm coming up with ideas and then shooting myself down, talking myself out of doing anything whatsoever. And I realised that if I wanted to live an incredible life, and I really did, that I had to get my mind to be on the same wavelength as me.'*

This was a game-changer for Carrie, and she hasn't looked back since, which really goes to demonstrate that it all starts in the mind.

The power of a smile

Have you ever woken up and dreaded the day ahead? I have.

When I face days like these now, where I am totally uninspired and feel like the world is an utterly unimpressive place, full of annoyances and hurdles, I transform.

I don't have time to be a sad sack. It takes work through. The first thing I do when I walk out of the building every morning is plug in my headphones and listen to some inspirational words from a motivational expert. This process helps me to stay humble throughout the day and reframes my point of reference to the world.

In time, this process has helped me to stop comparing myself to others, to be less focused on where others are going and to focus instead on my own path.

The second step I find gets me straight out of my funk is smiling like a mad man. I may look like a weirdo as I head down the escalator and on to the Tube to head into work but trust me, this works. By smiling my ass off, the number of good things that happen is insane. People literately respond to me in a categorically vibrant way, it's like I flip the game on myself and it magnifies the beauty of the world to myself.

> Gratitude is commonly taught as one of the most powerful tools that we can use to reconnect with the Universe, other people and ourselves.

There has never been a more impressively abundant time to be alive than right now. Access to the internet has granted billions of people resources for free that would have only been available to the minority in generations gone by.

I am responsible for my mood, and what I put out into the world. I strongly encourage you to engage in smiling when you are in the process of 'making it happen!' Set yourself goals, like, 'I will make eye contact with 15 people and smile at them regardless of the look I get back.' You'll be surprised how small shifts in your actions around smiling changes your physiology and, in turn, has you standing taller, walking with unstoppable confidence and kicking ass left right and centre.

Raise the energy, raise the bar

Energy is contagious. Have you ever noticed how some people can walk into a room and their presence changes the energy in the room? This can obviously work advantageously when it makes us want to up our game or become more focused, more aspirational, more powerful, more loving, and more caring, but it can also work in a negative way, causing us to feel more depressed, more restless, more defeated and more underwhelmed.

In order to go big, you'll need to bring this energy into your life on a daily basis and be the driving force behind your life. When we step out into the world, all manner of things can happen to us. The choice we have is how we react.

In my twenties, I travelled the world and met people from all walks of life. Some were travelling to escape corporate jobs they hated, some were searching for love, others sought adventure.

I find that when I travel, I have an easier time raising the energy bar. There is less tension in the air and fewer rules about what has to happen in a given day. By connecting in this way and acting from my freer self, I attract the very experiences that I'm in search of.

If things go wrong, I am capable of fixing them and see them as part of the adventure. Back in corporate la land, the hamster wheel can be turning so fast that we forget to raise our energy game, and miss out on the joys and experiences that it brings.

When we force the outcome by becoming narrow-minded, we reject the very things that the world is trying to show us or provide for us. It's like we're saying that we know better, and we haven't got time to listen. We don't even want to embrace the fullest versions of ourselves when we approach life in this way.

What's your excuse?

To work out if this is you, what's your go-to excuse for not getting shit done?

Are you an 'I never have any time', or an 'I am always so busy', or a 'Sorry I'm late', or even an 'I DON'T KNOW HOW YOU DO IT' person?

If this is you, then this IS a sign that you need to stop, get clear on what really matters to you and reprioritise. I urge you to listen to what you say repeatedly; your excuses will tell you where to focus and what needs to shift in order for you to get back on track. In all of the above examples, something needs to be cut or reprioritised in order for you to create time.

And remember, the perceived problem may be the cause of the actual problem rather than the problem itself. For example, you might say that a lack of time is blocking your success right now, holding you back and stopping you from creating waves. However, you need to uncover what's the underlying issue that underpins your lack of time, as it's not a lack of time that's actually stopping you, that's just the symptom. Is it the late nights, the unmotivating job, the inefficient process that your boss insists you follow, or a lack of training that is the cause?

Ray Dalio, Founder of Bridgewater, who is the most successful hedge fund on the face of the planet, says, *'Don't mistake a cause of a problem with the real problem. "I can't get enough sleep" is not a problem; it is the potential cause (or perhaps the result) of a problem.'*

He offers this solution: *'To clarify your thinking, try to identify the bad outcome first, e.g. "I am performing poorly in my job." Not having enough sleep may be the cause of the problem, or the cause may be something else, but to determine that, you need to know exactly what the problem is.'*

In continuation of the financial luminary theme, Warren Buffett, for example, is notorious for dedicating a huge portion of his day just to sitting and thinking, which is highly irregular for a CEO, especially one at the helm of the fifth most valuable company in the world.

Now that you've got your mindset right, we can begin the adventure of figuring out what the hell you're actually working towards.

Remember, no more negative, pessimistic, impossibility focused thinking. Your mind is a sacred place and it should be treated as so. It is your secret weapon and trust me, once you start to use it right there will be nothing that you can't overcome.

CHAPTER 3

KNOW WHAT YOU'RE WORKING TOWARDS

"Live your purpose from now on."

Mastin Kipp

O N THE JOURNEY to becoming the lion and making it happen, we need to have goals; a lion doesn't wake up in the morning and wonder what the heck it's going to do with the day or why it's alive. A lion is hungry, ambitious, it has a purpose and is driven by its goal. If you don't know your purpose or where you are going, how can you get there?

What am I working towards?

When I thought about what I wanted my life to stand for and what a meaningful life meant to me, it was using my gifts to help advance the world through coaching, proving it is possible, as well as helping others out of situations and places I knew there was a way forward in, even if they couldn't see it themselves yet.

To achieve these goals, I had to detach from the idea of a 9-5 job and live a life whereby I could choose the projects that I work on and where I do it. Life to me is about growth and pushing myself to become the best version of who I can be.

To facilitate this, I would ideally have a number of automated online businesses that granted me the financial freedom to live and work anywhere in the world and provide me with enough financial abundance that I could help change the lives of people who are less fortunate. This is what I am working towards creating every day. But I didn't always have the clear idea of where I was going.

For years, I felt I knew I could be doing more, and that there was something inside of me that could create a lifestyle I was more passionate about. I knew I wanted my life to stand for something, but I just wasn't sure what.

I'll be honest, it took me years and years of making the same mistakes and languishing in mediocrity before I finally understood how to complete the process of discovering what a meaningful life was and what it meant to have a purpose.

Let's not beat around the bush, it's a pain in the ass not to have a big vision.

Anyone you meet who's got it all figured out, well that's good for them, but their also really annoying and you'd rather they shut the f*ck up because it's not doing anyone else any favours hearing about how certain they are about their mission.

Well, I get it. I've been there and lived that relentless circle of trying (but not really succeeding) to find my purpose (whatever that is) and failing. It felt like an endless quest. I knew there should be more but I could not quite put my finger on it. I searched high and low. I looked for it in jobs, in girlfriends, in adventures, in shops, in entertainment, in everything but the one place I should have been looking, which was myself. Without a clear idea of this purpose, how could I build goals to work towards it? How could I channel my energy into the right places?

Below, I have outlined some basic steps that you can take right now to help define what a more meaningful life is to you. Here we are talking about a life where you are so totally pumped to be alive that you radiate with energy. You are literally buzzing with ambition, hunger and the need to contribute more to the world. As morbid as it sounds, remember you're going to die soon. We all are. And if it helps you jolt your consciousness into action then stay with that thought for a second, life will be over soon. What do you want yours to be about? What do you want to give to the world? How will you find fulfilment? Who will you become?

How to find your life of meaning

Step 1: Vision

Get the vision in your head. The best way to break this down is to get a vision in your head of where you would like to be at a certain point in time. For me, this was the age of 37, at this point in my life, I wanted to be financially independent and running my own businesses that helped in a major way to change people's lives.

- Have you got a vision in your head about what you would like your life to be like at a point in the future? What springs to mind right off the bat?

- What would you be doing if money were no object?

- What experiences would you be having?

- Where would you be having them?

- Who would you be with?

- What if someone gave you $1 million today – how would you spend it if you had to get rid of it all in 24 hours?

These quick-fire questions should start to trigger explosive thoughts of excitement, fulfilment and meaning, and give you a sense of what lights you up inside and where your passions lie. This is a broad-brush approach that forms the start of having a bigger picture of your direction.

Step 2: Timeframe

Now we need to break it down into much smaller steps. From the position of the big picture, we need to work backwards.

How old are you in your big picture vision? For me, I was 37 and 31 at the time I defined it. Therefore, I had 6 years to get from A – Z before I reached 37.

Step 3: Brainstorm

Now you have established your timeframe, write down all the things you would need to make your vision a reality. This is a bit like a brainstorm, so don't think about it too much, just write down everything that comes to mind about what you would need for your vision to be true. Don't hold back. Even if you think something sounds silly, write it down and make sure you're specific.

For me, it looked like this: owning a holiday home in Santorini, Greece; having the flexibility to work from multiple locations of my choosing across the world; helping people in developing countries who are less fortunate; coaching, speaking and writing about how to give more of yourself to the world; having passive income streams and freeing myself from the 9-5 lifestyle.

Step 4: Group

When you've got everything you can think of on the page, the next stage is to group these items into themes. Are some related to finances, jobs, careers, charity, entrepreneurship, health and well-being, investment, marriage, family, friends, travel, moving countries and so on?

Step 5: Complete the jigsaw

Then, once you've got your themes, begin where you are currently in life. Pull out a fresh sheet of paper and write down your age and how your life is now on the left-hand side, and your age and where you want to be on the right-hand side.

Draw a line between the two points and begin by placing the themes onto the line in order of priority with respect to the timeline. We are to put all the themes into some sort of order along the line.

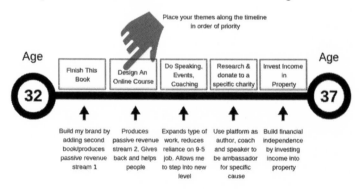

Place your themes along the timeline in order of priority

Age **32**

Age **37**

| Finish This Book | Design An Online Course | Do Speaking, Events, Coaching | Research & donate to a specific charity | Invest Income in Property |

Build my brand by adding second book/produces passive revenue stream 1

Produces passive revenue stream 2. Gives back and helps people

Expands type of work, reduces reliance on 9-5 job. Allows me to step into new level

Use platform as author, coach and speaker to be ambassador for specific cause

Build financial independence by investing income into property

It is almost like we are completing a jigsaw here, what would you need first to obtain so that you can move onto the next level and how would that thing support the mission towards the goal. For example, in order to have financial freedom, I need to have a product or service that I can offer to the world. Maybe that means I need to go on an app development course and learn to code, maybe there are other skills I need to develop. As you map out your themes, you should start to see an apparent order come to life before your eyes. Where there are gaps in between the themes and you can't see how they would link, add in a new theme; for example, if my goal was to start an ethical fashion label then, I would add research companies in Vietnam that ethically produce garments.

Step 6: It all comes together

Once all your themes have been mapped out on the line, sit with this for a day or so. Does the order make sense? Is the theme that is directly in front of where you currently are in life the best thing that you could be pursuing next in order to achieve the bigger picture goal?

What you have done here is break down the task of achieving your ultimate bigger picture and often overwhelming goal into smaller bitesize chunks. This process acts as a map and keeps you true to working on things that will take you forward in the direction that you want to go.

Hold on a minute, what if you're like me and you still have no idea what your bigger picture goal should be? What if you think that nothing inspires you enough to write it down and make a list and break it into small chunks? What if you never got that far in the process? Or thought that I'll just keep reading and see where he's going with this, then I'll figure out if this is something I want to partake in.

If this is you, then we are more alike than you think, and I understand your pain, frustration and curiosity that has kept you from not engaging in this exercise. But what I must press upon you is that there is literally no point in continuing to read this book if you don't complete this exercise.

Think about it, if you can't even muster up the ambition to go with me on this, then how are we going to go about changing your most destructive habits and overcoming big challenges?

This is your wake-up call.

This is it!

It's time to do something that your future self will thank you for. I know that comes across as some wanky motivational bullshit quote you'd find on Instagram, but if that's what it takes to get you to take this seriously, well OK then.

> The reason you need to stop what you're doing and focus on this for a few minutes is that by getting clear on what your goals are the whole orientation of your life can begin to shift towards fulfilment.

Without it, you are rudderless, just drifting, hoping that one day you will be washed into the port of your dreams and everything will become clear, but the risk is you spend a lifetime out at sea being knocked about by the waves and taken in directions that don't support your highest contribution to the world.

Now is the time to take control of your life, do you feel me?

OK then, that's freakin' awesome. I am glad you saw sense; we are in this together. To get clear on your big picture goal you need to observe what it is you're doing when you feel yourself light up inside, even if it is just for a moment.

Look for clues

For example, it could be reading a magazine article on interior design or watching a documentary on charting the length of the Amazon rainforest by canoe or it could be savouring the culinary genius of your local fine dining restaurant. Whatever your *raison d'etre* just go with it.

Whatever you notice of the next few days, pay attention to it, write it down on your phone and just observe that this could be a direction that you might like to move towards. Even if you have no idea how you'd open your own restaurant or start a design company, just know that this is the feeling we are looking for and it means something.

For me, every time I walked into a luxury hotel, I felt a deep sense of calm. I am sure everyone else does, but I knew I wanted the lifestyle that staying at a luxury hotel gave me. If I was someone who could afford to stay in a luxury hotel, what else might I be work on, who would I become? I realised the pleasure that I felt was the relaxation mentally that came with being more than fine financially, and I could let my guard down a little to relax into the idea of what I was truly capable of.

In the aura of a luxury hotel, I was free to explore what really mattered to me in terms of fulfilment and from there I could map out what an outstanding goal looked like. It wasn't that I wanted to open a luxury hotel, but I wanted to be the kind of person that could afford to stay at one. I also understood the projects that I would be working on if money was no object.

Therefore, it is important that you listen to yourself and think deeply about what these feelings are telling you. Is it the thing that you're excited about or what having that thing would mean to your life? Do you want to be the chef or just be able to dine in the restaurant? Are you passionate about helping other people to design their homes or do you want your own home to design? Do you want to trek in the Amazon jungle and complete the challenge of a lifetime or fight for the conservation of the rainforest itself by starting an awareness campaign? Noticing what it is exactly about what has come up for you in this exercise is the skill that you are practising here.

Don't worry if it takes you a couple of days or even a week to find your big picture goal, this is entirely normal, and it would be remiss of me to advise or advocate that just by picking up this book, the ideas will spring into your head after years of you trying to nail that sucker down.

It does require commitment and effort on your part to focus on it for a period of time, but if you just let it flow and follow your thoughts and feelings long enough, it will appear. Flow your energy; it is a great indicator of what you're passionate about.

If you didn't originally have a vision and weren't able to complete the steps above, then once you have a vision of it in your mind, go back and complete steps 2-6, including the line drawing exercise to break down the various stages of your road ahead. Then give yourself a pat on the back, you've completed the first step of being a lion and created the backbone of the process to achieve a more fulfilling life through meaningful contribution.

Mood boards

My strategy for really mapping out and picturing my ideal life was to create a mood board. I spent time fleshing out my ideas, my dream, and my vision and really connecting to the energy of what it would feel like if I had all that I desired. By collecting pictures, ripping pages out of magazines and taking screenshots of anything and everything that took my fancy over a few days, I was able to distil what I really wanted into a lifestyle.

When it comes to creating a mood board the key is it should propel you forward with such drive, vigour and force that you feel like nothing can stop you until you have achieved your goal. As you compile your mood board, notice the sensations you feel when you look at particular images. If an image makes you feel joyful, experience it, live it, relax into it. If an image makes you feel relieved, like a big weight has been lifted from your shoulders, then expand upon this feeling. Allow it to grow inside your heart and savour it.

To gain even greater familiarity, I stuck this mood board on the wall next to my bed to force me to look at it every day. I printed off the images and placed the mood board strategically within my home, where I would see it all the time, so that I could connect to my big picture vision with way more intensity multiple times a day. Visualisation is a key part of obtaining and building upon your goal. If you're someone who travels a lot, consider making your mood board the background on your laptop or your screensaver on your phone. That way, wherever you are in the world, you can check in with your vision.

Here's my mood board:

My mood board

As I have already explained, in order to keep myself on track, it was imperative for me to regularly find time to connect with my mood board. On top of that, I added to it as I experienced growth, both in my vision and in myself.

Are you ready to start working towards this?

As those of you with a keen eye will spot, part of my big picture life vision involves creating multiple streams of revenue and investing. However, in order to do that, I identified that I needed to move countries to Singapore to position myself for greater success, but more on that later... Sometimes the things we need to do to gain momentum in achieving our life's mission involve fairly big life changes. Don't be afraid to step these out and write them down. By acknowledging them as possible steps you will, in fact, gain more understanding around what it is that you want and why, and what you are willing to do, or not to do, to obtain it.

I'm sorry to say but once you've gone to all the trouble of figuring out what it is that you want, it's not good enough only to know what you want. This is unacceptable, you must work the plan into existence. That means you may need to experience a whole heap of new and unknown situations, so be ready to make some changes that might scare you and go for it every single day. What I am going to teach you in the sections that follow is how to channel your frustrations, anger and pain into creating a life of value, one in which you can be proud of your legacy.

Initially, we need to consider surrounding yourself with people that are ambitious high performers in the number one way. This will enable you to begin to shift gears and move your life in the direction of your dreams. You are ready to make changes and you mean business. Say this to yourself, "I am ready to make changes and I mean business."

If you're in a dead-end job or have a group of friends that are dragging you down rather than nurturing your inspirations, consider making some changes in this area.

This is your one life. Who you hang out with will have an influence on who you will become.

What I mean by working the plan, is making some adaptations and changes to your current plan that wasn't working. This could mean getting in shape, hitting a boxing class or joining a yoga group. It may also mean getting up earlier and creating the time to listen to podcasts and read more books.

This is what I did. I realised that the person I wanted to become craved this type of material in their life. I become deeply committed to learning and educating myself on the subject of personal development and growth. I get up at 5am and write for at least an hour each day, then I will go work out where I listen to anywhere between one to three podcasts, depending on the length, and this is all before sunrise.

If this type of shift is completely new to you, start by setting your alarm clock half an hour earlier and commit to getting out of bed as soon as it goes off, no matter what. Commit to try a new way of living, commit to not settling, and commit to giving yourself the opportunity to thrive.

For the plan to work you must live the life of the person you want to become, and it starts TODAY.

Trusting the universe vs. making it happen

When inspirational leaders and spiritual gurus talk about the Universe, it boils down to understanding that there is something bigger than us at play here, whether that be God, A Higher Power, Universal Intelligence, Universal Consciousness, The Universe, or The Creator. I will use these interchangeably throughout this book and lean more towards God and the Universe angle because this aligns with what I personally believe in.

Learning to trust that you are on the right path is a skill that takes practice and is especially hard when your stomach is all knotted up and you really aren't sure that you're making the right decision. It's important to look at the aspects that may be leading you astray

There are two ends of the spectrum, at one end you have the side of the Universe where everything that happens to you is meant to be and, therefore, your path is taken care of and on the other, you have the hustler who goes out there every single ready to face battle.

In actuality, I have found that these two are not opposing forces, nor do they even require different ways of behaving – they actually work in balance. For instance, it takes incredible strength to let go and trust that the Universe will deliver to your highest good; as much as it does to keep finding the energy and resourcefulness inside to face continual repeated rejection and resistance on a path that you know you must take, like securing a new job in a new country.

Strength and courage are engrained in both of these philosophies and I have found that when they are combined together, instead of seen as separate, you undoubtedly have the ultimate unstoppable force of life behind you.

Mastin Kipp, founder of TheDailyLove.com and inspirational number one bestselling author, speaker and creator of the Claim

Your Power program opens up on his Power+Purpose podcast[2] (which I highly recommend you subscribe to) that in discovering your purpose means, you must participate.

Mastin has dedicated his life to helping others find their purpose in life and runs multiple transformational programs for mind, body and spirit. Mastin states his programs are for *'ambitious, high-performers who want to live extraordinary lives aligned with their soul's purpose'*.

What he means when he says you *'must participate'* is that you need to put in the work, live it, breathe it, and be in it, not just follow it blindly, hoping it will all fall into place one day. It is through the process of consciously directed action that we can start to steer our lives towards the direction of our goals whilst understanding and connecting to the power of the Universe. It is the interplay between having a plan and allowing yourself to receive all the gifts that the Universe has for you along the way. Making it happen and trusting the Universe work both together to support your vision; they are not competing forces.

Having a plan is the single best way to get started and ensure that you reach your goal.

After all, if you don't know what you are aiming at how can you get there? It's difficult for the Universe to understand when you're sending it mixed messages, jumping from one ambition to the next or worse still, standing still, wanting all the nice shiny things out there, and doing diddly squat to draw them closer to you.

The Universe wants to help you, but it gets confused when your actions such as where you spend your time don't reflect what you are telling it.

We each have 86,400 seconds in a day to invest as we see fit; however, if we spend 56,000 of those seconds playing Xbox rather than working towards your vision, the Universe gets fed up. It doesn't know what to send you because you're giving it mixed messages.

---

[2] The Mastin Kipp Podcast (2017) https://itunes.apple.com/us/podcast/the-mastin-kipp-podcast/id1130708584?mt=2

Think of the Universe as your best friend. It wants to give you what you want. All you've got to do is show it, consistently and it will deliver the opportunities to you. And opportunities are like buses, if you miss the first one because you were too busy checking what Cardi B was doing at the weekend on Instagram and so didn't recognise the opportunity you've been waiting for was right in front of your face, it will send you another, as long as you are ready!

Let's stick with the examples for a while, as I want to make sure you really get it. For example, if your goal is to become a multimillionaire by creating a large business that scales so that you can ultimately help those living in poverty, *but* you have a rubber arm when it comes to going out with your friends every weekend drinking and getting up to mischief, then spend the next day lounging around in bed nursing your hangover and scoffing Big Macs, you're sending mixed signals to the world.

This will not work as a strategy as it is incongruent in extraordinary proportions. To play big, you need to make a choice. A choice to prioritise your goals ahead of instant gratification and to use your talents and energy to propel your ideas for the future into action now. Of course, the odd night out with friends isn't bad, but if it takes over your life and the occasional beer becomes nightly binge sessions, then you've got a problem as you have competing priorities.

Trusting universal energy

I had to trust the Universe when I realised that in order to make the move to Singapore happen, I needed to get super clear on what I wanted and then put it out to the world.

Once we had firmly made up our minds and set our hearts on making our home in Singapore, and had many months of attempting to land a job there, we made one important strategic decision that changed everything and created momentum. Where previously we had been focused on our current problem or barrier to overcome (not having a job) and fixing on the idea that we need to have a job in place before moving, we had not yet discovered the power of Universal Intelligence.

Think of Universal Intelligence like the all-knowing soul of the world, once you commit in your mind that something will happen and you remain absolute in your commitment to those thoughts then Universal Intelligence will go out there and start shifting things around to give you the opportunities that you need to make it happen. You just need to remain alert to noticing when they are coming your way and be open to receive them when they do. Acting on Universal Intelligence is a skill that can be practised. The skill comes from various sources, such as believing in your mind that you're already living in Singapore, desiring it with all your heart, and then following your intuition and the thoughts that come into your head. Universal Intelligence wants to help you on your way, all you have to do is be aware and listen. It's about trusting your intuition to follow hot leads, to connect with that person from school who you knew ten years ago, to send the cold email, to take the risk no matter how scary it might feel in the moment and then have faith that it will happen.

What changed everything for us was to book our flights. It was mid-December and I still hadn't landed a job despite multiple interviews and promising conversations. By not moving to Singapore, we felt trapped in a position both financially and mentally that we didn't want to be in, which only made matters worse.

One afternoon it all became too much. The desire to move to Singapore became too great and I just had to do something to move us in that direction, so I went online and locked in 3 one-way flights to Singapore in 3 months' time, on 5th March 2018. Once that was done it felt like a huge weight had been lifted from our shoulders. It was done, we were moving, no matter what. From then on, something changed in the mind; no longer were we handcuffed by the lack of a job. There was a shift in the types of conversations that we would have as a family and how we spoke about the process of moving to Singapore. We begin to put our stuff on Gumtree and sell all of the belongings that we did not want to take with us. Our world was transformed by our actions and our actions now aligned with our thoughts. It was like we were whole again and this act of booking the flights allowed us to see clearly again and get excited about our future in Singapore. We didn't know how it would happen yet; we just knew that it would happen and fully believed in it. We timed everything for our new life in Singapore, based on these dates. By setting a deadline and handing the rest over to the Universal Intelligence, a new energy was unleashed in both Sandra and me. We made sure that we said goodbye to all of our favourite beaches and enjoyed Manly with an intensity that hadn't been present for many months. We arranged to move our boxes and ship all of our stuff, closed down our accounts and let our landlord know that we would be moving out at the beginning of March, all still with having no job offer. We told the Universe what we wanted, and it listened and began to shift opportunities in our direction. It wasn't plain sailing and we had to take some crazy risks in the process, but we figured it out and made it through the challenge.

Jen Sincero, the bestselling author of *You Are A Badass At Making Money*[3], goes into awesome detail about this concept of telling Universal Intelligence what you want. She gives the example of a café to illustrate the point, *'You wouldn't walk into a café and order a sandwich by saying 'hey I want a sandwich', you'd rock up in there and give specifics, 'I want a cheese and pickle sandwich, mayo and the crusts off, lightly toasted.'*

The same goes for the Universal Intelligence. It is listening, so you'll need to tell it what it is you want, through your thoughts, through your energy, through your being. You need to focus on it, daily.

The think and grow rich formula

In *Think and Grow Rich,* Napoleon Hill defines one of the most important tools for getting want you want. He spent twenty years studying the habits and qualities of the world's most powerful and richest men of the early 1900s and interviewed more than 500 millionaires! Twenty years!

---

[3] Sincero, J. (2017). *You Are a Badass at Making Money: Master the Mindset of Wealth.* Viking

This included men like Henry Ford, Alexander Graham Bell and Thomas Edison. By examining what made them so successful and conducting in-depth interviews, he came up with a formula for achieving riches, as per the below. I include this, firstly, because it's an epic way to begin your journey towards financial abundance and secondly because finance is an area that people typically hold back from starting down the path towards an extraordinarily meaningful life. However, once you've put the following strategy into place, you can focus on getting started and taking action rather than worrying about money.

The Think and Grow Rich Formula

1. Fix your mind on the exact amount of money you desire. (It's not good enough to say I want to be loaded, it must be the precise amount of money you want to receive. This could be per year or it could be a lump sum that will allow you to carry out your vision.)

2. Determine exactly what you intend to give in return for the money you desire. (There is no such reality as "something for nothing". This should be every activity you intend to do, the amount of energy and time you're willing to dedicate and the idea's you're willing to put into action.)

3. Establish a definite date when you intend to possess the money you desire (you need a fixed deadline)

4. Create a definite plan for carrying out your desire and begin at once, whether you are ready or not, to put this plan into action. (You might find this part a struggle or daunting to begin with, but stick with it. You must commit to starting right away. Don't negotiate with yourself on this, it is done, and you will put this plan into action NOW. Those are the rules of the game).

5. Write out a clear, concise statement of the amount of money you intend to acquire, name the time limit for its acquisition, state what you want to give in return for the money, and describe clearly your plan to accumulate it. (See mine below for reference.)

6. Read your written statement aloud, twice daily, once just before retiring at night, and once after arising in the morning. AS YOU READ IT – SEE, FEEL AND BELIEVE YOURSELF TO BE ALREADY IN POSSESSION OF THE MONEY. (This step, which I have written in capital letters for effect, is paramount. Do this like your life depends on it!)

A simpler way to remember this formula is:

- What do you want?

- What will you give?

- What's the deadline?

- What's the plan?

- Write it down

- Speak it aloud daily, imagine you have the money already.

For example, you might decide you want to accumulate $2,000,000 by August 1st, five years from now, by selling a product or service as a salesperson.

Your desire statement could look like this:

By the first day of August 2023, I will have in my possession $2,000,000, which will come to me in various forms through employment, investments in property, investments in start-ups, book sales, online course sales, seminars, speaking engagements and windfalls.

Tim's Answers

- What do you want? *I want a $10m net worth.*

- What will you give? *In return, I will put my all into achieving wealth by paid employment, writing books, blogs, articles, speaking engagements and coaching.*

- What's the deadline? *By the age of 37.*

- What's the plan? *I will invest the revenues generated into start-up ventures, stocks, property.*

- Write it down – *see image below*

- Speak it aloud daily – *I do, imagining all the time that I have the money already.*

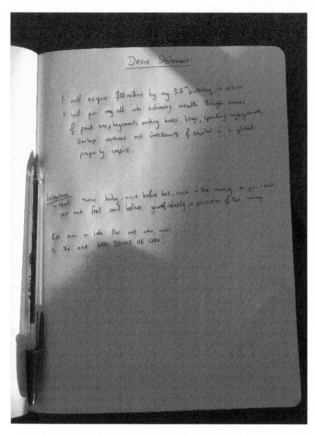

My desire statement

"The starting point of all achievement is DESIRE. Keep this constantly in mind. Weak desire brings weak results, just as a small fire makes a small amount of heat."

Napoleon Hill

In summary, after reading this chapter and completing the mood board exercise you should now know what it is that you want and what an awesome life looks like to you. You know where you're going, and you have direction. We are now ready to get into action mode and create. We'll spend the next few chapters looking at *how* you're going to get there. Hooray, you've reached the next level. Congratulations. I know this has not been easy but trust me, you're worth it. ;)

CHAPTER 4

PRIORITIES = PROGRESS

"Most people overestimate what they can do in one year
and underestimate what they can do in ten years."

Bill Gates

WHEN ARNOLD SCHWARZENEGGER was 20, he won the Mr Universe world title, a feat he achieved by spending 5-6 hours a day in the gym. What was different about Arnold though was that he did it with a smile on his face. There were plenty of other guys putting in the time, going through the motions and doing exercises but Arnold put in the work, mentality and psychically, and with a smile. In his mind, every rep, every jump, every lift was one more that got him closer to winning the Mr Universe competition. He was happy to lift another set, happy to do another push-up because he was focused on his goals. His belief in his goal and the determination to see it through got him over the finish line so that he beat the competition. That's not to say that he hasn't had setbacks or failures, far from it, but it was this mentality – that the work he was doing was taking him one step closer to the success of the final goal – that saw him do the work with 100% commitment.

Much like Arnold, who has dominated in many fields from bodybuilding to acting career and, more recently, politics and philanthropy, we need to get clear on our priorities and commit to doing the work.

We each have the same 24 hours in a day but it's what we do with them that counts and how we specifically focus our time on the things that matter, rather than procrastinate.

The reason it is important to know your goals and prioritise them because we make continuous incremental improvements through what we focus on day in day out and the small shifts we can make in the allocation of our time (e.g. dedicating one hour a day to reading).

Like dollars in an investment account that compound over time, our investment in our skills or our health and well-being compounds over time. Any investment that you make in self-development or dedicating to a side hustle or the development of an entrepreneurial venture or business can lead to remarkable outcomes in the not so distant future.

Success doesn't happen by accident

I hate to break this to you, but as important as it is to get your brain into gear, you don't just wake up perched on the plush balcony of your 5-bed mansion in the Hollywood Hills sipping on a freshly made skinny latte and deciding which Lamborghini you're going to drive today.

It doesn't work that way. Period!

I know, right, shocking!

Why can't *wanting* to be a success be enough?

The old saying by Jerry Rice, *'Today, I will do what others won't, so tomorrow I can accomplish what others can't,'* rings true.

Know your daily priorities

To dominate in action mode, it's about getting your priorities damn straight so that each day you can move forward. And when I talk about priorities, I mean getting the things that really matter right – the fundamentals, like your health, or spending time with family, defining and working on your personal goals (not those of society, or someone else, or what you think you're supposed to be doing) and living true to your purpose. If you are not clear on what you really want or what is really important it is likely you won't be allocating your resources towards those things, hence why the work you did in Chapter 3 was so vitally important.

Success is a process, and as correctly stated in *7 Habits of Highly Effective People* by Stephen Covey, you need to '*put first things first*' to start to create the life you want. This means sitting down and getting crystal clear on what matters to you, so that you can design an extraordinary life and then making sure you stick to the plan.

We need to work out what an awesome life looks like for you. Every person will have a different take on what this means to them. The key is not to get sidetracked or brainwashed by society or what others want but to focus only on what matters to you specifically. This is a sure-fire way to get closer to what will make you happy in the long run.

Ask yourself these questions by imagining your future life.

- What does an outstanding life look like to you?
- Is it going to the gym and working on your physical well-being?
- Is it having an awesome relationship with your spouse or partner?
- Is it travelling the world and meeting people from all cultures and walks of life?
- Is it starting a business and launching it on the stock market?
- What will your daily routine be like?

Tim's Answers:

- What does an outstanding life look like to you?

   A life where I am working in the field of my deepest passions, contributing to the world by doing meaningful work, operating the best version of myself and striving to continually improve for myself, my family, my friends and the world.

- Is it going to the gym and working on your physical well-being?

  Yes, I will also incorporate a workout session into my daily habits at least six times a week with one day off for rest and recovery. I do this because I know that mental and physical well-being is the foundation upon which I will form an outstanding life, and having a healthy lifestyle will enable me to go after my goals 110% with vitality, enthusiasm and energy.

- Is it having an awesome relationship with your spouse or partner?

  Indeed, it is. For me. the love I share with my spouse is fundamental to our well-being, the support we give to one another and the life we are building together. I chose to work hard on my relationship, to be the best version of myself in the relationship, and to be there for my spouse.

- Is it travelling the world and meeting people from all cultures and walks of life?

  Yes, at this stage of my life it is very much about travelling the world and embracing new cultures and realities so that I may serve in whichever way I am needed. I aim to take up opportunities to travel frequently and learn from other nations about the strategies and fundamentals of life. To me, travel lights up my soul and it is the people I meet along the way that give me the gift of new perspectives, love and understanding which shows me life's true intention.

- Is it starting a business and launching it on the stock market?

  I have started a number of businesses, although they are just fledgling ventures at this stage, I am committed to nurturing and growing multiple business and entrepreneurial offshoots in pursuit of my mission.

- What will your ideal daily routine be like?

Each day I will wake up at 5am. I step out on my bed and as soon as my feet hit the floor, I think of one thing that I am grateful for (usually my wife and child, depending on the number of sleep disturbances during the night). Following this, I will walk into my office or go outside. I will sit and begin to write in my journal, work on a project, or jot down everything that I am grateful for in more detail. I find that I am most creative in the early morning, and so if there is anything that requires deep thought or creativity then this is the time for me to tackle this. At 6am, I will eat breakfast and drink tea. At 6.30am, I will make my way to the gym, where I work out for an hour. At 8am, I head to the office and get my most challenging emails, calls, and work completed before anyone else comes in. At 12pm, I take lunch, and either dine with work colleagues or hit the gym for a second work out of the day. At 5.30-6pm, I head home to see my baby boy before bedtime and eat dinner. At 8pm, I jump back online and work through a few extra emails that might have come through and prepare for the day ahead. At 8.30pm, I listen to another podcast, audiobook or read. At 9.30pm, I try to fall to sleep and dream of how great life is.

*(Note: If a 5am start seems unimaginable to you, try setting the alarm 30 minutes earlier tomorrow and commit to getting out of bed when it goes off. The morning is **your time** to do the work that builds the future that you want to create for yourself, so take full advantage of it.)*

Tackling these questions in as much detail as you can should help you to build up a fairly graphic picture of what your ideal life looks like on a micro level. Don't worry if this feels unachievable now, small steps make amazing progress. Whereas in chapter 3 we focused on the big vision and purpose for your being here, in this chapter, we are concerned with getting the daily operations of how you'll build habits and stay on track.

If you're struggling to both keep track of all your daily activities and be aware of how you are spending your time, I recommend carrying a notepad with you through the day and writing down as best you can how long you spend doing each task. This will help to bring the picture to life and it's an easy way to figure out what is actually going on, rather than what you envisage to be happening with your routines. Habits and routines are sneaky because they are automatic; therefore, unless we do something to track them it can be hard to spot when they suck up valuable time or could be done more efficiently and improved.

The other aspect I would recommend tracking is the time you spend on your devices per day. To do this, I recommend downloading an app called Moment. This will give you the breakdown of your mobile or tablet usage on a given day, including how many times you pick it up and which apps you're using most. Understanding when you are using your phone (without even realising it sometimes), like on the morning commute to work, will increase your awareness around where you can claw back pockets of time to be used for achieving your goals.

If you find that your screen time is absolutely shocking and you're aimlessly dwindling away precious moments of your one and only life surfing Facebook, make sure that you address this now. If you go into the settings on your phone, there is an option under screen time that will allow you to place restrictions on apps and create downtime for yourself.

Once you've got clear on what an amazing life means for you, you can shift your time (your most important resource) from activities that take you away from your goals and vision for your life towards those that are going to bring you closer to it. This is easier said than done and will sometimes require a drastic change in lifestyle, and mean perhaps moving home, jobs, relationships or even countries to get aligned with the life you want to live.

It goes beyond talent

Looking at the world's most exceptionally successful people, like Warren Buffet, Beyoncé Knowles, Elon Musk, JLo, Jeff Bezos,

Oprah Winfrey and Sheryl Sandberg, it's easy to assume that they got where they are today due to talent. Of course, this played a part, but only a part.

In fact, overestimating the importance of talent in other people's success is a fairly common mistake. It's a dream killer because it allows you to slack off or rationalise that you're not successful because you weren't born talented, and the only reason others are doing well is because they have stacks of natural talent. When you consider the names above, they have all prioritised, overcome adversity, pushed through barriers of pain, fear and ridicule to get where they are today. It's important not to minimise the success of other people and rather to marvel at it and learn from it.

This ability to wear rose-tinted glasses when it comes to success, and specifically other people's, is a defence mechanism and a default human reaction in response to other people's success, and we can over attribute it to something outside of our own sphere of control, like talent or opportunity alone.

When you take a closer look at that though, exceptionally successful people are so damn successful, because of one or two vitally important things:

1. The ability to remove the unnecessary from their daily lives

2. The ability to focus on the core objective consistently over time.

Warren Buffet is famous for reading newspapers for five to six hours each day. Shane Parish, Founder of Farnam Street, says, *'Incredibly successful people focus their time on just a few priorities and obsess over doing things right. This is simple but not easy.'*

To give you a way to simplify your life goals and work out what's not needed, use Warren Buffet's 2 list strategy. It is an excellent tool that will show you how to master your priorities.

If you don't know what the goal is then it's incredibly hard to stay the course, let alone end up at the desired destination. This strategy is a real golden nugget and was uncovered during a conversation Buffett was having with his pilot on the topic of career priorities.

Warren Buffet's 2-list strategy

1. Write down on a piece of paper the top 25 goals you want to achieve in your lifetime.

2. Now circle the top 5 most important things of those 25. These 5 have now made it to List A, so write them down on a separate piece of paper.

3. The other 20 remaining items on the first list become your "not-to-do" list. This is now List B.

4. Ignore everything on List B, it becomes your "avoid at ALL costs" list. NOTHING on List B is to be touched until you've achieved your top 5 goals on List A, no matter what. (There is a degree of sensibility that needs to be deployed when using this strategy, for example, if you have noted down "pay outstanding invoices" on your list, make sure that you circle it as a top priority so it ends up on List A, rather than ignore it until you've had dinner with Brad Pitt on the top of the Eifel Tower, travelled around the world in 80 days, eaten sushi in Tokyo, solved space travel for the entire human race and saved a million people from famine. Make sure you pay your damn bills.)

This is the power of elimination at its best. Buffet's simple strategy eliminates wastage and forces us to direct our precious energy on only the top goals and priorities. You must be unwavering in your commitment to success and doing these top 5 items must become your ultimate objective. Keep both lists available and refer to them regularly. Anytime you find yourself straying from your goals on List A goals, shift your mindset to see this as sabotaging your chances of success. Keep referring to the lists often and keep yourself reminded of where you are headed and what you will be expending your time and energy on daily.

Successful people know how to focus on a small handful of goals. If you're thinking, 'Will I ever get to do the other 20 goals on

List B?' then the answer is yes. But I recommend that you do the 2-list exercise again after you've achieved everything on list A, as you'll have likely become a different person in achieving your top 5 goals, so you'll have a new list of priorities to go after. Redo the exercise and draw up your new 25 goals, then select the top 5 must do goals.

CHAPTER 5

MY STORY: THE $4000 COFFEE

"Today is brutal, tomorrow is more brutal, but the day after tomorrow is beautiful. However, the majority of people will die tomorrow night."

Jack Ma

HERE'S A TALE of persistence and patience, the latter being an aspect of overcoming obstacles and big challenges that I was less than proficient in. My tendency was to try and force things along with willpower so that the object of my desire (moving to Singapore, in this case) had no choice but to happen. What I learned in my quest to make my dream come true was that we have to trust in the bigger picture and have faith that everything is happening of its own accord at the exact right time. We have to trust in abundance and fight the temptation to moan or complain about things not happening. It's only when we leave this negativity on the shelf that we start to see the opportunities present themselves. This was a lesson that I had to learn and once I did, the results overflowed.

Wanting

My fiancé Sandra and I arrived back home in Sydney in June 2017 from a best friend's wedding in the South of France, and both felt the exact same thing as we stepped off the plane. Normally, we'd be ecstatic to be back in the land of golden sandy beaches, surrounded by places to get a mean coffee and avo on toast. But this time was different, we were both craving a new adventure.

Looking back, I was unprepared for the story that unfolded. I believed that the hardest part was over, making the decision and as we both knew exactly what we wanted, getting it would be easy, right? No. How wrong was I?

For a while we had been flirting with the idea of moving from the land down under to Asia or even Dubai, we figured it would be a phenomenal way to kick-start our savings plan, get help with our 6-month old baby, Levi, as we had no family in Australia, and streamline our lives so that we'd both have more time to invest in setting up businesses that could potentially earn us some passive income. This was step one in our big vision.

Plus, Singapore being a direct hub meant that we had more friends frequently passing through and we'd be living closer to both of our families in Europe. At this point, the thought of Levi not spending Christmas at home with his Granny and Grandad, unwrapping presents under the tree, surrounded by the warmth and love of family and friends was a sad one. As well as the fact that we were completely fed up with missing out on milestone events, such as weddings, engagements and birthdays, it just made complete sense and we knew it was time to get our asses into gear to make it happen.

On top of this, we wanted to explore. Singapore became the top contender, with quick access to Asia, a high standard of living and excellent schools it was an easy win.

Luckily, we both felt the same way and I began frantically applying for jobs on LinkedIn and messaging friends, recruiters and anyone I could think of to help out. The job hunt got off to a flying start and I had a number of first-round interviews lined up by August with some fantastic companies. To cut a long story short, none of them worked out for various reasons.

One company restructured so the role didn't exist, another one wasn't a fit due to the fact that my boss would have been an unbearably annoying and a grade A micromanager type, and another chose a different candidate at the final moment after convincing me to stay in the process when I'd dropped out because I didn't think it was a fit.

It was important for me to get a role that would support both my growth and our family financially, and not just accept anything that came up purely to solve a problem. It was incredibly hard to walk away from a final round interview and remove myself from the process because I knew that the culture or the role was not aligned to my values and skillset. It felt like I was being offered a key to everything that I wanted except it wouldn't have set us up for long-term success and had the potential to cause us even more instability further down the road. This was a skill I learned during the process, not getting too invested in the outcome and trusting that the right opportunity would appear.

As someone with a bias for action, I couldn't believe how slow the market was. Every day, sometimes every hour, I would search for jobs online, prospecting and reaching out to connections for help, gathering referrals, gaining introductions and setting up video calls over hangouts. It seemed that the prerequisite for getting a senior role was time spent working in Asia, which makes complete sense as any company is likely to choose someone who can hit the ground running and save them time rather than a candidate who may need three months to build a contact list before they could get going. I needed to find a company that was prepared to hire for cultural fit, skill and experience, not time spent in the market. In sales, you are bound by the constructs of the sales cycle, so any of these companies worth its salt should have understood that it would take a number of months for any new hire to gain momentum. Also, I was probably a catch because I could bring my experiences from the Australian markets as well as my connections into play. Alas, this logic was not shared by the majority of my interviewers. I came close at times to landing a role that ticked my boxes, but it was not to be.

Fast-forward to 23rd December 2017 when we were still living in Sydney with no job offers on the table. By this point, it had been 24 weeks of trying and our patience was wearing thin. We were getting frustrated because we wanted to be somewhere else and felt like we couldn't move forward with our lives, Sandra was still on maternity leave but couldn't look for employment in case we found jobs in Singapore and then had to leave. The sheer mental strength it took to keep us positive during this monotonous time was nothing short of an hourly process. We were unhappy, feeling stuck and wanting change.

At a certain point, I had to do something. We were still absolutely dying to move, so we sent out our commitment signal to the Universe and booked one-way flights to Singapore that were scheduled to leave on the 5th March 2018. With that act done, we set our intention and could focus on when I would hand in my notice and how we could best wind down our lives in Sydney. There was a lot to do.

Shortly after this, I was approached by work to go on a business trip for a sales kick-off conference in the second week of January and, as luck would have it, it was to be held in our Singapore office.

Taking action

Upon hearing this news, I decided this was it! I needed to leverage this opportunity to the full. The conference was only 3 days, but I began right away planning how I could take full advantage of this little stroke of luck.

I hit the gym, a place where my mind relaxes and gets creative. Ideas seem to flow right between lat pulldowns and tricep curls. It struck me that I needed to take charge of the opportunity once again and put it all on the line.

We were stretched financially, having lived on one salary for 8 months while Sandra took care of Levi, and with our impending wedding fast approaching, the pressure was beginning to mount. But the more I thought about it, the more I knew that any extra time I could spend in Singapore was worth its weight in gold. It was going to be a game-changer.

So, I asked the question. I texted my boss and asked cheekily if I could have seven days off after the trip. I didn't say for what. I just asked the question. She agreed, which meant that I now had seven full business days in Singapore to line up meetings, coffee dates and absorb the culture of the place.

At the time, I got a sense that this was an important turning point. Rather than focusing on opportunities that had not been right in the past or ones that were had got super far down the line only to fall over right at the last hurdle, I needed to think positively. This was possible. This was about creating the opportunity. I needed to draw line in the sand. The past was the past but the future, that's where we create what we are after.

Despite all the meetings I had lined up, I had this niggling thought that the trip could still be made better, and that maximum value had still not been reached. It came to me on a walk at sunrise, as I was striding out of Manly and down one of the many cycle paths leading to Fairlight. Manly is spoilt for walking routes that follow the beachside and go along the ocean.

I realised that I wanted my family to come with me on the trip. They had never accompanied me on a business trip before, but with this one being in Singapore it made so much sense for them to come and soak up the atmosphere of the place too, especially as we were serious about moving there. Rather than have them waiting back at home in our small studio, with Sandra taking care of our baby on her own for 12 days, we could all stay together and have an adventure.

This decision now made the trip full value and allowed them to experience what it would be like to live there. It also gave them the opportunity to fall in love with the place and see it for themselves, rather than me trying to convey everything that happened and what it was like on my return.

We leveraged this opportunity and went hell for leather setting up apartment viewings. We stayed in different hotels all around the city in various locations and had over 10 meetings with recruiters and potential employers.

Achieving

Then on day 4 of the trip, it happened! The $4,000 I spent on the trip paid off.

Momentum was in full swing; our energy was overflowing and we were in the midst of another jam-packed day full of coffee meetings. An introductory meet and greet with a recruiter in a coffee shop quickly led to an interview in just 60 minutes time!

It was as if the planets had aligned. There was a role on offer at a company just launching their Singapore office. It was to be their Asian hub and they were looking for a Sales Director. In another stroke of luck, the managing director's lunch meeting got cancelled, meaning she had time to conduct an interview with me before she flew back to Sydney that evening. Right away, I was ushered into a side office of a traditional shop house above the bustling din of Telok Ayre Street, here I was handed a laptop and told to prepare for the meeting. An hour later, I was sat patiently waiting for my interviewer to arrive. We got on like a house on fire and ended up chatting for well over 90 minutes, which was a good sign.

The initial interview went well and swiftly led to a second-round interview, which was scheduled at 6am, four days later, where I met the founder and the COO. Fast-forward to 4 days later am I am sat in my hotel room on a video call to the Australian office facing a panel, including the CEO. I am in flow and loving the questions and the direction it's going.

Later that evening, after presenting to 120 people at the sales conference (the one I had come to be in Singapore for), I received a job offer. Life could not have felt better in that moment. Finally, we had done it, we had cracked the code and our new life was about to begin. The ecstasy of relief and the joy that Sandra and I experienced when I put down the phone after accepting the role poured over us. We had fought so hard to get to this point and waited so patiently.

Luckily, we still had 3 days left in Singapore, so we were able to explore some more. That feeling of knowing that we had done it and we would be returning to Sydney to pack up, hand in my notice and start our new adventure was incredible. After 7 months of trying, we had finally cracked it. We told the Universe and then we showed the Universe that we were committed to getting this and making it happen. The Universe responded, and it was sensational.

The detail

To break this down, my meeting with the recruiter was just a coffee to put faces to names. That coffee meeting invite triggered a thought in the recruiter's mind and she put me in touch with her colleague who had a role going that she thought I'd be interested in. There was a time pressure because the Managing Director of the company was only there for 1 day, so they hustled to try and get me in to see her straight away. Funnily enough, her lunch cancelled and we were able to meet at a local coffee house for nearly 2 hours. We hit it off right away.

In that initial interview at the coffee shop, we discussed 30/60/90 plans, so rather than wait for the second round, to see if it was required, I worked morning and night to pump out a stellar sales plan. (A 30/60/90-day plan is what businesses use to articulate what they plan to achieve in those time periods. In this case, I was being asked to formulate a plan for the Asia market and how I would get up to speed, over-achieve on sales targets and learn how to do business in a new market. I find that a well-thought-out plan can be the difference between a successful second round interview and not. Sending it early is also an excellent way to show you have initiative and are passionate about the role and the company's success. When we extend ourselves slightly we can often create a memorable impact and as I will show you further on in the book, there are some specific ways in which you can do that to increase your chances of success (in my case, by demonstrating my core competencies and blowing the other candidates out of the water). When designing a 30/60/90 plan, I ensure that each objective or deliverable is a SMART goal, meaning it is specific, measurable, achievable, relevant and time-bound.

Once I had drawn up a kick-ass plan, I got it across to her the following day and then began working on my people strategy for Asia. As I was new to the market, I'd found that employers were slightly hesitant because I had limited contacts. I needed to demonstrate how I could leverage being new to market as an advantage and not a disadvantage in order to meet new, influential folk.

To counteract this objection, I put together a people strategy document detailing who I already knew who would be key to extending my network in Singapore and ramp up the growth of the business. By addressing this head-on, I showed I was aware it could be a potential obstacle and also demonstrated that I had a structured plan in place to overcome this and had a path to follow. I did this in order to pre-empt any reluctance they might have had or desire to go with a safer option, e.g. someone with more business contacts or years of experience in the Asian markets.

I sent off my people strategy too; remember, this was all before the second-round interview had even happened, and before I had been asked for it. Then I got up at 5am, prepared for an hour and had a 6am interview over Skype with the global management in Sydney.

What I learnt from the $4,000 coffee

When we want something, we must go for it with no holds barred – even if that means flying your fiancé, 6-month-old baby and yourself to the market, and you have very limited funds and a number of responsibilities to manage. As I'm sure you'll have gathered by now, the purpose of this tale wasn't the discovery of the world's most expensive cup of coffee, but rather the pursuit of a dream and how courage and ingenuity are required to craft an appropriate response to the world's opportunities. After all, opportunities like the business trip to Singapore will present themselves, but it's what we do with them that counts, and how far we are willing to push the boundaries of our own limitations – even if it costs us $4,000 or more to put ourselves in a position where we are having a coffee with the right person, at the right time.

It's also about being comfortable with being uncomfortable. I was uncomfortable to ask for the time off as it was short notice and I knew I'd be using the time to create new employment options for myself. But there is a massive upside to asking and getting the time off. It enabled me to create the opportunity for my family and me to go and test out the market, and even more crucially, it allowed the Universe to work its magic and solve this problem for us.

So, I would say, focus on the bigger picture, don't get caught up in the day to day. What is the worst that can happen? They say 'no' and you come up with another option? The rewards outweigh the costs. We just have to get over ourselves and what others may think of us and ask the question.

If I had stayed focused on my lack of comfort, my image at work or our financial position, none of the above could have happened. **I would have been playing it too small.**

To create real change we need to play big. Not only do we need to think big, we must also be open to living big by receiving and partaking in all manner of experiences.

Ultimately, this means juggling multiple responsibilities, handling objections and pushing for the things we want, despite the setbacks and no matter how many times it takes. It's like being a ninja – things keep getting thrown at you, others try to tell you that you should stop, you can't do it or won't master what you wish to do, and it's your job to block them and protect your path to the future.

Self-help books generally refer to this as resilience, and like a muscle, it can be built upon and expanded so that your ability to deal with a heavier load is increased. As well as resilience, one must possess incredible amounts of faith. In order to succeed, you must have faith in abundance that your goal can and will be achieved; perhaps not in the way you might have imagined, but achieved nonetheless.

A note on abundance and lack

Whoa there, Nelly! If you've just sped past the word abundance without contemplating it's inordinate and infinite ever-expanding greatness, let's take a moment to recognise and explore this pillar of truth in all its glory, from the self-help and ideological growth sense of the word.

Abundance derives from the Latin verb abundare, which means "to abound or to overflow". Life itself is abundant, nature is a fabulous example of just how abundant and giving the Universe can be. Think of the billions of blades of grass on the planet or the drops of water that make up the ocean; abundance is all around us. When we become consciously aware of just how abundant our world is, we notice everything that we have and gratitude for its abundance flows out of us. As a result of this grateful thinking, we manifest more abundance. We trust wholeheartedly that the world will provide and lead us to the path of our highest good, putting our skills to use in the best practical way possible.

The opposite of abundance is lack, which is essentially focussing on what is not there rather than appreciating what is. A person consumed by lack gives up their energy and focuses solely on what they don't have or becomes stuck in a repetitive and tired pattern of comparison with others. It is easy to spot a person operating from the lack vantage point as their consciousness is sucked into a vassal state and operates at the mercy of everything they cannot control. This behaviour is draining and, trust me, it doesn't get you closer to what you want, far from it. It turns you into a complaining machine and transforms the way you interact with the world into a low energy state. Nothing of substance can be created in this state.

These two things, complaining about what we don't have and why it isn't fair and constantly comparing your lives to the lives of others will take you off course. It's so easy to do and that's why it's so important to your mission that you stay on the right side of it. When you have a purpose, you don't have time to be concerned with what other people have or complain about why life is so unfair. If you're reading this and think this might be you, go easy on yourself, I've been there. With the Singapore mission, all I wanted to do (and did do at times of weakness) was complain about why it wasn't happening and moan about how easy it was for others to get what they wanted. This lack mindset tempted me every single day, multiple times a day, in fact, when I was indulging a bit of self-pity. Deep down, however, I knew that the more I complained the more it drained both my energy and time away from creating opportunities for my family to move to Singapore. And even though I was well aware that complaining was killing my focus, I still indulged in it. It took a mammoth effort to stop this cycle of lack, but by constantly telling my mind that I refused to think like this, I overcame it.

What I want you to remember is that it's not about being perfect, it's about striving to be better.

One way to overcome lack is to find your purpose and then live it. You'll shift to the side of an abundance mentality once you have a purpose that is so compelling, it requires you to use your unique gifts to be of service to others.

Whilst we're on this topic, let me highlight another form of the lack mentality to watch out for, which is subtler but no less prevalent in today's society. In fact, it's become an epidemic of colossal proportions. This is the constant need for the world to align with our expectations. We fixate on the way we believe things should be and try to control it, and the more we do this, the more we detach from the abundance of the world.

This is driven by the continual, monotonous observation of other people's lives, which has been exponentially increased by social media. The tools in our pockets enable us to check-in 24/7 on lives that have been edited to perfection, which not only gives us unrealistic expectations but also leaves us feeling that we don't measure up in some way.

It may seem ironic that the abundance of communication and connection created by recent advancements in technology can also lead to us experiencing less abundance if it's misused.

So addiction to this phenomena is something to watch out for.

> Comparison and complaining are two of the fastest ways to deviate from a life of abundance, so let's nip this one in the bud right now before it gets out of control.

Abundance is your friend; it is to be celebrated and witnessed. For example, take money. This is a topic which houses so much emotion and governs people's lives according to silent rules and thought patterns that are entangled in shame and guilt, consumerism, and pain from the lessons learned during in childhood. According to the law of abundance, there is more than enough money for everyone and so if you receive an increased share, it does not decrease the amount another person receives. However, nine times out of ten a lack mentality is the default choice for people when it comes to the concept of abundance and money.

But what happens when we have an epiphany and experience a seminal shift in consciousness away from the lack mentality and embrace fully the abundant nature of the world? We move our thinking to believe in the overflowing goodness and positivity in the world and, as a result, experience more of it.

The abundant mindset draws experiences, people and opportunities to it that would be unavailable to those with the lack mentality as they would be too closed-minded and preoccupied with comparison and complaining to notice the valuable opportunities available.

Hopefully, by now, you are starting to get the picture that abundance is a beautiful thing and it is all around us. The more that you can operate from this level of consciousness, especially at times when you are channelling your lion to overcome a big obstacle, the more you will invite in positive opportunities.

°If you had told me before when we flew out to Singapore that I would be returning with a job offer I would have been elated, over the moon, on cloud nine. The next time you are facing hardship and adversity remember this story; after all, your $4,000 coffee could be right around the corner. The question is, will you do whatever it takes to put yourself in the optimal position to go after it and simultaneously let the Universe work its magic on your behalf? Or will you sit at home moaning how about how much easier it seems for everyone else? Let me guess…

CHAPTER 6

MY STORY: THE $7,000 MEETING

"It's the possibility of having a dream come true that
makes life interesting."

Paulo Coelho, *The Alchemist*

APPARENTLY, MY EDITOR says I can't start another chapter
with a similar title directly after the previous one, as you
might think I have become lax in my approach or given up on my
promise to provide a structured manual that is so strong it keeps
you nourished to the end. But I want to share this story with you as
it highlights another experience where I put it all on the line to get
to a place I had never been before. My goal here is to help you see
the correlation between things you would like to do (big vision)
and doing something you think at first is absurd (the unknown)
in order to make it happen. This is about being the brave lion and
taking that step into the unknown.

Wanting

So there I was, staring at the computer screen, looking at an
opportunity of a lifetime to meet one of my all-time favourite
heroes from the sales world. Sandra and I had been watching Ryan
Serhant on Bravo's *Million Dollar Listing New York* over the last
7 series for as many years.

We had seen Ryan get up to all his antics on the show, pull stunts to
get clients to turn up to his broker's openings and even shut down
the whole of Times Square to propose to his fiancé. But most of all,
we loved Ryan's application of fun to sales and his unapologetic
methods of getting the best deal for his clients. Sitting on our sofa

in our tiny studio flat in Manly, Australia, we had formed a bond with him, although Ryan didn't know it yet.

And then came the opportunity. For Sandra's 40th birthday, I was planning a trip to New York City, NYC, a place she had always wanted to visit again. It would be our first time to the Big Apple as a couple.

I had faith that the money would come and we had all the money we would need. I JUST KNEW IT HAD TO HAPPEN. I had to make it happen for Sandra. This was her 40th and we needed to start living our life for us. It didn't matter if it felt like we couldn't afford it, or the timing wasn't perfect, we had to say, 'screw it, let's do it,' in true Richard Branson style.

As I was contemplating booking the NYC flights, I saw that Ryan Serhant was launching his first book, *Sell It Like Serhant*[4], and as an incentive to turbocharge sales, he was offering anyone who pre-ordered 100 copies a 1-hour sit down meeting with him at his offices in NYC.

What are the chances? How awesome would that be if we could have a sit down with Ryan Serhant – the man himself – during the surprise trip for Sandra?

Taking action

I had faith. I followed all of Jen Sincero's badass financial advice. I booked the flights to NYC. (For those of you who aren't familiar with Jen's work, her badass advice is best explored in her book, *You Are A Badass At Making Money*[5], which covers the full spectrum of how to master the mindset of wealth). I trusted that we already had the money we needed somehow and it would come to us. As soon as I had booked the flights, I had doubts about how I was being reckless and putting my family in financial danger by indulging in a whim. I was leaping into

[4] Serhant, R. (2018) *Sell it like Serhant*. Hachette Books.
[5] Sincero, J. (2017). *You Are a Badass at Making Money: Master the Mindset of Wealth*. Viking

the unknown and didn't really know how this was going to pan out.

I was worried it might not happen or that it was a hoax, but I held my resolve. It took two more weeks of mulling it over before I finally hit buy on Amazon.com and placed the order for one hundred of the finest copies of Ryan's sales book. It was a fairly big investment at $25 a pop.

Achieving

As soon as the email receipt from Amazon swooped into my inbox, I forwarded it over to Ryan and prayed for a response, which I knew deep down was coming.

We were almost 10 months out from the date when I was requesting to meet with him. It was a long way off, but now the flights were booked, the books were ordered and all we needed was for Ryan to agree and we were home and dry.

In true Ryan fashion, he came back to me within two hours of the initial email, cc'ing in his assistant Jordan to arrange to get a date in the diary and set it up.

Faith

I WAS OVERJOYED. When you put faith in and trust your intuition – your gut, your deeper self – when that something is niggling you, and you are afraid, but you know that if you do it, you will be living big and upping your game, then go for it.

Deep down, I knew that in order to be the person I wanted to be, I needed to act like that person. This involved making big uncomfortable moves financially, mentally and physically in order to step into the unknown and take the risk, come what may. I had to commit to the process of moving forward by listening and then acting on my own instinct to make it happen. Taking action is about who we become in the process. The cost of not taking action is too great.

What could that opportunity to meet with Ryan create? What new adventures could it reveal? If we just do what we have always done, then we will continue to get the same results. By actioning this strategy and having a sit-down meeting with a man who has taken the real estate business by storm in the last 10 years, reached the very pinnacle of success on a global scale, has two prime time TV shows on Bravo, has a media company and grown an empire with very audacious goals year on year, and is on track to do over $1 billion in sales this year, I was doing it differently. This was attracting the means necessary and seizing that opportunity to play it big, knowing that the Universe would provide the way.

One day later, after an email came through confirming the meeting with Ryan, the money for the NYC trip appeared in my bank account via another means. I got an unexpected bonus payment from a previous employer that I had forgotten all about. I hadn't even counted on getting as I had put it fully out of my mind. But the money arrived nonetheless, as if drawn to the fun of it all.

If that's not meant to be, I don't know what is. I couldn't believe it.

What I learnt from the $7,000 meeting

I had faith, followed the intuition the Universe gave me and cleared the way to allow once unobtainable experiences to flow into my life, but then I needed to trust and take action.

Seize the opportunity, even if it seems odd, farfetched or out of reach. Nothing changes unless you do.

Connect back to your *why*. Why are you doing this? What is the driving force and motivator behind it? Could this new experience lead to new and interesting roads? Could it open life-changing new doors and be the exact right thing that you need to do to get to the next level, or transform your business, or make that contact? Take a moment to gather perspective and bask in the knowledge that you could be one call, email, click, promotion or meeting away from that big break that transforms your business and helps it go stratospheric.

Think about your legacy. What do you want your life to be like? What experiences do you want to have? When you're lying on your death bed and you're looking back, do you want it to be full of regrets or to be able to say, "I went for it," "I owned that fucker," "I did it." Time is ticking away, every second is one you won't get back, and it is an illusion to think that opportunities will come when the time is right, the time is never right, it's about what you make of them when they do come that counts. Don't wait for perfect.

How bad do you *really* want it? Are you sure that you really want it? I mean, you say you do, you talk about it all the time so put your money where your mouth is. Are you willing to fly across the world for a 1-hour meeting in the hope that it will offer more value than you're currently able to gain in your present circumstances? Are you willing to follow the signs that the Universe has been putting on your path for you to follow, even when they look like gigantic, scary, inconvenient, unknown, reckless risks? This is a test of faith. Believing that your purpose and your goals are worth achieving and you won't stop until every stone has been upturned and you have become the lion.

When we put it out there, the Universe will follow. I realised from this experience what Tony Robbins means when he says, "everything you want is on the other side of fear". Fear is just energy and if you overcome it you are transferring energy into joy. There is also value in the ability to say "no" to your mind and tell it how you want to feel about a certain experience or thought. Once you reach this level of control over your thoughts then fear becomes something to move towards not hide from. And I'm not talking about legitimate fears like running across a train track or seeing a stranger in a dark alley. I'm referring to overcoming those fears that you know you should be focusing on, deep down. The ones you know you should address but keep putting off, like making that cold call, quitting your dead-end job, ending a damaging relationship, pitching to that big shot client, doing the community event, going to the out of reach interview, and having that difficult conversation with a loved one. When we take action, the Universe will move to support us.

CHAPTER 7

TIME MANAGEMENT & OUTSOURCING

"Being busy is a form of laziness – lazy thinking and indiscriminate action."

Tim Ferriss

THIS CHAPTER IS dedicated to one of the most important parts of overcoming challenges and making it happen. In it, we will take a look at the aversion you have to outsourcing time-consuming, low-value tasks and how to go about this, so that you have the time to redirect your energy to bigger and more meaningful activities, like transforming your business from being good to great.

I'll also give you the frameworks that I used to ensure I became a high performer and could gain control over how I both allocated my time and operated my daily routine.

Effective time management is one of the most fundamentally life-changing aspects of being the Lion that there is.

Learning to manage your time and what to focus your attention on requires discipline and commitment. It isn't easy, but once mastered, the rewards are so vast that we need to make sure we have this stuff nailed early on. I'll let you into a little secret: time management is the number one thing you can do to outperform your competitors. I'm talking about how you can approach and structure your day to squeeze the absolute most out of it.

This is about outsourcing the tasks that are holding you back and getting super clear on where you need to be focused so that you can allocate time to the things that make the difference. You get it, this is important. Let's quit this introductory waffle and begin, after all, time is of the essence.

> "Discipline is the bridge between goals
> and accomplishment."
>
> Jim Rohn

Zone out all distractions

Now I want this book to be as hard-hitting and game-changing as it is both personal and relevant to overcoming the struggles and big challenges. That's why I don't want to sugarcoat this, it requires an absolute commitment to your goals. This means working weekends and locking yourself in the office after your day job every night for months on end and working on your side hustle. It means making this the norm, not the exception.

I do this regularly. I will check into a hotel on a Friday night and you won't see me until check-out time 12pm the next day. In these hours, I am anywhere between **creation**, **conditioning**, **certainty** and **connection**, depending on what I need. I have worked weekends for 5-6 years now and it's amazing what you can achieve in the personal development and growth space – the books you can read, podcasts you can learn from and the ideas that will pour out of you, as you build and create the vision for your life.

The main goal is I am giving myself what I need in order to stay focused on my mission. This could be planning and reorganising the chapters of my next book, preparing for a life-changing interview, building a digital course, or getting some shut-eye.

My schedule during the week will dictate whether I need this time and what its purpose will be.

Unclog your diary

Now I want to ask you a question and it answer honestly, I will know. Do you sometimes do things for other people that you don't care about that much because you think you have to?

Let me give you some examples to make it easier to answer. Do you go out for after-work drinks when you really don't feel like it or attend random functions just because they are on or hold off doing something you know you should?

I'll be frank, all of these things are holding you back. In order to get your game face on and be the Lion, it's important that you are clear on what's important and what will give you the momentum you need to accelerate towards your dreams.

I want you to prove it to yourself. Think of something that's achievable, yet off limits because it takes at least 10 hours of concentrated work. For example, rewriting your CV, completing an online course, setting up a website or online store, selling your belongings on eBay to raise funds or booking tickets and planning that trip South Africa. That kind of task. We all have something on our list.

Now, have you got the task in your head? Are you imagining it?

Right, I want you to commit to ticking this off 7 days from now. To be a goal crushing machine, to be a lion, it requires that you put all the small stuff on the back burner. It means you adopt habits that will take you further and push you to your limits because that's what inspires growth and expansion.

I promise you that once you start crushing your goals and making the slightly impossible happen, you will start to expect more from yourself. **Remember that your only competition is you, and you are competing with what *you* are capable of.**

One way to build confidence is to get closer to what scares you. So, if going to South Africa, setting up your online store, recording your podcast, investing in your future, finding the right partner scares you, it's the right thing to do.

Once you get used to overcoming challenges on a regular basis, challenges that you once thought were a stretch will become very achievable. You will test your challenge muscle by using it. Just like going to the gym, it will get stronger.

To achieve in big ways, you need to do things that might seem strange, like checking into a hotel in your home city. But it's not about the hotel, it's about getting quality time to invest in the planning, strategy and thinking that's required to work with unstoppable force.

High performers' time management hack

Have you ever met someone that you would consider to be a higher performer? Did they just seem to be able to do everything all at once?

The reason is because they knew which tasks are important and therefore what to prioritise and what to ignore and outsource.

High performers are high performers because they have eliminated everything that doesn't serve their goal and is categorised as a time waster.

This allows them to have a sixth sense when it comes to the important tasks. They can fully tune into what's going on around them and remain open and on top of the changes. Being highly effective is much more important than being busy.

Let me bust the myth that being busy equals being an efficient and high performer. It is not the number of tasks you personally attend to that makes you successful, it is the choice and distinction of which tasks you choose to apply your skills to that does.

Being able to take time out and step away from the business is VITAL for success. It goes hand in hand with results and creativity. High performers are comfortable with making decisions and have absolute focus, conviction and a commitment to the end goal.

But knowing what to prioritise, especially when everything changes all the time, is not always easy...

Get busy with the Eisenhower Decisions Matrix

This little matrix might not look like much, but when you are in the thick of it and your brain is going at a million miles an hour with all the tasks that you need to complete, a love-in with this guy may provide you with much-needed clarity on what's important. Remember, as I covered in chapter 1, if you aren't sure of your priorities, you are likely to spend your resources inefficiently.

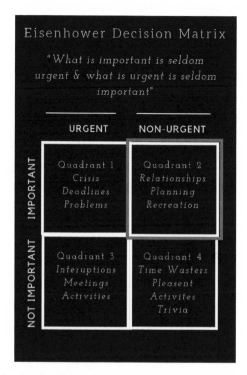

This matrix simply divides up all your tasks into one of 4 quadrants based on the level of importance and urgency. The principle behind the matrix is that focusing on the items in the **important non-urgent** category will allow you to spend time and energy on those items that will produce maximum results before they become important and urgent.

To start with, focus on completing the important urgent tasks, do the important but not urgent tasks later, outsource the urgent non-important tasks and completely get rid of the not important non-urgent tasks. Banish these non-important non-urgent time wasters from your life.

For example, of the items listed below, which do you think goes into what box?

1. It's coming up to the end of the year and you know you need to do a review your annual sales strategy for the business.

You know it's the right thing to do as it will help you be more effective and capitalise on successes from this year.

2. Your friend has just announced on Facebook that they are moving to a new house.

3. You have a deadline coming up for an important client project at work in 2 days.

4. You're required to attend a call with the London office once a week for an hour and a half. You aren't sure why but it's 'the done thing' and everyone else does it so you don't want to rock the boat. You don't contribute much as it's not relevant to your department.

Answer:

No peeking if you haven't given this at least 60 seconds thought.

1. This would go into the important non-urgent box because it is strategic work that will help you assess the strengths, weakness, threats and opportunities, as well as devise a plan of action for the year ahead. This will help you to deploy resources effectively, understand the trajectory of the business and avoid the pitfalls because you know what to look out for. Ultimately, this is where your focus should be. By taking the time to analyse the results and optimise for greater performance, you are able to outmanoeuvre the competition and build a business that is prepared and ready for the future.

2. This would go into the non-important non-urgent box. A go-getter like you doesn't have time for Facebook, you've got way more value creating shit to do. Ignore it and congratulate them later.

3. This would go into the important urgent box. A deadline of this nature for a valuable client is career-defining and should be dealt with immediately. Time pressures like this, if left unaddressed, need to be managed ASAP.

4. This would go into the non-important urgent box. Calls like this have a way of appearing in everyone's diary.

If it's not adding value, then avoid it like the plague. You have better things to do with your time than sitting twiddling your thumbs on a call that doesn't involve you, just for the sake of it. Your time is valuable. You are a creator. Go create.

I have broken down the classifications with some extra examples below to give you more of a sense of what I mean and where tasks should be allocated.

Important/Urgent – The action here is to *Manage*

- Deadlines
- Problems
- Crisis planning/fixing
- Pressing issues
- Putting out the fires

Important/Non-Urgent – The action here is to *Focus*

- Product updates
- Strategy and prevention
- Review of results
- Relationship building
- Planning
- Recreation

Non-Important/Urgent – The action here is to *Avoid*

- Frequent interruptions
- Distractions
- Calls
- Meetings

Non-Important/Non-Urgent – The action here is to *Eliminate*

- Facebook
- Procrastination

- Time wasters

- Some emails

- Junk mail

The key thing to this being a success is your ability to distinguish between how and where your time and attention is allocated currently, and where it should be directed.

This is fundamental to the art and science of making it happen, you need to be able to decide which box, items and tasks should go into. This must be done on the fly, at speed, in the midst of everything else that is going on around you.

As you are more than aware, the world is not a static place, things change, and as such we need to be able to reprioritise when an item moves from the non-urgent/important to the urgent/important, paying careful attention to this shift is where the high performers excel.

So next time you are in the thick of it and the world is pulling you in a million different directions, pull out your Eisenhower Decision Matrix and start categorising all of the tasks at hand. I know it can seem counter-intuitive to stop work on ticking something off your list and take the time to stop and organise your to-do list, but trust me, it's a game-changer

In order to have time, we must create time.

It may seem simple, but it often gets overlooked. When you add up the amount of time in a day that we spend cleaning, washing, cooking and attending to admin there are a good few hours that can be salvaged. Yes, it costs money to outsource these tasks and there will be some of you who have a mild aversion to the thought of paying money for something that you can do yourself but trust me, this is nothing compared to the wasted opportunity that you are saying goodbye to by not pursuing your dream. Quit siding with reluctance to change and embrace it. This is your new life calling; come and get me, Lion.

Here are a few of the different examples of tasks you can outsource:

- Washing
- Ironing
- Finances
- Investments for retirement
- Payment of bills, accounting, bookkeeping
- Cooking
- Cleaning
- Dry cleaning
- Driving
- Childcare
- Food purchase and preparation
- Holiday planning
- Booking travel
- Organising parties
- Gardening

Here are but a few of the ways you can outsource these tasks:

- Food delivery services
- Concierge Services
- Babysitting
- Automated payments
- Helper services
- Cleaners
- Uber

We are so incredibly lucky, the world has never been more abundant than it is today. Connectivity to the internet and the rise of start-ups means that you can outsource and automate practically anything. There are so many apps that can help you outsource anything.

Are your views on outsourcing outdated?

Let's be clear, this is not about self-indulgence or thinking that you are above doing the task yourself. And I don't mean you should give up the tasks you enjoy; maybe ironing is your way to destress in the evening or balancing the books yourself helps you sleep better at night.

Optimise your life and improve your time management now by removing the tasks that don't serve your big goals and just outsource them. This goes hand in hand with ensuring that you strategically position your life to focus on the important things, so you can get the most out your time on this planet.

Each and every day that ticks on by is another one that you aren't going to get back. Why shouldn't we aim to live our best lives?

A few decades ago, the world looked very different, and with that came some views about what you can and can't do yourself, what you should and shouldn't do and how you should be proud to take care of business yourself. People judged those who outsourced, deeming the act as a wasteful, gluttonous and irresponsible.

This mentality emerged from a time when things were different, opportunities were different, there was economic depression, extreme lack and much hardship. It was a post-wartime mentality in which digging in and doing absolutely everything and anything mattered greatly.

However, the world has advanced now, we are in times of huge abundance and beliefs such as these no longer serve us, in fact, they hold us back.

Beliefs that we should do everything (ironing, cooking, cleaning, website design, investment, video production) ourselves actually limit us because they cause us to focus time on the wrong things and motivate our actions from a place of guilt, or self-righteousness for making another person do it, or we feel we don't deserve to live 'the good life'. The truth is you are only hurting one person. YOU! And, as a result, you are denying being of service to others by developing your greatest gifts.

"If you deprive yourself of outsourcing and your competitors do not, you're putting yourself out of business."

Lee Kuan Yew, First Prime Minister of Singapore

This is a trap that most start-up/entrepreneurs fall into, thinking that they need to take care of or be good at everything. Remember, it's not your job or responsibility to be good at everything nor will you be. Learning to delegate and outsource should be your greatest virtue. This is your responsibility. If you're a fashion designer who is terrible at accounting – don't beat yourself up about it, get a bookkeeper and focus on what you're good at!

You need to make peace with beliefs that were most likely passed down to you by your parents. What's wrong with living as fully as you can?

Get rid of the guilt

You don't have to do it all. Where did this idea even come from that outsourcing indicates a self-indulgent, lazy and wasteful character? It likely stems from the era of our grandparents or great grandparents back in the 1900s when the world faced drastically different circumstances than it does today.

However, as we are well aware, the world has changed rapidly over the past century. In years gone by, it was frowned upon to outsource a task that you could quite easily do yourself, especially in times of severe austerity, like during the war. Back then the ability to be self-sufficient was very important. Being thrifty and hands-on was a required skill for survival during this era because many faced a constant struggle to survive.

We have inherited this mindset, which affects our ability to adjust to the vast abundance of the world that is readily available to us. This is because our parents raised us with the lessons that they learned from their parents, who did an amazing job of pulling together in times of economic depression.

The reality is, real wealth comes from inside. Real wealth is the love you feel for your spouse, self-love, living your purpose, the freedom to choose, and the knowledge that you have the ability to achieve anything that you put your mind to.

The pattern of guilt-driven action described above is not chasing the dream. It's rooted in the same belief as the lack or scarcity mentality (the voice that says 'if you want a job done right, you must do it yourself'), or the judge mentality (the voice that says, 'I am not good enough unless I do all the tasks I can possibly do' or 'I am not enough unless I have the latest BMW').

But let's get real for a second. Your time is valuable. You are enough, and you don't have to do it all. We have an unfathomable opportunity to be alive at this present moment with the advances and innovation that have taken place over the past few decades. There has never been a better time to begin living your purpose and to give the gift of your talents to the world by serving others (not getting bogged down with the tasks you don't enjoy). Your mission is too important not to outsource elements. This shame and guilt around not being in control and not doing all the tasks is holding you back from activating your higher purpose, especially true at the most challenging times. If you are up against it and the chips have not fallen in your direction, you need to outsource like crazy to claw back your most valuable resource, your time, so that you can focus on what you do best, what you were put on this planet to do.

Put yourself first

To flip the switch on the guilt-driven pattern, you must start putting yourself first and get comfortable with taking care of yourself. It's tough, especially if you came from a strict household where there's a lot of shame attached to putting yourself first.

Why do it?

It's because you must take care of yourself in order to take care of others, and to help others flourish, you must be on the same path yourself.

It's not selfish to put yourself first so that you can be the very best version of yourself and provide the very best example for those you love. Mastin Kipp says, "The greatest burden for a child is the unlived life of a parent." He suggests that the greatest gift you can give them as a parent is to be an example of how to live life fully aligned to your purpose. If you have kids, this can be a difficult one to contemplate and put into action, but it is true. By being an example of a life well lived you are setting them our children up for success, as you are teaching them how to approach the world with curiosity and explore their own unique talents and gifts.

Understand that by letting go of some of the tasks and allowing yourself the opportunity to perform at a higher level, you are one step closer to playing it big.

By outsourcing tasks such as the ones listed above, you claim back time in your life to do more of what you love and give more.

It may not come easily but stick with it. Each time you feel doubt, remember why you are doing this.

- To help others
- To give your gift to the world
- To be the very best YOU that you can be
- To live life fully
- To be a shining example to the world of what is possible when you let go of the guilt and focus on love

Your time is precious

Now that you have this time you've gained by outsourcing, you must guard it like precious treasure. There's no point freeing up all this time to spend it watching season 8 of *Game of Thrones*. This time is yours to use wisely.

To begin with, ensure that each day you spend at least 45 minutes immersing yourself in an activity that grows you mentally, such as:

- Listening to audiobooks (I love audio because you can do two things at once, like workout in the gym, and double up my output)

- Inspirational books (biographies of people you admire, self-help, stories that pique your interest)

- Online courses

- Lectures

- Thought-provoking and inspirational events

- Podcasts

The reason I am prescribing this mandatory 45 minutes is that by focusing on growing the mind, you open yourself up to new realities and possibilities. Using your time to increase your understanding of what is possible for you is like going to the gym for the mind.

Get as close as you can to the world that lights your fire. Put yourself in the same circles of people who are going places where you want to go. This time is for you. Do this consistently, every day. Like F45, this is 45 minutes of success training. Treat this as your most scared sanctuary. Above all else, use this time to get inspired and move your goals forward.

The zone of fulfilment

I'm not stopping yet, not until you well and truly get the picture of how important time management is to achieve your goals and live your vision of life.

Finding time to do the things that truly matter to you is number one.

What you focus on is what you'll get more of. For example, if you focus on lack, you'll get more lack, and if you focus on abundance, you'll get more abundance. If you're serious about getting more out of your life by discovering your purpose, then direct your focus on the things that matter by creating a plan to achieve.

Tony Robbins has also created a hybrid model based on Eisenhower's Decision Matrix which operates across the dimensions of distraction, delusion, demand and THE ZONE.

The idea behind it is you spend 60% of your time doing things in the zone of fulfilment, much like Eisenhower's model.

Again, in this model the activities are categorised as:

Distraction = social media, Netflix, WhatsApp, Facebook.

Delusion = paying bills, that never-ending to-do list.

Demand = texts, Emails, calls, anything that interrupts the important state of flow when you are on a roll.

The Zone of Fulfilment = you are completing tasks that are important but not yet urgent. Time spent here is where you accelerate towards your life goals. This is where you launch that podcast, open that online store, write that book, develop that course, and share your gift with others.

This is my interpretation.

The way to use this tool is to track yourself for a day. Make a note of all the activities that you do throughout the day and how long you spend doing them. For example, if you use social media on the bus to work for 20 minutes write this down. If you spend

4 hours at the recording studio working on your demo track, log this in.

The idea is to hold yourself accountable as you go through your day so that you get as accurate a picture as possible of how you are spending your time. At the end of the day, go through your list and assign a dimension to each of the activities (either delusion, distraction, demand or the fulfilment zone). Then add up all the time you have spent in each dimension so that you are left with four numbers. Add them to the first row on the column below, labelled Time Spent (minutes).

Next, add up the four numbers. This is the total amount of time recorded doing things. Add this to the Total column on the first row. Then divide each number by the total amount of time. This will give you the percentage of time that you've spent in each zone. Add these figures to the second row for each of the respective dimensions. For this to work, it is not imperative that you put something in each box, the goal is to get a clearer idea of how you actually spend your time. There may be some people that have 50% in the fulfilment Zone, 40% in distraction and 10% in Demand with 0% spent in Delusion.

Daily Time Tracker

Dimensions	Distraction	Delusion	Demand	The Fulfilment Zone	Total
Time Spent (minutes)					
Percentage of Time				*	100%

* Remember the ideal should be 60% of your time is spent in The Fulfilment Zone. If this is isn't you right now, fret not, this is what I'm here for. Be glad that you have uncovered it and brought awareness to this area of your life.

Now that you're aware of how you are currently allocating the time in your daily life, look at the time spent in the Zone. If it's below 60% then vow to change this and repeat the process one week from today.

Reflect back on your previous scores; hopefully, there has been some improvement. It's important to keep checking in on your time management and focus to ensure that you stay on track. Don't be afraid to conduct an inventory of your daily routine at random times throughout the year. It's tools like this and staying conscious of any big changes in your life that might be causing you to deviate from the ideal path that will keep you focused.

Week 2 - Daily Time Tracker

Dimensions	Distraction	Delusion	Demand	The Zone	Total
Time Spent (minutes)					
Percentage of Time				*	100%

CHAPTER 8

ACHIEVE YOUR 10-YEAR PLAN IN 6 MONTHS OR, BETTER YET, NOW

"Don't wait. The time will never be just right."

Napoleon Hill

"YOU SHOULD TAKE your 10-year life plan and ask, why can't I do this in 6 months." This is a quote by Peter Theil, author of *Zero To One*, venture capitalist and the co-founder of PayPal. Just pause for a second and take it in. How would living with this objective at its core impact your life? What would you do differently than you are now? What risks would you take? Resting or relaxing into the idea that we have all the time in the world means we take longer to achieve our goals.

The point of this chapter is to move your thinking from a place of dreams and hopes to a land of conviction and action. If you only take one thing away from this chapter and even this book, it is this, action will be the greatest and fastest route to success. In order to become the fullest sense of ourselves we must act rather than think, and in order to expand into our own reality and push the boundaries of what we know to be possible, we must act.

Taking action, no matter how uncomfortable, leads us to our destiny, and we need to do a lot if. If you have a feeling about something and you are wondering, 'Hmmm maybe that would be a good idea,' just go for it and dive right in. Make that big old call to Forbes or show up at your favourite entrepreneur's hotel and see if they have time for a coffee. We only get what we want in life by having the balls to make decisions and choices.

Needing to catalyse my growth

Moving to Singapore was a transformation point for me. I was surrounded by new and exciting possibilities, new routes to work, new friends, connections and activities. Alongside this shift, I noticed myself being drawn to the path of accelerated growth more than ever before.

For the previous 6 months, I had focused solely on reading all I could about how to build wealth. At the back of this book is a selection of the books that I really recommend if you wish to take charge of your financial future. It was now time to put this knowledge into action.

What brought me to this way of thinking and focused me on the abundance that is available to us all was twofold.

1. I had a strong feeling I could be doing more with my skills, resources and gifts that I had been blessed with.
2. I started to think: what if I died tomorrow, or in 6 months? How would I approach today if I knew that to be true?

If you have thoughts rattling around your brain, take notice of them, because your life-force is trying to tell you something.

The key thing to note here is that this wish to blast your life into a new realm of possibility and abundance should not be confused with panic, anxiety and a rush to do everything you haven't done yet because you might die soon. That is a fear-based mentality. Instead, what we are talking about is an abundance filled mentality.

By thinking of life and its events through this 'What if I only have six months left?' lens we are able to access our habitual choices on a moment-by-moment basis, rather than go along with our autopilot, semi-boring, routine response.

It's like you zooming down a highway then all of a sudden being stopped by a toll booth. This toll booth is your new '6 months to go check in', it allows you to take a brief pause from whatever it is you are doing and check in with yourself to see if the decision you would normally make when on auto-pilot actually aligns with what you really want. The 6 months to go philosophy will push you to make decisions in distinctly new directions. No longer will you have the luxury of coasting along the motorway of life. The benchmark for success has changed. We sometimes rest on our laurels and say things like "one day I'll do that" or "next year we'll go there" but the glaringly obvious point is WHY NOT NOW? Of course, it's easier to stay in your cute 4-bedroom home rather than sell up and move to Africa and start a school, but if not now, when?

Our habits define us, but when you connect to what you actually crave it will not only puncture the routine decision-making process but also help you to question your deeper motivations.

A tool like this will do just that.

A quick note on doubt

Reprogramming our thinking in this way allows us to take giant leaps forward and to move away from fear (such as, 'what if it doesn't work?' or 'what if they say no?' or even 'what will my parents think?') and think about the biggest outcomes of what you might possibly achieve.

So much of our external reality is controlled by what we think internally, which comes from how we were raised and what we were told back in the day when we were growing up.

The silly thing is, we cling to these mantras and messages even though they don't apply to us as adults. We know exactly what our parents would think about spending $4,000 on flights to New York to meet a person they had never heard of and ordering 100 of their books to secure a sit-down meeting. We experience the emotions as if they are right there with us, telling us that we are being stupid or wasting our time, not to mention our hard-earned cash.

What's even more concerning, is that by listening and then acting upon these emotions from our childhood, we are robbing ourselves of the opportunity to find out what would happen if we listened to our intuition.

We have to take action based on how we, as adults, as the people we want to become, would act, and not on how we felt as little kids when we were being scolded for not eating all of our food at the dinner table.

The amount of shame that we carry around as humans is unbelievable, shame about things that don't matter. This baggage can either hold us back from going out, making our stamp on the world and achieving our best lives or it keep us holed up wondering and dreaming in the land of 'what ifs'.

My 'What if I only had 6 months' challenge

We've all seen episodes of *Friends*, where Monica gets her credit card stolen and then gets super jealous of the way the thief is living their life, or *YES Man* with Jim Carrey. These are just movies and sitcoms but they're amazing examples of what I mean by changing your thinking to 'I only have 6 months left'. I would even take this one step further and change your thinking to what can I do NOW! Today.

The more I started to think about this "what if", the more clarity I got. I set myself this challenge: to be all that I can be in the quickest amount of time possible. Remember I was doing this not from the position of lack and panic but from one of abundance.

This meant frequently pushing myself out of my comfort zone; in fact, much more so than I would like to admit. This had an impact on the decisions I made with my investments, the risks I was willing to take, the calls I was willing to make, the conversations I had, the money I was going to spend in order to invest in myself through experiences, meeting new people, and taking my A-Game to 100%.

To stay focused and on track, I made sure I kept my mind coming back to the principle of 'What if I only had 6 months' every day by writing this question in my phone and answering it back to myself.

My 10-year plan in 6 months.

- Become a multi-millionaire in six months ($4m)
- Live the best version of my life (make good decisions, live fully)

I started thinking about the changes I would make if I really did have only 6 months to achieve this. Who would I surround myself with? Where would I spend my time and what would I do differently?

So, this one question about what I would do if I had 6 months left quickly became several. I added notes in my phone whenever I felt inspired or whenever I felt that the Universe was trying to get me to understand some profound and different messaging.

I consistently pushed my ideas bigger and forced myself to go big in my thinking, which spilled over into my actions. I wrote all my ideas down, no matter how wild or outrageous they seemed to be, and ticked them off, one by one. I didn't doubt myself, despite the temptation to delete things that seemed way too ridiculous.

In case you're reading this and thinking that you'd struggle with this, or that you would be instantly embarrassed for thinking that you could do something outrageous and have a temptation to play small, I feel you.

It's not an easy thing to believe and do, but the more you start to think about it, the more your ideas will begin to flourish and the more comfortable you'll become entertaining them. The key is to write them down. It doesn't mean that you have to do every single one right now in this moment, but by committing them to the page, it gets you to flesh out what's inside. As a result, small actions you could take towards actually making it happen will appear.

Like emailing Necker island and asking for the prices to spend a week there next year. Easy to do, harder to execute. Somewhere, deep down, I know I'll get there in my lifetime. I dream of spending a week on Necker playing tennis, wakeboarding and relaxing in the Great House with Branson, sipping on some tea and watching the sun go down. What a day that will be! And I can't wait for when it happens, because I KNOW it's coming. It doesn't matter that the price for a week on the island is well over my current annual salary. What matters is that I've followed my intuition, taken the first step and can now go about making it happen, and with this new perspective. I just might get there in 6 months rather than 10 years.

What changed?

What I found was that in embracing this philosophy, I grew super-efficient with my day job, pumping out 20 emails in 30 minutes (which would normally take me half a day, if I allowed myself to get carried away with all the distractions of life).

This then meant was I was able to choose how I spent the rest of my time, because I was already performing at a high level in my job and didn't need to stay late, which was usually due to compensating for indulging in inefficiencies, like chatting with co-workers, getting coffee, or browsing Instagram. When I got into a rhythm rather than approaching each email sporadically when I felt like it and blocked off half an hour and tackled them all, one after the other, I found I could smash them out, which worked wonders for my sales results and my personal life. Not only was I getting more done efficiently, I also had more time to invest in self-help and my own personal development.

All up, this new way of thinking led me to want to live the best version of my life possible. I could feel the fire burning inside of me, pulling me along to do more, to think bigger and to go for it like never before.

Living like this also makes it perfectly clear what we don't want in our lives, and what's not serving us. I mean if you only had 6 months left, how would you really want to spend it? Going out partying Thursday through Sunday every weekend? Maybe. But you might also want to ditch that in place of trekking through the mountains of Chang Mai, experiencing the canals of Venice by gondola and witnessing the Northern Lights in Norway.

For example, in my mid-twenties I took a trip to Goa in India with my best friend Ryan. It was a defining trip for Ryan because he met and fell in love with his now wife on a beach during our 10-day jaunt. We were both 27, single and up for an adventure. Unfortunately, towards the end of the trip, due to my over exuberance in trying the most dubious-looking steak I have ever seen, I ended up coming down with giardia, which is a waterborne disease caused by a microscopic parasite. It's not pretty and affects your ability to properly digest anything, so I became very weak and severely malnourished.

At the time though, I partied on, not fully understanding the implications of such a parasite. I left Goa a day early to return to London and attend a gigantic house party that was sure to be off the charts in both scale and hilarity, leaving Ryan to woo his fair lady. Landing back in Heathrow after a number of connecting flights through Mumbai and Bahrain I did not feel good. In fact, I felt horrendous.

When I got home, I crawled into bed and slept for two hours. Jetlag had kicked in and the giardia made sure I felt even more terrible. Nevertheless, after 2 hours of sleep, I arose determined to make it to the house party I had just flown 18 hours to attend. It was February, so freezing in London. I threw on my finest Indian clothing, which I had purchased at the Anjuna flea market days earlier, and made my way over to Brixton in a cab.

Arriving at the party, I was so happy to be surrounded by great friends, I put my feelings of malnourishment, dehydration and jetlag behind me and threw myself into the party spirit. It was amazing to be back home and see everyone again. I was able to regale them with tales of our Indian adventures and discuss how Ryan was still in Goa and potentially had a new girlfriend.

The party wound down about 3am, and by the time I got home, I started to feel bad, really bad. Like I had contracted a tropical disease. My head was spinning, and it felt like I was hallucinating. I was so dizzy.

I didn't know it then, but it took me over a year to get better and properly recover. I never gave my body the chance it needed for long enough to get back to full strength. The dizziness was relentless and after tens of trips to hospital for examinations and exploratory tests of my aching stomach, they still couldn't find a cure for it.

What I want to highlight here is that by not listening to my body and pushing myself too hard, even when I was ill, I made the situation worse.

I just couldn't see that by focusing on short-term pleasure, instead of resting and giving myself a chance at recovery, I was taking myself further away from my goals. Had I only had 6-months left to live, well, I would have wasted it.

Looking back, if I could give myself some advice it would be don't eat steak in Goa, and more importantly, sacrifice what you want to do for the sake of your higher purpose. Back then, I didn't really have a compelling purpose, which was part of the problem as it stopped me from seeing how much time I was wasting by not prioritising my recovery and trying to carry on with my life like I was invincible. My focus was to party, to be with my friends and to hang out. I'm not saying that's bad, far from it, but had I known how to live a life with meaning, fulfilment and high stakes achievement, I would have been able to use more willpower and improve myself so that I could do more with the time.

And this applies to anything, it could be your friend's birthday party on Saturday night. You've known each other since primary school, and now you do play dates together with your kids. You want to go out and celebrate, but you also want to spend Sunday working on your new music business.

Fast-forward to mid-afternoon on Sunday and you're hungover, watching *I'm a Celebrity Get Me Out of Here* on TV, sprawled on the sofa hungover ordering a pizza from Domino's. You most definitely aren't in the mood to take action on your new recording studio idea now.

Result: no action taken, no progression, no momentum.

Excuses 1: You 0.

Now that's a harsh example because it was a friend's party and it's an easy situation to find yourself in, and trust me I have been there, multiple times. I have put events, parties, nights out, social occasions above all else, for years.

But don't kid yourself, not working on that business idea, writing that screenplay or applying for that UX course is holding you back from operating at your highest potential. Instead, it is keeping you fixed in the same spot, pinning you to the same routines and limiting the action that you can take on producing results.

It's all about sacrificing the short-term temptations for long-term gratification and when you put it all on the line that extra vodka lime and soda doesn't have the same appeal.

When you connect to something bigger than yourself and a vision of how your life could be, or your focus shifts towards who you could help, the drivers that motivate you will move your life in a different direction, towards your purpose.

Sometimes when we know a certain thing is beneficial for us or needs our attention, we hear the nagging in our mind, but somehow drown it out with thoughts like, "Yeah, but I'll go to the gym tomorrow instead" or "I'll stop eating junk food next week." These thoughts rely on you having a good supply of time in the future. But what if that doesn't exist.

I used to have plenty on my list of "things that are good for me, I'll get around to someday," but then something clicked and one day I went straight to my local GNC and stocked up on probiotics. I had heard they were good for you, yet despite knowing this for years that having a healthy gut is important if you want to improve your quality of life, I never did anything about it, even after the run-in with giardia in India. I purchased the most expensive 100 billion probiotics on the market and took them for one month to see if I felt any better. The result was that I've never looked back, and they are now a constant in my daily routine.

When we reprioritise what is important in life, we give more love to our families. We leave work early, hang out with our spouses and enjoy some luxury together.

We can do this because we stop wasting our time and money on things that don't matter and don't support us.

We stop worrying about the future because we are in the present.

The past doesn't matter either, because we only have 6 months left, and we're going to make damn sure that we squeeze every drop of life out of them.

We connect with the world and it rewards us for this. Remember the world and the Universe is a place of infinite possibility, and the energy you put out is the energy you receive. By giving you put out the energy of love, abundance and freedom into the world, which the world will pull back to you in droves. This is why many of the top success coaches will tell you to give freely.

Just try it. When you spot the opportunity to help or give, even in a small way, go make a difference and see how your life changes. Remember, it's about a way of thinking. The more we can tap into our life-force when playing big and be connected with the Universe in this way, the bigger we can play.

CHAPTER 9

ACTION HERO: SIR RICHARD BRANSON, "SCREW IT, LET'S DO IT"

"Life is a hell of a lot more fun when you say yes rather than no."

Sir Richard Branson

Meet Richard

Richard has clearly done a heck of a lot during his 69 years on planet Earth. Kicking off his entrepreneurial hot streak at the age 16, Richard now constantly tops the list as one of the 100 most influential people in the world. He's got a breadth of experience across multiple industry sectors, tenacity in business, and more importantly, a deep understanding of the most pressing issues that challenge society today. We can learn from Richard's approach to problems and how he tackles adversity by living life to the fullest. Richard's life is packed to the brim with adventure, philanthropy, solid business decisions and some really epic parties.

He bases his philosophy of 'screw it, let's do it' – spoken like a true billionaire – on finding opportunity in a problem, taking the risk, doing it anyway and bringing fun to business. You too can apply this simple yet effective philosophy to everything you are going through on a daily basis, in the relationship you have with your spouse, girlfriend, boyfriend, gardener, cleaner, even the cashier at the supermarket. Bringing the fun into the situation literally transforms the world around and will light you up inside.

In this chapter, I will breakdown the secret to Richard Branson's success and how he lives a fulfilled life. I will also give an example of how I've applied this mantra to my own life and share a few ideas on how you can adopt a similar approach. This chapter is fundamentally about learning to overcome your fears, finding new ways to solve problems and pursuing opportunities so that you can reach your greatest potential in life.

Richard's philosophy

The reason I have chosen Sir Richard as our action hero is the outstanding number of business ventures he has under his wing (Virgin Group 400+), as well as his record-breaking feats, being knighted for his services to entrepreneurship by the Queen. The plethora of organisations and people he has helped, inspired and changed is remarkable.

Screw it, let's do it

When it comes to taking action, we could all take a page out of Richard's book sometimes and say, 'screw it, let's do it.' This isn't a philosophy based on throwing caution to the wind and going for it whatever the outcome; rather it is about finding innovative ways to achieve bolder outcomes, which are sometimes daring and calculated. Richard is always pushing the envelope just that bit further, expanding mankind's mark on the world and allowing us to think big even when the situation (like space tourism) is a relatively unknown frontier. This type of attitude to decision making is one that I want you to take note of. By exploring ideas, you are giving them the space to evolve and take on a different form, which gives the Universe the opportunity to provide in ways that would seem incomprehensible if we relied on just logic alone. By welcoming the challenge rather than pushing it away, avoiding it or seeing it as an opponent, you are taking calculated risks which use fun as a lever to create bigger and better outcomes on multiple levels. This philosophy in itself is innovative. In a world of practicalities, we need a presence that pushes the boundaries and explores the fringes of current possibility. My hope is that you will take a moment to reflect on how you could approach the situation differently when you're faced with your next big challenge, and how you can will the outcome into existence by saying, 'Screw it, let's do it.'

The key takeaway is that when you are faced with a problem, obstacle or an adverse situation you would rather not be in, such as your flight getting cancelled when you need to be somewhere for a really important meeting, you need to consider what would Richard do. He'd most likely pool everyone together who'd missed the very same flight and charter a private plane using the collective funds (like he did in the Caribbean, pre-billionaire days). It's about thinking outside of the box for new solutions that are possible but seem so out there that they aren't normally explored. When you tweak one element of the decision-making process (like pooling the funds of a hundred people to make it affordable) and then say, 'screw it, let's do it,' you can overcome the problem.

Richard's approach to problem-solving

A key part of being a problem-solving whiz is being able to imagine potential new ways to meet the objective and produce outcomes, rather than getting caught up in the drama of the immediate annoyance of the cancelled flight, for instance.

By tackling the specific route cause of the problem with a fun and inventive solution (e.g. getting a group of people together to solve it as a collective) you can meet the challenge head-on.

If you look at what Sir Richard has achieved so far in his lifetime, it's incredible. He's gone from failed attempts to sell Christmas trees to selling budgerigars, to starting a student magazine in 1968, to creating a record label, to trains, to airlines, to cruises, to holding numerous Guinness World Records, including both the first trans-Atlantic and Pacific ocean crossings in a hot air balloon, to buying an island and turning it into a magnificent luxury resort. Now Virgin Galactic is moving into space tourism by offing private flights into outer space! And that doesn't even begin to cover all of it. There's philanthropic work with The Elders, working with various nations for causes he believes strongly in and supporting his family with their endeavours.

Sir Richard is an astute businessman, he has a way of making business decisions at the right time that capitalise on underlying market dynamics, as well as address a consumer need to improve a particular product or service far beyond its current capacity. He is also a maverick who is willing to go all out in pursuit of his vision. The Atlantic balloon crossing caught his eye, not only as an interesting challenge and adventure, but also because it provided a vehicle to raise awareness of the Virgin brand and, more specifically, Virgin Atlantic. *"We needed to come up with fun ways of promoting the airline, getting Virgin on the map,"* he explained[6].

> But I believe the real secret to Sir Richard's success is his ability to say 'yes' to life.

If you spend time studying Sir Richard, it's clear that his ability to say, 'screw it, let's do it', to the opportunities, even in the face of tough decision making, has made him successful. For example, when he sold off his Virgin Megastores to keep his other venture, Virgin Atlantic, afloat. Sir Richard applies the "screw it, let's do it" philosophy to help him problem solve. He is willing to wrestle with ideas, find a way through the mud and the dirt, and forge on when many others would give up.

He has made the tough decisions by looking at life through the lens of what would be the most fun and what he could get away with. This doesn't mean that Richard is a rash or flippant decision maker, or that he makes decisions lightly, far from it. He takes time to weight up all the options, looking at all the information and hearing out his expert team. However, the thing he does above all is listen to himself. He trusts his own intuition and is willing to take responsibly for the outcome. When he says, 'screw it, let's do it,' he has accepted and made peace with all the possible outcomes and is willing to play the odds that it is worth taking the risk, as when he broke the world record for hot air balloon flying. Just two

---

[6] *Don't Look Down*, Netflix, 2016. https://www.netflix.com/title/80141261

days earlier, a Japanese man had attempted the same thing and tragically died.

"Screw it, let's do it" is committing yourself to find a way forward. This might mean calling up Nelson Mandela and pitching him the idea to start a community called The Elders, then jumping on the next flight to South Africa to continue the conversation, or doing whatever it takes to persevere in the face of really challenging stuff. You might sit there and think well that's easy for him, of course, he's got piles of cash and friends in high places, and, and, and… Quit being a victim and get real. Sir Richard built his business skills from the ground up and he uses the same fundamental principles of being open-minded, seeing the possibility in things, taking calculated risks and looking for the fun to be as successful today as he was when he was first starting out.

Don't make decisions based on fear

Before we start to dig into this too deeply, you need to know the enemy of this process is fear, so let's get that guy out the way first…

If we can transform how we interact with life, the real question is why do we hold ourselves back and limit what we are truly capable of?

It's a thoughtful question that stems from how we have been conditioned in society. We are told from a young age to fear anything that is out of the norm. We are taught to fear and reject that which deviates from standard practice or goes against the grain.

This means testing out new strategies or following our passions gets, at the very least, muddled or, at the very worst, inhibited completely. In essence, we are taught to play it safe.

What Sir Richard has consistently done is treat life like it's an adventure and look for ways to take the unconventional, less trodden, unpopular route, even if it's sometimes unpopular, in order to activate his passions and marry them to new, innovative ways of doing business.

If you take a look at human history and think about living way, way back, the skillset that was required to survive was vastly different to what is needed in the world today, but we still carry around those same protective traits and habits, even though they are not essential for survival anymore.

I grew up in Nottinghamshire, England, in a small town located 3 miles outside of Sherwood Forest, home of the legendary heroic outlaw Robin Hood. Robin's claim to fame was that he roamed around Nottinghamshire stealing from the rich and giving to the poor, wooing his fair lady, Maid Marian, and duelling with his arch nemesis the Sheriff of Nottingham. You might have seen the Walt Disney version where Robin is played by a fox, if that helps jog your memory.

The skills that would have been required to survive back then in the 13th–14th Century, during Robin's day, were horse riding, building fires, archery, hunting, and conforming to the King's rule was the accepted practice.

If you did anything other than learn these skills and abide by these laws you were ostracised, like Mr Hood, and forced to live in the Major Oak (a large Oak tree found in the centre of Sherwood Forest that is rumoured to be Robin Hood's home).

Of course, Robin's philosophy was in direct contradiction to that of the King, i.e. 'take from the rich and give to the poor, so that might also have had something to do with it as well. But the point of the message was go along with the norm, know your place or face being banished as an outlaw.

Today, we still hang on to the very same survival skills that we have had held for thousands of years. These mental schemas and ways of thinking, even unconsciously, hold us back from achieving what we are capable of. The anxieties, the fear and baggage hold us firmly in place, not wanting to push too hard or too far.

I have come to believe that deep down the root cause of fear is love, or specifically, our fear of not being loved.

For example, you may have a burning desire to run your own business or to quit your day job and travel the world, but *wanting* to do something and *doing* it are two very different things.

What holds us back is fear, fear of the unknown, fear of looking stupid, fear of losing money, fear of not being good enough. Fear, fear, fear, so many different forms of fear! But it all boils down to one thing, and that is the fear of being rejected by others or ourselves. I am taking this one step further and suggesting that this ultimately stands for fear of not being loved by ourselves. If you want to go stratospheric and put what you're truly capable of out into the world, you'll need to summon the courage to make bold moves that see you overcoming your fears time and time again.

Tim's steps for conquering your fears

Step 1: overcome doubt and fear

Developing strategies to overcome sluggishness, doubt and fear is one of the most important factors to progress. If one strategy doesn't work, then try another, and then another, and another. Keep going until you feel your fire build inside of you until it's about to burst out of you.

1. **What would Richard do?** Remember Richard Branson's 'Screw it let's, do it' approach to life? How could you apply this motto to the situation and fear you are feeling right now?

2. **Take a deep breath**. Remember the randomness of life. You are spinning around on a tiny planet in this massive universe worried about X (e.g. my new job, my finances, my health), breathe deeply and remind yourself that it will all be OK.

3. **Focus on something you appreciate.** I do this every time I'm nervous and anxious over an upcoming business meeting, event or have to face something that I consider to be a big deal. Each time I have to overcome this and need a quick boost, I think of how lucky I am to have Levi and Sandra in my life and that I get to go home to them tonight. Redirecting focus away from the thing that's causing you stress and on to something that you appreciate it an excellent way to transform your perspective and quickly overcome the feeling of fear.

4. **Move your body.** Studies and research show that you can literally change the way you feel by changing how you position your body. If you're fearful, sit up straight, imagine you are a lion, push your shoulders back, your chest out and walk proudly. You might not feel like a lion, but this is a proven method of reducing the power that fear has over you. A subtle change in your physiology changes your psychology and the chemicals that your body releases.

5. **Smile.** By smiling you active the release of the feel-good neurotransmitter's dopamine, endorphins and serotonin which are natural chemicals produced by the body and heavily correlated with success.

Doing these steps might not seem like much, but they will program your mind and body to achieve success through better decision making, being courageous and overcoming your fears, doubts and worries.

Now you can go and create; create through the love that you give out to the world. Through your belief in other people's dreams, plans and goals. Give by supporting others and adding as much value as you can to the present moment.

If you are looking for a new job but feel anxious and frustrated, don't fall into the trap of focusing on what's not right, e.g. the current job. This actually creates a whirlpool of doubt, which sucks you further and further in. This is a massive time waster. To counter the pull of this whirlpool you will need to change the strategy. Play that song that fills you with joy over and over on repeat. If that's not hitting the spot, get out for a run. Still no fire? Treat yourself to a massage or help someone worse off than you.

And finally, if all of the above doesn't work for you, **'Don't be afraid to try what you're not qualified to do.'** This is from Tim Ferriss[7], the self-help guru, lifestyle coach and bestselling author of *The 4-Hour Work Week*. I'll admit it, I absolutely love this one. It gives you an ultimate license to go for it on any scale. It's limitless. Keep this philosophy in mind when you encounter your

---

[7] https://www.tonyrobbins.com/podcasts/the-tools-of-titans-tim-ferriss/

next roadblock, or an unbelievable opportunity presents itself. Then go for it.

> "If somebody offers you an amazing opportunity but you are not sure you can do it, say yes – then learn how to do it later!"
>
> Richard Branson[8]

Step 2: recognise your landmines

The second stage is learning to cope with the reality of the situation as it is, learning to thrive in an environment that feels like it's full of minefields, pulling you back, keeping you fixed on the spot not knowing which way to turn for fear of being blown up.

The reason that landmines feel so restrictive is we can't control where they are. This lack of control leads to learned helplessness, a psychological condition where the subject accepts their fate and gives up trying. Instead, they accept the negative situation as their only option. By opening your mind to the potential size of the opportunity rather than focusing on impracticality, fun is given room to breathe.

The way to remove the landmines is to begin with a brainstorm. Here you need to look at the situation as it really is (not how it feels in your head but how it is in reality).

Start by focusing on the problem, get clear about what's working, what's not working and what could be better.

- What is it about your current situation that could be better?
- What is it exactly that makes you tick?
- Go deeper, what's hiding under the surface – is the problem really your boss?

It's important to keep in mind that when you get a new job or enter a new situation, you are still you – you still have all the same problems and hang-ups, so it's better to figure out why you are feeling a certain way now so that you can take steps in the future to feel differently. Otherwise, you will get

---

[8] https://www.virgin.com/richard-branson/y-yes

frustrated when you're sitting in your new job feeling exactly the same way about it as you did in your old job because you've moved a problem rather than solved it. You have removed your landmines.

> Adversity is painful, can shock the life out of you and it sucks, but it's also an opportunity for growth if you seize it.

Sometimes the situation happens in such a way that there is literally no choice but to move forward. The only option is to learn how to deal with the landmines by carefully removing them and disarming them. These experiences of growth can transform us into the people we want to become.

Just like diamonds are created under pressure, humans who go through hardship change. Those who can take something fundamentally hard and turn it to their advantage have a gift. It also helps you to connect with others and see inside when you have been through something tragic that you never thought would happen in a million years, or when you have conquered a problem you once thought impossible. After that nothing can hold you back.

By being the one who creates joy in other people's lives, you are operating from a place of gratitude. It's pretty awesome that by doing something rewarding, you can also help yourself.

Step 3: Cultivate creativity and fun

The way to do this is to move through the ideation phase; these ideas could be potential solutions but to understand if that is the case, you must get to the stage where you are taking actions, like a scientist in a laboratory you need to experiment.

First, get as many ideas out on the page; throw them out there, no matter how random. If it appears in your mind, get it down there. By opening your mind to the potential size of the opportunity rather than focusing on impracticality, fun is given the room to breathe.

Try bringing the *screw it, let's do it* philosophy into your own life and apply it to your ideas. Try all of them and then figure out what works.

Here are some strategies I use to inspire **creativity and fun** in my life:

- **Get a Massage** – this clears the mind, relaxes the body and increases the creative thought process

- **Listen to Spotify** – I have a set Be The Lion playlist* filled with uplifting, emotion-creating songs. I will often play one song on repeat for as long as it takes, 10 or even 20 times, until I reach a state where ideas are firing and I am itching to express myself on paper, take action, and be of service to others. *You can find this playlist on my website www.tcastle.net/bethelion

- **Running** – rhythmic motion interrupts the normal mental and physical state and produces endorphins

- **Brainstorming** – fill the page with all your crazy, wonderful ideas. Get a plan and then work out how you will achieve each one of your goals. This will bring more control back, reduce fear and increase your go-getter attitude.

- **Learn something new** – climbing, body pump, salsa, swimming, basketball. By stimulating the mental muscle, we force the brain to form new neural pathways as it adapts and changes to different stimuli. Neuroplasticity, which is basically our ability to change our thought patterns, is strengthened when we challenge ourselves with new activities, like skiing or boxing, that our brain isn't used to. So mix it up. Not only is it a great way to meet interesting people and make new friends but it will also increase your mental agility, making you sharper and more on the ball. You'll find that with all of the recommendations in this book, there isn't just one benefit, it's likely that by adjusting on one dimension you'll also experience benefits in multiple other areas of your life.

- **Meditate** – I struggle with this one, but I know that a high proportion of the world's most successful people build in mediation or mindfulness as a part of their daily routine. In any given day, they find time for it. Therefore, although I personally find it challenging to prioritise time for meditation, I understand if they can do it, with everything they have going on, then I really must make it a priority. The reason meditation has become so popular isn't because it's a fad. It's been around for thousands of years, but the benefits are only just becoming widely documented to the mainstream. Meditation acts as a mental reset allowing you to let go of the external world and tap into your deep stream of consciousness. In this state, you are able to connect more deeply with your core. Benefits range from experiencing a greater sense of self, less stress, decreased cortisol, improved ideas, increased confidence, more centeredness, connection to the Universe, increased gratitude, happiness and love. And that's just to name a few; mediation is really a gift to yourself.

- **Smile** – at everyone, like a maniac. Do it, you'll see how your life changes. A smile is a gift, so if someone flips you off, walks into you, pushes in front of you or ignores you, rather than getting in their face, try approaching the situation with a smile. It's a small and simple change, and the benefits are all yours, baby.

- **Do the opposite** – if you never go for a swim, go for a swim. New horizons, new experiences shake the mind, body and soul out of the set patterns of standardised, predictable routines. By doing the opposite, you'll shock yourself out of the pattern. For example, if you're single and never ask people out, today is the day, my friend, it's happening. Take the bull by the horns and ask that hot guy at the bar out for a coffee.

- **'Enjoy the absurdity'** – I'm stealing one from the Tim Ferriss playbook. He says that in order to enjoy life, we must sometimes create the absurd. Tim is one for doing this right. He will sometimes go to the airport wearing a white cowboy hat, just because, or lay down in the middle of the floor at Starbucks to check out the complete and utter look of bewilderment on people's faces as they come in. In doing so, Tim is breaking the cycle of monotony and creating his own fun through absurdity. I can fully imagine the looks on faces and how I would feel. You can't help but laugh at the situation yourself, even if you're the one who created it.

- **Writing** – after doing any of the above, I am usually in a state where ideas are flowing. This could be a little while after. I frequently wake up at 3am and write for a couple of hours (and trust me when I say this, 'No, you won't remember them in the morning.') or on the train. It doesn't matter when the inspiration hits you, just get your words down on paper. The ideas that bubble to the surface are absolute gold. Make the effort to jot them down. These ideas are your way forward!

What I learned from Richard

Screw it, let's do it.

What I believe Branson has got so right about life is that he sees the challenge as the fun. He can make a difference to a product or service by going after it with all the intensity and passion of someone with a mission, instead of getting annoyed with the status quo. He matches passion with solutions to solve interesting, big problems.

Sun Tzu, the famous military strategist and author of *The Art of War*, said, '*Opportunities multiply as they are seized.*'

This is incredibly true. When you take action in the direction of your ideas, opportunities begin to flow. As you grow by taking actions that align with who you want to become and follow your instincts, the size of the opportunities that present themselves increase too. The key is to be aware that they are opportunities in the first place.

The perfect job could be staring you in the face, but if you are so focused on what's not right with your current status instead of being determined to try new strategies, you will fail.

As mentioned before, if one strategy doesn't work, try something new. Don't keep on applying tactics that haven't worked, move on! This is no time for hoping. As Tony Robins says, *'Life happens for you, not to you.'* This applies to both the bad and the good.

Who knows, not getting that job may lead to you getting an even better one. Being dumped leaves you free to find your soulmate. Losing the house gives you the skills to rebuild. The best financial experts in the world reckon that if all the money of the top 1% was equally distributed to everyone else in the world, it wouldn't take long for the once wealthy to get it back again. This is because of who they have become while learning how to master the art of making money.

The same goes for every situation you are facing. If you want to learn from the best, find someone who's been through it before and ask them how they overcame it. Write down what they tell you and then reflect on how you can apply their lessons to your own life. If you feel drawn to a certain city, person, lecture, event or company, make the call and follow this instinct.

This is what it means to live in the present, to take advantage of your very humanness. By listening to your inner guidance, you end up closer to where you should be. Branson knows how to operate successfully because he trusts himself. He's an opportunity spotter, he listens to himself and seeks out what he doesn't know from other wise individuals.

The next time you are facing a super-sized challenge that you would normally shy away from or think is impossible, remember to go back to the drawing broad and throw all your ideas out there, no matter how whacky or crazy they might seem. You never know, they might just be the one that gets you saying, 'screw it, let's do it,' allowing you to continue where others have stopped and charter unknown territory for yourself. This action alone will build new confidence within you and unlock a deep resolve that, when it comes to tackling big problems, you are a force to be reckoned with. Go make it happen! I KNOW YOU CAN DO IT!

CHAPTER 10

DECISIONS AND ACTION

"Decisiveness. The ability to make a decision in the face
of uncertainty."

"If you get in your head, you're dead."

Tony Robbins

YOU GOT TWO quotes for the price of one there, but I love them so much. If you get in your head, you're dead. How right is that? (I am aware of the irony of starting out a chapter on decisiveness with two quotes that I can't decide between but sometimes it's just a two quotes kinda chapter.)

OK, now that you've got a clear picture of what it is you want to achieve from the previous few chapters. You've also learned the importance of making time to work on it and how to push past your fears that are holding you back from success. Now it's time to take on this beast of a topic: decision making. Once you're on board with the idea of working towards your goal, you are inevitably going to face some tough decisions. I don't want that to put you off, so I'm going to share some superstar techniques for effective decision making.

When I first heard about the power of decisiveness, I was listening to the Tony Robbins podcast, and also reading *Think and Grow Rich* by Napoleon Hill. When you listen, read and immerse yourself with enough of what the best minds in the world say, you'll see that certain techniques, lessons and key themes crop up time and time again and continue to resonate, reverberating across the world by showing up in other philosophies and mantras.

It's funny, I didn't realise it, but I have been using an amazing strategy that both of these gurus share. **This strategy puts you front**

and centre of your own life by giving you no way out. It just has to happen. There is no other option, therefore you will make it so.

The captain's story

Both Robbins and Hill draw on a famous story that goes like this. Long ago, a captain of a ship was sailing with his men to fight in a battle for an island. They were entering enemy territory and had no idea of what they would find. All he knew was they were significantly outnumbered, 5 to 1, so it was going to be a tough battle. His men knew this and he felt that if there was a way out they would lose due to the impulse to retreat. Any split or divide in the mentality of his small army would make them weaker and they would operate less like a unit, and so lose the battle, first mentally and then physically. To have any chance of winning the attack needed to be coordinated, tactical and strong, just like the mind of his men. In effect, the battle would be won or lost in the mind.

So, what did he do?

When they made it to the shore and were about to go in search of the enemy, he gave the order to burn the boats! There was no way back. They would either succeed in battle or die. Either way, his men now fought with more passion, strength, vigour, and their minds were focused only on winning.

This strategy gave his men no way out, so that they had to win at all costs, and fight all night if that's what it took. As a result, they took action with every ounce of their strength, wit and might.

There are times in life when we need to 'burn the boats' and back ourselves into a corner in order to operate at peak performance or just change the record. For instance, you might be working in a job that you loathe and have tried to find alternative employment, but the days, weeks and months have kept dragging by, one laborious second at a time, so you end up feeling like you're on a hamster's wheel, well and truly stuck. If this is you, it's time for a radical change, and this sometimes requires you to burn the boats, giving yourself no choice but to succeed and find a new path. For example, you could just hand that notice in.

Can you think of a time in your life when you've burned the boats?

If so, good on you because you're more entrepreneurial, creative and go-getter than you might have thought, and you're already operating on timely principles that have been passed down and retold by the world's best personal development coaches for decades.

If you haven't burned the boats before, maybe you're facing a situation right now that is getting out of hand or is simply unmanageable. Think about how you might burn the boats and then rip that band-aid off (caveat: if it makes sense). What I am offering here is not a quick fix, but a strategy that you may not have realised is an option. It may not be your preferred option, but sometimes, in order to move forward, we need a push that only comes from putting ourselves in the firing line.

As the subtitle of the book states, this is one way in which to begin the journey of overcoming big challenges and making it happen, but this is not the journey. This is just the catalyst for starting the journey, overcoming the big challenges and making it happen is still ahead of you, and that is what we need to figure out.

Case study: my visa crisis

I once had a major job interview lined up at Facebook, Singapore. When you make it through the first couple of rounds of interviews at Facebook, they do what they call a full circle, This is where you spend 4 hours being grilled by different members of the team and take a tour of the office. It gives you an opportunity to get a feel for what life would be like to join the company. It's an effective way for you and them to get to know you, plus it's way more convenient than taking random half days off work to go to the 'dentist', aka Facebook interview rounds 2-6 every other week.

When I heard the news that Facebook wanted to take me through to the full circle round, I was pumped. I knew deep down that this was it. The only thing standing between me and the job was 4 rounds back to back, and perhaps an interview with senior leadership. I was up for the challenge. In fact, I relished it. The HR process at Facebook was impeccable, keeping me informed at every stage of the process and preparing me for what was about to happen so that I had all the information and could prepare to put my best foot forward.

As it got close to the interview day, my excitement grew. I was 2 days away from the full circle Facebook interview and I was currently in the United States on a business trip that had annoyingly been scheduled the week prior to my Facebook sojourn in Singapore. I needed to get back to Australia and take my flight to Singapore that Facebook had laid on.

I was all ready to board the plane back to Sydney via LA when I got to Denver airport, but I was told by a rude and less than helpful attendant at the check-in desk that I wouldn't be boarding it as I didn't have a valid Australian visa. I'm not sure if you've ever had to deal with a check-in attendant with an aversion to being helpful. I certainly hadn't had the pleasure until then. They made it ultra-difficult to engage in any basic communication, avoided all eye contact and would not acknowledge the fact that I was stood in front of her asking how I could fix this situation.

"Can I just take the flight as far as LA and then sort the visa when I arrive?" I asked, with an upbeat tone, unwittingly inviting no response from the attendant.

"Am I able rebook a one way to ticket to NYC or LA, any of the major airport hubs, it doesn't really matter where I just need to get on a flight tonight…"

"What if I don't fly to Australia? Can I please book a flight to Singapore?"

Nothing, nada, zilch. She did not utter one word or flinch from her concentrated stare at the screen in front of her.

She was clearly having a bad day, but this level of disregard was just plain rude.

My blood was starting to boil, and I began to get frustrated. I hadn't prepared for this. In my head, I'd gracefully fly back to Sydney, stop in at home, say 'hi' to my family, take a quick shower, head out to catch the flight and smash the Facebook interview in Singapore.

A few quick calculations told me that I had to leave Denver that night in order to get across to the other side of the globe in time. I needed to head either to the West Coast or East Coast, it didn't matter which, I just needed to get myself to a bigger airport, but this interview-blocker was in my way.

There was one thing I did know, I had to make that interview. There was no other option, it just had to happen. There was too much at stake. I had waited all month to get this in the diary and it could have implications for my career.

Cue, the change of plan.

When life doesn't go the way that we had envisioned it, we must engage our resilience and resolve to make it happen. For me, this involved a series of decisions followed by swift action. I started my adventure by calling practically everyone at the United Airlines call centre and was passed from person to person as the flight departure time inched its way closer. The long and short of it was that there was little they could do without the proper authorisations at my end, as it was my company that had arranged the flight, and with it being a Friday night, I was out of luck on that front.

This led me back to the check-in desk. There were three attendants on duty that night, including the interview-blocker. As I moved further down the queue that snaked around the departures area, and I got closer to the desk, I realised I was playing attendant roulette. Would I get the interview-blocker again or would I get my shot with someone fresh? This would dictate my fate.

After what seemed like the most painful wait in the history of waiting, and with only 45 minutes to go before the plane to LA took off, I was in a race against time to get someone to care about my situation and help me book a fight out of there.

Boom, a couple on my right completed their check-in and I reached the desk again and began running through the same conversation with a different person, this time describing what had happened. Ah, refreshing. Hopefully, this time I could look forward to an understanding soul, a little witty banter perhaps, surely nothing could be as bad as what I had previously experienced. I was wrong.

Nope. This guy was just as bad and did little to understand that I didn't care so much about my Australian visa situation right at this second and all I wanted to do was get to LA or New York pronto. The visa situation had thrown them off guard and distracted them, just like when you give a dog a new toy. I was getting nowhere, again. Then, after another 8 minutes of trying to wrangle any useful information out of him an older man, who'd been listening in to the whole conversation, swooped in and took over.

He instantly smiled and said, "I'll take it from here." He quickly ran me through some options but there was only one that made real sense, which was for me to repurchase my seat on the plane and pay an additional fee so that I could board and go direct to LA rather than carry on to Sydney. I was really up against the clock now. By the time all the transactions, cancellations and rebooking had been processed, I had less than 25 minutes to go through security and make it to the gate before take-off. This was going to be tight!

After spending a small fortune on another seat to LA (don't ask why I had to buy two seats, it had something to do with not being able to change the first ticket because it was connecting on to an international flight), I was told by the older gentleman that I probably wouldn't make the flight as it was about to leave. Oh, now you tell me, upsell, cross-sell and then leave me high and dry, hey. I felt completely used.

This information led me to super-charge my mindset. I found myself running full-pelt through the airport like a man possessed, or the kid from *Love Actually* (if you haven't seen that movie, it's the part where Liam Neeson's son goes charging after a girl at Heathrow Airport in a last-ditch attempt to say goodbye before she flies to America). As luck and determination would have it, when I got to the gate the plane was still there. I only made the flight because it was 30 minutes delayed (and thank God it was). After all that, I don't think I could have faced a night in an airport hotel waiting to go through the same ordeal again in the morning. LA was going to be a welcome sight, or so I thought.

When I arrived in LA, it was gone midnight. I got my bags and headed straight to departures. I wanted to get on with the next leg of the journey. There was a huge storm in Miami, and it was disrupting many flights. I reasoned that it would be best for me to try, if possible, to get out of the US in case the storm started to come in my direction and I ended up trapped in the City of Angels. Not that it would have been a bad thing. Under different circumstances, I would have been excited to be there but all I wanted to do right now was to fix the current issue and start making my way to Singapore.

I phoned Sandra again and gave her an update that I was now in LA and looking to go direct to Singapore rather than come home first. She agreed that this would be the best way forward, we were in this together. At times like this, when you feel alone and like the world is out to get you, or at least trying to throw your plans off course, it's important to connect with people who will understand. I also let my best mate Richard know what was going on. Richard has always been one of those guys that is great at finding information fast on the internet. No sooner had I told him about my predicament, a flurry of news and weather updates started to come through on my WhatsApp. Richard was now my point person on the storm and with that delegated I could now focus on locating the Cathay Pacific check-in desk. It was now 12.30am and I could see from Skyscanner that there was a flight leaving at 1.30am bound for Hong Kong. This was it! This was my ticket out.

I made my way up to the check-in counter and asked how much. It was around $1,500 which I thought was very reasonable for a last-minute deal to the Far East. However, there was a problem. Cathay had run out of meals for the flight and that meant that they wouldn't sell me a ticket on the plane. "I'll go without a meal," I protested. After some back and forth with her superiors it was unfortunately a no. They were unable to let me fly because it was against their policy and as an airline, they could get into serious trouble for this. Realising I was getting nowhere, I figured I would just come back in the morning, so I needed to find some place to get my head down for a few hours and get online to figure what the next best plan of action would be.

I relented, and then I made a mistake. Instead of asking how the airport worked and where I could find the nearest half-decent hotel, I just walked off assuming I would figure it out. As check-in desks and other counters (like the information desk) started to close down for the night, the airport turned into a dead zone. It was weird, and I felt frustrated and alone.

I had never been to LA before, but the airport is massive and inconvenient, you need a car to get around. After walking and walking for about an hour I realised it was a bad idea to try and search for a hotel by myself.

I remember finding a 7-Eleven and stocking up on vitamin drinks, a random selection of chocolate bars and a banana as if I was gathering supplies for an epic marathon across a dessert. My mind was beginning to panic. I was tired, drained, fed up and unsure how I was going to keep my energy up to find a hotel and figure out my next move.

Eventually, after returning to where I had started, I found a shuttle bus outside that was going to the Hilton. By this point, I didn't care what it cost. I had some points in my Expedia account and thought to hell with it. I needed to put my head down on a pillow and sleep.

Once at the Hilton LA airport, I checked in, had a shower and started to feel a little more human again. It was 3am now and I still felt on edge, like I couldn't really concentrate until I knew I had a flight booked that would take me to where I needed to go. So, I powered up my laptop and went about booking the exact same flight, only 24 hours later. This would get me to Hong Kong the morning before the interview and then I'd jump on a plane down to Singapore and it would be show time! I reasoned that this would give me time to get my energy back, focus on writing the presentation that I still had to prepare and go through some final interview preparation.

I woke up the next day around 12pm and felt much better about my situation, although I still had this nagging feeling that this wasn't what I had planned. It was deeply frustrating because I had been so looking forward to seeing my family after the week away. I spent most of that day on the phone trying to figure out how to resolve my visa situation and figure out what on earth had gone on. In the heat of the moment, I had been completely preoccupied with getting myself to the Facebook interview on time that I hadn't really let the gravitas of the visa situation sink in. As it turned out, it was quite a big deal.

Australia takes visas seriously, and even though I had been living there for the best part of half a decade, I had inadvertently flown out of the country without informing them. I was in the process of applying for a partner visa and one of the restrictions of this is you must inform immigration when you want to go aboard. Once you do this, they give you a 90-day window to be outside of the country. As long as you're back before this deadline, you can go in and out as many times as you like. I had done this 93 days earlier for the family trip to the South of France for a friend's wedding and because this was a quick work trip that had popped up out of nowhere, it hadn't even crossed my mind to check.

I was 3 days over the deadline, which had automatically triggered immigration cancelling my work visa. This meant that not only was I now unable to work but I was also considered a tourist. This was a problem. I had an apartment, I was the sole breadwinner and I had a family to take care of. This made the Facebook interview even more high stakes now. If I got the job, then none of it mattered, but if I didn't, then what a mess we'd be in.

It was now Sunday afternoon and I was due to fly out that night. The interview was first thing Tuesday morning, and being a Sunday, there was nothing I could do to contact immigration or my visa agent as Australia had closed for business. As I counted down the hours, I tried not to think about all the potential outcomes and focused instead on only things that I could control, like eating, sleeping and writing a damn good presentation.

Finally, it came time to fly and I felt a wave of relief as we took off. There was heavy turbulence throughout the flight, but after going through so much it didn't faze me too much, although I do remember thinking I didn't want to die this way. I could imagine the headlines. "Man tries in vain to make Facebook interview, beats all the odds but got stuck by lightning en route." Luckily, 22 hours later, I landed in Singapore via Hong Kong ready to face the interview panel at 9am in the morning.

After a few hours of the finest sleep ever in the world's most comfortable bed at the Marriott South Beach Hotel, thank you Facebook, I woke with a sense that I should have a suit jacket to really make that all-important first impression a cracker. The problem was I hadn't brought a suit jacket with me.

It was 7.30am and the interview was in 90 minutes, what could I do? Shops in Singapore don't open until 10am. *Nah too late, lah. What else? Come on Tim, think of something!* I turned to my network and texted a friend who lived in Singapore, somewhere, who might possibly be my jacket size.

It was now 7.50am and the jacket had to happen. Jetlagged as I was, my focus and the fun of it was kicking in. It was an adventure, and I had done everything possible to make it happen so far. I wasn't going to let not having a jacket stop me from progressing. I convinced a passing cab driver to take me where I needed to go. He already had a booking but couldn't turn down the extra $20 bucks I was going to pay him to get me to my buddy's condo on the other side of town.

Man, oh man, was that a cab ride. Going at 120km an hour around the streets of Singapore in the morning traffic, it was like being in a Clint Eastwood movie, while I headed further and further away from where I needed to be for the interview.

The Facebook offices in Singapore are right next to the hotel that they had kindly put me up in, yet there I was travelling at the speed of light in a mad man's taxi to a friend's house that I had never been to before. There was now just 53 minutes to go until I needed to present myself for inspection at Facebook HQ and I didn't know how I would get back there.

After what felt like much longer than the 10-minute drive I had been promised, I arrived, thankful to be alive. Now I needed to find the right condo. My friend lived in what seemed a jungle of them. There were towers everywhere. I mean multiple towers; left, right and freakin' centre.

As much I was enjoying checking out the palatial views and gigantic infinity pool, surrounded by the most impeccably manicured palm trees, I hadn't taken this risk just to leave empty-handed. I wanted that damn suit jacket. On went the data roaming, always a painful cost when jetting into a new country with no local sim, but time was money in this instance and needs must.

After running around 3 towers before I found the right one, figuring out how to work the intercom system and navigating the stairs, I arrived at my friend's front door. I had made it. Not just to get the jacket, but from Denver to LA, then reprogrammed my whole trip, before heading to Hong Kong and Singapore, and now I was even going to look the part as well. Could this day get any better? Well, yes it could. With no idea of how I was going to make it back to the centre of town, Chris and his wife Al offered me a ride in their Uber, which was picking them up in 4 minutes and going right past where I needed to be. Boom! All I needed to do now was nail the five hours of interviews ahead of me, and we'd be home and dry.

When I walked into the Facebook reception, I couldn't help smiling with glee at all the adventure and the hustling I had done to get myself there. It would have been very easy to give in, stay in LA a couple more days and figure out what the hell was going on with the Australian visa but no, not today sunshine. This interview was going to take place, it just had to. I had done everything in my power to make it happen, and I was going to give it my best shot. The visa drama would have to wait.

The modern-day captain

Now let us come back to the present day. You might currently be toying with the idea of starting your own business, but don't want to take the plunge for fear of failure.

The question is how hard would you try to get your business off the ground if you had no choice? No alternative? What would you be comfortable doing if you had no choice?

> What kind of life do you think would be more interesting to live? One where ideas stay as ideas, or one where they are put in play and taken for a spin?

Sometimes, the only thing holding us back from making a decision is the fact that we are too comfortable. We have the comfort of choice, the choice not to do it and to blame it on waiting for the right moment.

Sometimes, the way forward is about backing yourself into a corner in order to force yourself to do something, to make a decision and go after your future potential with all you've got. And don't kid yourself here, not doing anything is still making a decision. It's not doing nothing. In fact, it's going backwards. You are deciding to tread water, which in today's society means you are being left behind.

I'll give you an example, I want to give seminars, presentations, and workshops to help people optimise their daily habits and routines, understand what steps to take next to launch their ideas and to put together a plan for hitting their goals and needs. I know the workshop concept has the ability to help people. I know I can create the content, and I know I could create the time to develop the material if I wanted to.

But I'm still holding myself back. I'm 97% of the way there, but 3% is keeping me from pulling the trigger. Is it because I feel I need to know more? Maybe. Is it that the truth though? No.

I've read enough, talked to enough gurus to put something meaningful together, even if it's just a skeleton framework.

I'll tell you what it is. It's the fact that I need to balance making the decision to do something with the fear of failure. I need to be OK with making a commitment to creating a workshop, trying and then failing. Maybe I'll put 50 hours of preparation into my workshop and no one will turn up. Maybe it's the pressure of family, friends or colleagues expecting greatness and possibly judging me from the sidelines. It's scary putting yourself out there, even if your idea is great.

And that's really the reason why I'm not at 100% yet, but one day soon I will get the extra 3% it takes to put the workshop in motion, but for now, I'm in a holding loop.

Even though I know my workshops could be the ticket to financial freedom, I still haven't pulled the trigger. If I lost my job today, this is what I would do – create success workshops, seminars, webinars and give lectures in universities. I would write the life optimisation course and then use my sales skills to sell it.

So here we have something I am passionate about and believe would add massive value and generate a substantial income for my family, yet I'm still sat here stewing over small questions, like 'How it would begin?' and 'Am I qualified?' It's laughable really, and of course, I now know I need to take taking my own advice, get to it and create the damn workshop J. By telling you, I have given myself no option to go forward. I've burned my boats.

I give you this example to show you that we can all be just 3% away from our big break, but unless we become committed to making decisions and acting on our intuition when we get these game-changing ideas, then we will always stay at level 1.

I take my hat off to you, my fellow creators. This is it; this is how the game is played. You've got this far, but if there is a burning desire you carry around with you, I encourage you to burn the boats. No, I implore you to do it. You owe it to yourself, don't let the time slip away. Time on this beautiful world is a mirage, it's not a given. As we get older, day by day, we move closer to the end.

> Don't let your gift get buried with you, get it out into the world and give others the opportunity to experience joy created from your gift.

Perfectionism vs. test and learn

"He's so mad, but he won't give up that easy? No.
He won't have it, he knows his whole back city's ropes"

Eminem, Lose Yourself

The other issue that holds us back from making decisions is feeling that we need to have it all figured out perfectly before we start. This is a contradiction – you will learn by doing it, you cannot know it all before taking the plunge. Testing something and learning from that experiment is how you create knowledge. The most successful apply the test and learn theory to everything, they don't wait for perfect, they get writing, get emailing, get into action mode.

Taking action is 100% THE BEST THING YOU CAN DO FOR YOURSELF.

The illusion is, 'If I consider this for one more week, it will be even better', and then one week goes by and we still haven't done anything to move it forward, or we make excuses.

If you've ever watched *The Apprentice* in the UK or the US, you'll have seen ten young corporates parachuted into different tasks each week. What the show is really testing is who can get out there and make it happen, who's got the initiative, who can listen to a brief, understand the objectives and get into action mode to create sales. It's through the application of this test and learning a methodology that huge gains can be made, and hundreds of meaningless hours saved. Remember what Tony said, 'If you get in your head, you're dead!'

Cultivating an action-oriented mindset is one of the best skills you can encourage yourself to develop. Try to get into the habit of thinking big and taking action in the moment rather than deliberating. Ask yourself what you could do to test it out right now.

As Ray Dalio puts it in his book *Principles*, time is much like a river and it is carrying us forward downstream towards events in our lives. Yet, it's the decisions we make when we reach each of these events that ultimately lead us to experience very different results.

The decisions we make when we reach these junctures are super important. Ray is a big believer and promoter of the idea of meritocracy and he readily encourages his ideas to be thoughtfully challenged. In fact, he has attributed the incredible success of his company Bridgewater (the largest hedge fund in the world, $132.8 billion in assets under management) to this way of dealing with information and decisions. This is exactly how Ray wants it because he understands we can't know everything.

If we can't know everything then we shouldn't get hung up on making a decision, we should consult with people that have differing views to understand how they see the world and then make our choice and move forward, learning from our mistakes.

Don't play small

"Shoot for the moon. Even if you miss you'll land among the stars."

Norman Vincent Peale

If you want to leave your competitors in the dust, then test, learn, and refine as you go. Where most people typically fail is they play it too small, i.e. they only go after a small vision. This inadvertently helps to create the reason why they don't follow through on their ideas, which I will explain in a second.

The next thing they do is migrate all of their focus and thinking towards the problems that they would encounter and need to overcome in order to succeed. These problems can seem overwhelming and gigantic in size and volume and doubt starts to set in.

The problem is it is difficult to get motivated or even started if the underlying goal or vision is too small and the number of perceived problems too large. This is because the overall payoff is not that appealing to warrant the effort. This then stops us from taking action. As you can see, it's cyclical. In this scenario, our thoughts and feelings drag us further down, away from our potential.

In contrast, it's the ones who get started who learn the most. And in life, those who aim for the moon and cultivate a gigantic vision often win big and see their reality change as a result.

There are lessons, insights and learnings that can only be accessed by trying to bring your ideas to fruition. You've got to be relentless in the pursuit of your mission. There is a treasure trove of information waiting to be discovered on the other side of taking action.

The action cycle

In life, the ideal action, results, learning cycle that you want to operate in looks like this…

You are in control of your own life, but you must commit with absolute certainty. Find a path and test it out. Results are born out of decision.

"Life isn't happening to you, it's happening for you."

Tony Robbins

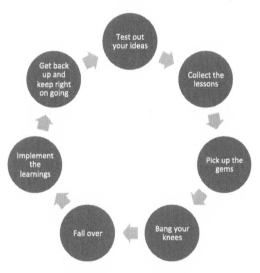

The action cycle

In the world of a go-getter, decision making and action taking are both inseparable and interlinked. It's like they're married, where one goes, the other is close behind. This means that once you've made a decision, you should immediately take some form of action to move your life in that direction.

One of the simplest mistakes people make is to wait too long on sidelines after making a decision without taking any action. This is a dangerous pattern that is to be avoided.

Instead, trust that you're the creator of your life and everything happens for a reason. Take a binding action to commits yourself to follow through on your decision. This could be booking the plane tickets, submitting that manuscript, enrolling on that course, signing that lease or calling that person you know could help.

I want you to fall in love with the cycle of decision making and taking action. May it be a union of joy for you and may you find the strength in its power that's required to open doors and bring you closer to your goals than ever before.

CHAPTER 11

MAXIMISE YOUR STRENGTHS

"The key to success is to fully understand how to apply
your greatest talents and strengths in your everyday life."

Gallup, *Unleash Your Talents*

I AM A huge believer in playing to your strengths. Whether you're naturally talented at something or have spent ten thousand hours practising to reach a level of mastery, your strengths are a core competency that should be maximised. To be great at anything, you need to practice, even if you are talented. Even the most gifted sports players spend many hours practising every day, even if they're world number one. Being aware of your strengths is like getting the keys to the kingdom. Once you know where it is you can move mountains, leverage this all-day long.

Tim Ferriss believes that 'the most successful people usually maximise one or two strengths'. A common mistake is to try and grow skills in so many areas you don't get anywhere with a single one of them. This is about focus.

During an interview for the Tony Robbins' Podcast[9], Ferris was asked which of the top strengths he had mastered had

---

[9] The Tony Robbins podcast: *Talking with Titans* (2016) https://www.
tonyrobbins.com/podcasts/the-tools-of-titans-tim-ferriss/

fundamentally transformed his life, enabling him to move from the dark days when he was contemplating suicide to becoming a super-successful entrepreneur, investor and public speaker with multiple bestselling titles.

His answer holds incredible value, and that's why I want to share it with you today in more detail. I have highlighted a few select segments from this amazing Q&A below to give you a sense of the nuggets of the gold that Tim Ferriss outlined.

Tony: 'What would you say are the top strengths you have maximised that have made your life so much different than back in those dark days?'

Tim F: 'They're all related to asking questions, and what I've realised is that studying questions and improving questions, is improving your thinking.'

Tim F: 'I've become better at asking a handful of questions. Ask absurd questions.'

1. 'What is the worst that could happen? Then going through the process below:
   • Write down what you're considering doing.
   • Make a column, using bullet points, of all the worst things that could happen if you do that.
   • In the next column, write down what can you do to minimise the likelihood.
   • How can I get back to where I am now?'

It's Tim C interjecting here. This is an example (below) of the table to give you an idea of how this works. In this scenario, I am considering a move to Spain.

What am I considering doing?	What are all the worst things that could happen if I did that?	What can I do to minimise the likelihood of this happening?	If each of these happens, what can I do to get back to where I am now as quickly as possible?
Moving to Spain	Run out of money	Limit the amount of money spent, invest, create new revenue streams	Keep my old job open, earn more money beforehand, as a buffer
	Get mugged	Buy insurance, go with a friend, learn self-defence	Move to a new town, buy CCTV, get a dog
	Get sunburnt	Take copious amounts of sun lotion	Buy aloe vera after-sun

2. Figure out 'What are the assumptions and how can I test them? If I'm stuck, or I feel like I've hit a ceiling with something, what are my assumptions right now, including the stories I'm telling myself? How can I stress test them?'

3. 'In x situation, what if I did the opposite just for the next 24–48 hours.'

Tim Ferriss gives the example of doing this when he was his first job, cold calling. He thought what if I didn't do a 9-5 day like everyone else, and started calling offices early in the morning and after work instead?

With this in mind, he made sure he was smiling and dialling by 7.30am each day, and very often get connected straight to the VP's or even the CEO of the company who would answer the phone, circumnavigating the PA. By taking this action, he started to book the most meetings as a result.

This raises an incredibly valuable point I want you all to take note of about questioning how you are approaching a problem or the process.

For example, is this the only way to make sales? Or am I doing this just because it is the norm? What could I do differently to get results?'

Tim F: 'When you ask yourself these types of questions it productively breaks the framework and the lens and everything you've been using to try and solve your problems up until that point, because they're incompatible.

Treat your brain as you would your body, take some time to dedicate to these kinds of practices.

Mindfulness – 'putting yourself in a state where you become more aware of your thoughts and emotions and you can steer them in a particular direction.'

There is so much value in this short 51-minute podcast. I truly recommend that you jump on and give it a listen. https://www.tonyrobbins.com/podcasts/the-tools-of-titans-tim-ferriss/ Tim's books, *The 4-Hour Work Week* and *Tools of Titans* are also overflowing with advice from world-class performers, as well as coping strategies and mechanisms to achieve more from life.

What's your talent?

We each have been blessed with individual talents that can be engaged to their maximum potential if we so choose.

Ponder on the questions below for a moment, giving yourself the time to yourself to investigate and explore with curiosity what comes up. Spend 15 minutes at least on this, and write down what comes up for you.

1. What are your top three talents?

2. What makes you so excited that you willing to give it your all for?

3. What would you do if nothing was impossible?

4. What fears are holding you back?

5. Are they life-threatening?

6. What's the worst that could happen?

7. What action could you take right now to make your vision happen? If you don't know, what would you do if you did know what to do?

The cliftonstrengths assessment

In every job I go into, I always get my team to complete the CliftonStrengths exercise, which is a self-assessment tool designed to 'identify an individual's specific "talents" so they can be harnessed and leveraged for maximum benefit'.

The CliftonStrengths assessment is an instrument made up of 34 strengths (themes) that are categorised into 4 domains (Executing, Influencing, Relationship Building and Strategic Thinking).

It was created as an online assessment instrument by American Psychologist, Don Clifton who was honoured by the American Psychological Association with a Presidential Commendation as the father of strengths-based psychology.

I highly recommend that you take this assessment as a method of mapping out your own unique strengths. Humans are a diverse bunch, as the CliftonStrengths research shows the odds of two people having the exact same top 5 themes are 1 in 33,390,000.

The research has also shown that people who take the test are 6x more likely to be engaged at work, 3x as likely to have an excellent quality of life and 6x more likely to do what they do best every day. That last statistic is the one that stands out for me. If we can get closer to aligning with our strengths, it gives us an opportunity to maximise them and take our potential to the next level.

From a workplace perspective, this exercise not only helps individuals to learn about their own strengths, but it also makes it abundantly clear how the team can get the most out of each other as a collective, which is why I love it

"There is no more effective way to empower people than to see each person in terms of his or her strengths."

Donald O. Clifton

At the end of the exercise, we all go through the results in a debrief and discuss our answers to questions like the following:

- You get the best of me when...

- You get the worst of me when...

- You can count on me to...

Each person then reads through the 29 themes that did not come up in their top 5 and identifies one theme that they wish was more dominant in them or that they envied in others.

This process uncovers incredible value.

CHAPTER 12

PERSISTENCE

"If there are nine rabbits on the ground, if you want
to catch one, focus on one. Change your tactics if you
need to, but don't change the rabbit. There are so many
opportunities in that you cannot catch all of them. Get
one first, put it in your pocket and then catch the others."

Jack Ma

THE FINAL THING I want to teach you about taking focussed action is you have to keep doing it, all the time. When asked what's the most important advice to an entrepreneur, Jonas Kjellberg, co-founder of Skype, answered:

"Commitment, get out of bed, look yourself in the mirror
and say this is going to be the best day of my life, put on
that smile, and try to change the world, because doing
that every day will take you places."

Jonas Kjellberg, Co-Founder of Skype

Persistence is the ability to move forward in spite of the setbacks. It's having a bigger vision for your life and maintaining focus on it so that the bumps along the road don't distract you from the overall picture and direction that you want to go.

It also has to do with connecting to your drive and your ability to see more and do more.

Persistence is having the drive and hunger to follow your map, which is created from the information that is revealed, no matter what it takes or how long the journey.

Persistence pays off

When launching my first book, *The Art Of Negotiation,* I was my own hype man. As I was self-publishing, there was no agent to promote the book for me or get me any media gigs. It was actually part of the whole writing a book experience that I was looking forward to. Given that I work in sales and business development for a living, I couldn't wait to start hitting the phone, emails, and to take it to the streets; whatever it took, no matter how random, I was up for it. Trying out different strategies to get contacts, produce sales or develop opportunities is my bread and butter.

I started out by making a list of all the publications that I wanted to appear in, who I wanted to read my book and where I wanted it to be available.

I sent copies all over the US to titles like *SUCCESS Magazine* for a book review, and then I followed this up with my blog posts, which were specifically crafted to match the style of the these titles and to appeal to their audience.

I emailed, tweeted, tagged, and hustled so that I could try and get my book in front of the decision makers, and it worked.

My objectives allowed me to take action on the things that I wanted to achieve. After getting the email configuration to the editor at a certain magazine or blog, I engaged in a dialogue and moved the conversation forward to see how I could a) add value to the organisation b) become involved and help in some way. Each day, I took small actions to move through my list of objectives that I had written down.

Approaching Branson

One of the people I most admire, both in business and in life is Sir Richard Branson, and I started on my mission to make contact with him back in 2016. My aim was to get a recommendation for my book *The Art Of Negotiation* from him or work with the Virgin brand in some way.

This is what it took to get in front of Sir Richard Branson:

- I wrote down my goal and put together a plan

- 1 x Christmas Card sent to Necker Island sent in December 2016 (deliberate strategy, I know Richard prefers handwritten mail)

- Response received on 4th March 2017 in the form of a lovely email from Amy, his PA on Necker, thanking me. The card had made it! From this, I knew two things: it was possible and the address had worked. I had crossed the void. I was now only one degree of separation away from Richard, and I was closer to making an impact

- 1 x copy of the book sent to Necker Island in search of Sir Richard Branson, April 2018

- Fantastic response via email, received on 23rd July 2018, sent by Hayley, his new PA on Necker. The book had made it and was sitting on her desk ready to be passed on to Sir Richard.

- 2 x copies of the book, plus a personal letter outlining my hopes to work with Richard, sent to Virgin's London Headquarters, April and July 2018

The process and time taken to get a copy of my first book in the hands of Richard Branson: 2.5 years.

Feeling: indescribable.

The lesson here is how important it is to write down what you want to achieve and make a plan to achieve it. Take small actions each day to move your way closer, try multiple angles. Notice I didn't just stick to one strategy. I thought about it at first and decided I would take a long shot by sending a Christmas card to Necker Island. My thinking here was, less mail is probably delivery to the island than the London office; therefore, there the Christmas card or book may stand out more if it reached this destination. I hypothesised that there could be lower barriers to entry, just like Tim Ferriss did when he decided to buck the trend in his first job and make calls during off-peak hours and ended up frequently getting direct contact with the CEOs and owners of the companies. This strategy had the same principle behind it.

Know and remove the blockers

Blockers are negative fear-based thoughts that hold you back. I want you to get out a fresh sheet of paper now and brainstorm for 5 minutes on the topic of your blockers. What is holding you back from great success? What is stopping you from being all that you can be – the most authentic, value creating, badass version of yourself?

You were put on this planet for a reason and you're not helping anyone by not reaching your full potential. I want you to really go for it when you write your list. Don't edit it, just write it all down, free flow, and see what appears on the page.

This exercise is designed to get you firstly into awareness mode and then into action mode. By focusing on the blockers and how you can remove them once and for all, you are strategically moving your plans for world domination forward.

It's so easy to blame others as to why our big break hasn't happened for us yet or fall into victim mode. It could just be because you aren't taking enough action in the right areas or you are holding back because, deep down, you fear judgement or ridicule from your friends and acquaintances.

The reality is, you are giving up on your dreams for the satisfaction of not having to deal with others' opinions. I mean, that is sad, and just plain crazy when you really think about it. You are giving up on your chance to be all that you can be in your one life on this planet, all because you don't have the guts to remove the blockers.

Once you've identified your blockers, the next step is to find solutions. For example, here are some common blockers and solutions to starting a business.

- **I don't have the right tools to carry out the job/do what I need, e.g. a portable laptop** – *solution* – rent the equipment, borrow the equipment, take out a loan to buy the equipment. Get creative, often you know someone who can help, maybe a friend of a friend will have what it is you are looking for.

- **I don't have time** – *solution* – discipline. Lack of time is never the reason. Create time by outsourcing lower priority responsibilities and rearranging your schedule, e.g. fewer meetings, shorter meetings, delegating responsibilities, waking up an hour earlier, going to bed an hour later.

- **I get distracted** – *solution* – learn to cut off the noise, leave your phone in your bag, go somewhere that you won't be disturbed. Train yourself to focus on the task at hand for 20 minutes. You'll find that the more you decide to commit to completing a task, the better you will become at finishing. Carry a notebook to write down amazing (potentially distracting) ideas, record a voice memo, meditate, realise that your distraction is a form of giving up on getting the life that you dream about.

- **My friends will judge me** – *solution* – find a channel to test out your idea away from prying eyes and judgment. By removing the blocker of social judgement you allow yourself the opportunity to move forward in big and daring ways, uninhibited. For example, rather than posting it direct to Facebook, shoot a video and post it on YouTube. Build up your audience, gather feedback, and enjoy the ride away from your friends and family. Find some place to do what you do without holding back due to social pressure, doubt, what your friends and family might think, or filtering what you want to give to the world.

When you are ready, you can introduce your friends and family to your business, content or mission. The goal is to get the work done, rather than stop or limit yourself. There's a magnificent array of channels out there from members-only communities to forums, so just staying quiet about your idea while you test and build.

- **What if someone writes a negative comment on my new blog post** – *solution* – lie down in the middle of Starbucks. No seriously, in order to move past a point of not caring what others think, you need to be comfortable with the uncomfortable. You need to be able to continue on despite the setbacks, and people that would see you fail. When you are truly working on something that is bigger than yourself, the cost of not moving forward is greater than stopping. Now, I'm not suggesting it doesn't hurt a little to get negative, mean or downright ugly comment for all to see, but it is par for the course. Research shows that we need five positive experiences in a relationship for every one negative for it to be considered amazing. When you put your work, ideas, prototype, business and self out there for the world to see, it takes bravery and guts, so it is a daunting experience at times. But that doesn't mean there aren't ways around setting yourself up for a beating. Ignore it, delete it, embrace it, write back constructively and show your strength of character. Inspire others to do the same, be honest about it, report it, own it, post about it. The world is filled with people who have been hurt and are looking for healing. Show them that it happens to the best of us and how to move on courageously, regardless. Then you will have not only developed your tenacity and grit, but you will have also helped another in the process. Let your healing be their healing.

- **I don't have any money** – *solution* – get a loan, borrow from friends and family, reduce your costs elsewhere in your life, negotiate costs, move to a cheaper apartment, as rent typically makes up a large sum of outgoings, hack together a solution and do it anyway. Don't let not having the cash be the reason you never get started, take a second job, create another income stream, rent out a room on Airbnb, there is always a way.

- **I don't know what to do next** – *solution* – find a mentor, someone who has done what you want to do with a great degree of success. This is probably the most valuable advice given in this list, if not in the chapter. Learning from and replicating the steps to success from someone who's been there and done it before in the area you're trying to break into can save you a great quantity of time and money.

- **I'm not a technical person** – *solution* – outsource, go to night school, train yourself via YouTube. My preference is to outsource. This frees you up to focus on other aspects of the business or problem you are facing, such as sales and marketing. There are plenty of sites out their touting services for website design, custom integrations, and technical know-how. Ask for referrals, this goes back to my point about getting a mentor, someone who has been where you are right now. They will typically have a black book of contacts and done the leg work previously to ensure that contractors are vetted and can get the job done. This can save you time and money without the stress.

Ready to find solutions for your blockers? Fill out the grid below (or make your own version of it). Add in your blockers on the left and the actions you could take to remove the blockers from your life on the right.

The goal here is to get creative with the actions that you can take and demonstrate the numerous ways in which blockers can be banished.

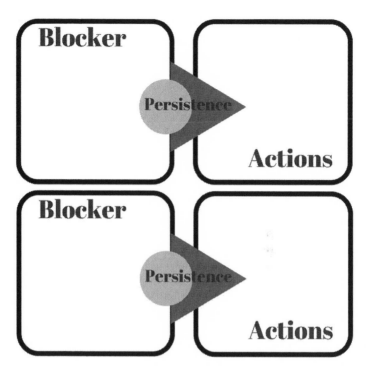

Your blockers and actions

PART 2

CONDITIONING (MIND & BODY)

INTRODUCTION TO PART 2

"I saw the angel in the marble and carved until I set him free."

Michelangelo

WE'VE TALKED ABOUT the benefits of taking action and delved into detail on a plethora of action inspiring mechanisms that are geared to get you up off the sofa, out of dreamer mode and into the ass-kicking goal crusher that you are.

In this section of the book, I'll show you strategies and techniques to condition your mind and body for success. These will enhance your ability to get into your peak state to really go after what you want and draw it closer.

Conditioning your mind and body is a core area that you must master to become the lion. Amazingly, it is often overlooked, possibly because it takes long-term commitment. It's not a quick fix or shortcut but the results are phenomenal. Conditioning does not happen overnight. Much like taking action, conditioning needs to be worked on daily. The attainment of a conditioned mind and body is sustained through daily practice of habits and rituals that leave you effective, alert and ready to spring into action at a moment's notice.

It's something that's taken me years to get the hang of, and I am far from over in my quest to understand, improve and maintain proper conditioning of my mind and body. When I was younger, I disregarded the importance of having a daily mental and physical routine and didn't understand that I could actually achieve more by sticking to such a thing as a plan. I didn't want to spend time working on my mind and well-being when I could be delving into some action. But as I mentioned, this approach is unbalanced. Just like for the lion, the benefits of having a sharp mind that is constantly fed with interesting material and a physically fit body that is in shape and can take advantage of any opportunity at a moment's notice is paramount to peak performance.

I cannot stress enough the importance of being both mentally and physically in shape. This a huge benefit to you as an individual; not only are you more able to tackle anything that comes your way, but it will also have a knock-on effect that spreads across the other areas of your life. When you apply the discipline, commitment and hard work it takes to get yourself fit by consistently working out 3–5 times a week, having a daily mindset routine with primers to help you stay aligned with your vision and aim to be the very best that you can be, it will open you up to see new opportunities and enable you to take on responsibilities and situations you never even thought possible before.

Whilst it is true that I now have a more measured approach to the food I eat, work hard to cultivate a mission-driven mindset and look after my mind and body better, I could still improve. I am by no means an expert in this area, but the changes I have made have been really transformative. I want to show you what you can achieve just by committing to a few simple yet effective changes.

Be warned, this section might challenge you. If you thought you were being pushed into new and unknown situations in Part 1, then that was just the start of it. Get ready to go deeper into the 'be the lion' philosophy and get primed to be our best selves. This is not the time to rest on your laurels, so put down that second biscuit and hold on because we're about to get ripped, both mentally and physically.

CHAPTER 13

MIND AND BODY HERO TONY ROBBINS: FRESHEN UP YOUR MORNING ROUTINE – TONY ROBBINS STYLE

"I can get up at 8am and be rested, or I can get up at 5am and be President."

Jimmy Carter (39th President of USA)

Meet Tony

TONY IS A force, and on top of this, he has business interests in over 30 organisations that do over $5 billion in revenue each year. Tony has little time to waste and so outsources what he does not know about nutrition, exercise, health and well-being to experts who plan his routines. Of course, over time Tony has built up a deep understanding of his own body and its capacity to endure physical exertion and stress. It all starts with the morning routine.

In this chapter, I will breakdown the secret to Tony Robbins' morning mastery and show you how having a consistent daily routine is a fundamental path to success, enabling you to achieve more and staying in tune with what really matters. I will also demonstrate how I have applied these techniques in my own life, as well as the results I've achieved and the pitfalls to avoid, as this will help to transform you into a morning routine machine!

Even on the bad days, and everyone has them, taking elements from this chapter will help you navigate stressful events more clearly. So, get ready to supercharge your mornings...

Tony's philosophy

Ah, the good old morning routine. It's often overlooked. Tony Robbins has revolutionised it for millions of people, but it took me a while to take notice. I didn't think much of having a morning routine until it was pretty much the only option left on the table. I tried various strategiesx to get more energy, from upping my caffeine intake by drinking 3–4 cups of coffee a day, to listening to fist-pumping music and getting a boost from eating sugary cakes. As I am sure you can imagine, none of these worked in the long term; in fact, they made my life worse in all respects. I got fatter from all the cake and semi-addicted to the sugar rush. Mid-afternoons became hard and I started wanting to sleep at my desk, the excess caffeine I was drinking throughout the day gave me heart palpitations and made me anxious, and the music made me view life as a constant nightclub. When we try and apply quick-fix strategies to solve a lifestyle problem, they never work. We need to take decisive, sustainable action.

The energy sinkhole

One morning, I woke up completely knackered. I mean absolutely pooped. The funny thing was I had just had a solid 7 hours the night before, which for the dad of a one-year-old is always classed as #winning.

As I sat on the edge of my bed, contemplating how the hell I was going to tackle the day, I realised I didn't want to continue in this way – always shattered and continually operating at a mediocre level. I could barely make it through the day without falling asleep at the gym or going to bed right after dinner at 7.30pm. And then there were the dark thoughts that you get after weeks of interrupted sleep patterns. I was just surviving, and that wasn't good enough. Working in sales, the energy and enthusiasm you bring to each encounter go a long way to connecting with potential buyers and selling. I needed to figure out how to feel more alive, revitalised and raring to go on a daily basis.

I realised that I wanted more energy, as a human, as a man, and as a person who is only 32 years old. I felt I should and could have more energy in my life.

I totally understood how this energy void had resulted from a combination of the ongoing sleep deprivation that comes with having a child and full-on days at work. Both of these factors together created a sort of rhythmic never-ending roller-coaster.

For months, it had felt like someone wanted something from me every waking minute of my day, which I was more than happy to give. However, I had just started to wonder, what if I can't keep this up?

Enter Tony

Then I got to thinking, who's the most energetic person I can think of? Who's that person that just doesn't stop? Who's older than me but has more energy than the energizer bunny? Of course, Tony Robbins popped into my mind. The guy literally does not stop. I follow his Instagram and he's everywhere all at once, throwing the same amount of dedication, passion and enthusiasm into life, every single day. He's like an omnipresent energizer bunny helping people and saving the world, one fist pump at a time.

I wanted that. 'I shall be like Tony,' I thought.

Visualise Tony

So, for the next few weeks, whenever I felt the energy sinkhole appear or I felt myself being dragged in a million different directions by work, family, friends, myself, and even my mind, I paused and visualised Tony Robbins on stage, giving it his everything.

This brief pause allowed me to connect with the deeper purpose of what I was doing, and by holding Tony in my mind, it also stopped me from going into victim mode. Tony is a big masculine dude. He's also a role model and someone who I admire; someone who would keep me from drifting back into thoughts of 'why me?' 'what now?' and 'why do I need to go?' These were all excuses, basically. Plain and simple, I was wasting my time on feeling sorry for myself, which only perpetuated the very situation I was trying to avoid. Instead, I should have been staying positive, with go-getter phrases in my mind, like 'bring it on,' 'I'M READY,' 'here I come,' and 'I'm going to give it my all.'

Our mind is like the most powerful muscle in our body. It literally changes how we perceive the world, and this controls whether it is a place of inspiration, or a place of suffering and chaos.

Our minds must be kept focused on how we want to experience life. We must become experts at controlling our thoughts, so that each thought reinforces the fantastic life that we want to live. It all starts in the mind.

I would think about Tony on stage carrying the crowd of thousands who depend on him to show up and deliver. If he is flat, deflated or not giving it 110%, the audience will know. He has to have his energy on full beam.

On top of visualising Tony giving his powerful motivational speeches, being the lion on stage, I was intrigued to find out more about him. I did some research into his daily routine to see if there was anything else that Tony could teach me about having an abundance of energy.

A quick Google search revealed that Tony has a plan, and this plan allows him to maintain momentously high energy all day, even with little to no sleep and no stimulants like coffee or alcohol. *I mean come on!* Anyone with that much energy and no coffee must be doing something, right?

At its core, Tony's morning routine comes down the habits he has formed, and his commitment to repeat these strict habits consistently, day after day.

Tony's 3 steps for improving your morning routine

Step 1: Embracing the cold

The first thing you need to do to live like Tony Robbins is to jump headfirst into an outdoor plunge pool after waking up. If – like most people – you don't have one of those in your mansion, you can opt for the cold shower option, whatever you find the most exhilarating and cost-efficient.

Talk about commitment, this guy has multiple homes around the world and each one is equipped to take care of his needs. He is committed to having more energy and recognises how important this is to him in his daily life.

If on the odd day he does not feel like using the pool, he'll jump into his full body cryotherapy tank for up to 3 minutes. This involves stripping down and being surrounded by super-chilled air (which is 150–290 degrees Fahrenheit). Its benefits are said to include improved sleep, pain relief and the mitigation of depression.

The sudden drop in temperature causes the body to react by sending an army of endorphins surging around the body. These affect us the same way as opiates like codeine, morphine and heroin, but are stronger and not addictive; it's like having your own natural pharmacy inside your body.

Endorphins are released at times of stress and fear. If they overdo it, they can leave us an anxious nervous wreck. They are released to help us deal with pain, but they are also present in huge quantities at times of pleasure, like in the throes of hot passionate sex, closing a deal, gambling in Vegas, times of connection and attraction, or when your team is winning the game.

Endorphins are also produced during exercise, childbirth, meditation, controlled breathing and even eating chilli peppers. The hypothalamus is the command control centre in your brain that regulates when you should get a hit of endorphins, just like it regulates when you should eat. It sends a signal to the pituitary gland (the pharmacy) which doles out a dose. This then surges around the body, eventually hitting your brain's opioid receptors, making you feel on top of the world.

When I tried this, I was reluctantly curious. I'll admit that I didn't want to do it, but I wanted to experience the blast of endorphins, so I stepped forward into the waterfall cascading from the shower. It is brutal at first. The cold water felt like ice against my skin and my mind automatically wanted to switch it back to the luxurious warm water again, but as the moments wear on and you hold yourself in place, the body relaxes into it. The mind begins to calm and the water strangely feels less invasive than it did seconds earlier. After a few more seconds, it begins to feel almost pleasurable. Of all the rituals in the book, this is the one I need to psych myself up to do.

One aspect that was distinctly different to taking a regular hot water shower was the increase in neural activity I noticed. My brain felt more creative, more alive. It was like every droplet that hit my head fired up more cylinders, and more synapses were connecting in joyous rapture and frenzied celebration. This I realised was part of the endorphin rush.

I tested it a few more times over the following days and can safely say my body handles hot water by relaxing, which is perfect if I want to snuggle down into bed and go to sleep, but instead, I wanted to feel awake, revitalized and ready to go.

Over the coming days of experimentation, I settled on going for the cold-water option and found that my creative mind awakened again and that I felt more focused and able to seize the day.

I'll let you into a little secret that I know helped me slightly, which is quite possibly cheating. The cold water isn't super cold in Singapore, in fact, I wanted it colder. If you're reading this in Sweden, however, I wish you luck.

Step 2: Priming

After you've had your cold-water blast and got dressed, the 'priming' stage is next, which involves 3 minutes of deep breathing exercises combined with thinking thoughts of gratitude.

For this to have the optimal effect, you need to find somewhere comfortable where you cannot be uninterrupted. Sit in a seated position with your eyes closed. This could be on your bedroom floor, the balcony or even the garden. Just find a spot where you feel a sense of calm. Next, raise your arms above your head and breathe in through your nose slowly, then lower your arms and exhale in a short powerful blast. This practice comes from an adaptation of Kapalabhati Pranayama, pronounced kah-pah-luh-bah-tee prah-nah-yah-mah, which cleanses the respiratory system by cleaning out the waste and promoting the rejuvenation of body and mind. It dates back to texts written in 150 BC and is also sometimes referred to as light skull breathing.

There are multiple benefits to this type of breathing exercise, including strengthening the abs and diaphragm, cleaning out the airways and preparing the mind for meditation and other tasks that might require a high degree of focus. I know what you're thinking; it might look weird to sit there puffing out air like a raging bull with your arms flailing around, but trust me, this stuff works. You not only feel more alive, when you combine it with focusing on all that you are thankful for, you also open up your mind and our heart to the universe. This could be your family, your friends, your money, your life, the sunshine, your pets, your health, or anything else you may be feeling thankful for. This process allows you to attract positive energy and draw in opportunities.

Thanking God or the Universe and generally being grateful for what you have on a daily basis is one excellent way to shine.

After 3 minutes, switch it up and focus your attention on wishing good things for your friends, family, clients and asking for strength. This direct and concentrated process takes a little over 6 minutes in all to complete but has the power to rejuvenate your life and make you feel alive. Give it a go and see how refreshed and energised you feel.

This simple process goes like this:

- 3 minutes – cold shower
- 3 minutes -- deep breathing and thoughts of gratitude
- 3 minutes – of wishing good vibes for others and asking for strength

As Jen Sincero says, 'We're on this planet once, and to spend it doubting yourself and thinking that you can't create what you desire is no way to go, I mean, why not just go the whole hog and see how awesome you can be?'[1]

---

[1] Sincero, J. (2013). *You Are a Badass: How To Stop Doubting Your Greatness And Live An Awesome Life.*

The whole routine is done and dusted, including the shower, in under 10 minutes flat and sets Tony up for the day ahead, no matter what he has to accomplish.

Step 3 Change your state

As Tony says, *'motion creates emotion'*. Tony gets himself into peak performance before a show by changing his state through movement. This includes incredible amounts of jumping, shaking his arms around, fist-pumping and shouting affirmations. If you've ever experienced one of Tony's live courses, like *Date With Destiny* or *Unleash the Power Within*, you'll witness him jumping up and down on trampolines. Tony changes his mental state by changing his physiology.

To give you some insight, Tony does around 50 events a year that can sometimes be up as long as 12–14 hours a day and continues for five days and nights back to back. Dr Jacob Wilson and his team at the Applied Science and Performance Institute measured Tony's body when he was doing one of these events and what they found was astonishing. In any given 12 to 14 hour show, he burns over 11,300 calories, which is the equivalent of 2.5 marathons! In addition to this colossal feat, Tony also jumps over 1,000 times in a show, which is on par with playing 2 full basketball games at the level of an NBA player. And most surprisingly of all, the lactate content in his blood was an unfathomably high 14.1 (4.0 is typically enough to cause most people who are exercising to not be able to speak!). Tony and his shows are electric!

Being in the right state and adjusting your philological response to the world, so that you can produce incredible results, is not just something that Tony talks about in his seminars, it is also something he embodies as a way of life. Tony uses his body to show his authenticity. That's why people can connect to him and will open up in front of thousands of strangers. Tony is a leader. He demonstrates vulnerability and humanity by showing his emotions when listening to the stories told by members of the audience or when sharing stories from his own life. In doing so, he gives others the platform to give themselves permission to be vulnerable too. Bringing this emotion to the forefront is where big breakthroughs can be made. If you get the privilege of being able to attend one of his shows what you'll witness is Tony breaking through boundaries, not just in his interventions but in the way that he conducts himself and the high standard he holds himself to. If you can watch how he adjusts his movement and body to match the situation, it is the work of someone who's attained mastery.

When he's working with a group of top senior executives as a coach, Tony gives the example of a presenter. He'll ask them to change their state of energy to improve their body language and delivery.

When a presenter stumbles it's because they are out of their comfort zone and haven't raised their energy state to meet it. He suggests practising the presentation at the new energy level, clapping, fist pumping, jumping to get in the zone and rock it!

This idea of changing your physical and mental state to meet the circumstance is phenomenally powerful and shouldn't go unnoticed. This is literally gold right there.

How did I put this all together and apply these principles in my own life? What did I change in my life, after exploring Tony's habits, that helped me to turn things around and give me more energy than ever before, and did it work?

In short, the answer is 'yes'. Now every time I take a shower, I am reminded of Tony's routines and the standards of excellence he holds himself to. I realise that if I want to experience the best start to my day, I should nudge the temperature down a few notches and just force myself to do things my mind tells me that I can avoid. Gaining this control over my mind has helped me no end, and I encourage you to find a morning mentor. It may not be Tony, but find someone who's morning routine you admire and stick to it for a few months to see how your life changes. Working in sales, I have incorporated a number of Tony's techniques into my routine. This gets me more primed for action rather than haphazardly hoping that I'll feel up for the day ahead and ready to perform. The system works, if you work it.

In the next section, I share a few more tweaks that I've made that allow me to bring my A game consistently.

What I learned from Tony Robbins

A structured morning routine is the way forward

My morning routine is now the bedrock of my existence, and much of my success in the other 4C areas, like the ability to experience sustainable **Creation** and **Connection**, results from this practice. Even if I do nothing else throughout the day, I always make sure I do my morning routine. My mind and body actually crave it now and I feel disappointed if I miss it.

Instead of rolling over and grabbing my phone to flick through any WhatsApp messages, texts and emails that might have come through overnight, I now take a very different approach.

Every morning, as soon as my bare feet touch the floor, I take a moment to connect with the things I am grateful for in my life before I do anything else. This practice centres me before all the energy depletes and mood-altering thoughts come rushing up (like paying my bills, all the meetings I need to attend, and the emails and calls I need to get through). So, before all the noise starts, I get grateful. I find this helps me to get centred on what really matters.

Honestly, it felt weird at first, just sitting on the edge of my bed and pausing like this. I used to occasionally struggle to immediately come up with things that I am grateful for, but now when I sit there for a few seconds, a rush of answers flood into my consciousness and I am overwhelmed with gratitude. This practice has slowly got easier and my gratitude now flows more easily. I noticed was that gratitude started to show up in my daily life, not just in the morning, and it felt like the gratitude was travelling with me throughout the day. As a result, I began to recognise and appreciate much more around me, such as a smile from a checkout person at the supermarket, the security guard saying 'hello' as I entered my building, the way the sun catches the leaves on the trees, and an abundant sense of just how lucky I am to be alive.

If you're struggling with low energy and want to feel a zest for life again, I recommend that you start this practice every morning *before* you check your phone, *before* you go to the toilet, *before* you do anything. Sit on the edge of your bed and think of something you are grateful for in your life. Then repeat the phrase, 'Good things are on the way, good things are coming my way today'. I learned this from Idil Ahmed's brilliant book, *Manifest Now*. Manifesting is the process of thinking things into existence. It might sound whacky or unrealistic if you aren't familiar with this practice, but it's all to do with energy. When you align your thoughts and centre them on a particular specific outcome by visualising or speaking, it causes the energy to vibrate at a certain level. By doing so you are able to draw outcomes that you want towards you. You can't control how it happens, but you can be sure that it's on the way. Don't worry if you're confused, this is just a very simple explanation. I will go into greater detail about manifesting and the powerful effect it can have on attracting outcomes in your life in Part 4 of the book on Spiritual (**connection**).

Next, if you can (and I know you can because you're motivated to operate in new ways of thinking and open to experiencing new levels of success) don't reach for your phone. I know it's hard, and it gets harder in week 2, 3, 4 and 5 when you want to have a sneaky peak. But resist the urge to pick it up and check social media or your email inbox. Instead, use this time to fully wake up and go into your space. I recommend that you dedicate a specific area in your home like your study, balcony, garden or porch to be your sanctuary, where you can sit without being disturbed. Now write down what you are grateful for. To make the most of your early hours' retreat, I recommend choosing somewhere with limited distractions. The aim of the game is to connect deeper with your inner self and to do that it's probably best that you go somewhere private, but it's completely up to you, we all work differently.

For example, every morning I go to my study and sit down and write about how much love I have for Levi and Sandra, and how grateful I am to be here in Singapore, using my skills, strengths and gifts to go after new and interesting challenges. This is completely different to the type of gratitude you feel when your feet touch the floor after waking up that I spoke of a few paragraphs ago. It might seem like gratitude overload but trust me, waking up and feeling grateful for being alive and all that you have in your life is the best way to maximise your abundance.

Then, when I am ready, I write out all the things I will do with my newly manifested $10m (the amount from my Think And Grow Rich statement, please feel free to change this sum to your own manifested amount). This process gets me to focus precisely on what I am going to do with my talents, skills and financial abundance. It makes it more real and helps me to visualise the stage after acquiring the money. It also steers me away from negative thinking and moves me into a zone of possibility, which is a fantastic place to be at the start of any day.

I often remind myself that it is not *what* we know that is the key to success but *how* we apply it, and that's ultimately driven by our *belief* of what is possible. If we don't think something is possible then we won't try it. In turning our back on trying, we are saying no to the miracles and opportunities that show up all the time and help us move forward.

Keeping a fully open mind and using the power of my imagination to understand what I would do with $10 million, sets me on that course. This is because the clearer the heart and mind become the more the mind goes to work to make it happen.

My attitude towards change dictates how change affects my life.

The other thing that I've changed (and this will resonate with all the parents who are reading this or anyone who's been woken by screaming or loud noises during the night, drunken party goers, building work, and generally has interrupted sleep) is my attitude to when I'm woken by Levi or I find myself awake at 3am and can't understand why.

Instead of immediately getting annoyed and frustrated that my beautiful REM sleep cycle has been broken and trying to solve the problem by forcing myself back to sleep, I work with the problem and just get up.

Instead of resisting it I go with it, and the way I work with it was simple. By just getting up out of bed and going into my study, picking up a book and reading or writing or listening to an audiobook changes the feeling of annoyance to one of acceptance.

By shifting and not obsessing over my goal of falling back to sleep and seeing the time as an opportunity to expand and grow takes the negative emotion out of the situation, and so being woken up no longer has any power over me. This means that I no longer become annoyed when I get woken because I now look forward to being productive and continuing my development.

By looking at the problem in a different way, I was able to achieve much, much more. I was able to prepare for my day ahead hours before anyone else. I even had clients in Hong Kong who were still working that I could do business with and expand my sales pipeline.

One time, as I was walking Levi at 2.34am around the grounds of our apartment block in the hope of getting him back to sleep, I received a message from the Head of Marketing from Singapore Airlines. As we were both up, we were able to move the conversation forward and set up an important meeting. So, what might look like a problem on the surface can, in fact, be an opportunity to yield unbelievable results.

Any time that you are up before the rest of your household, claim this time as your own and get your mind ready for the day ahead. Make sure you follow these steps and you'll see the benefits quickly.

Because I was getting up at 3am, 4am and 5am, I could be out of the door at 6.30am and at the gym working out. This made working out an automatic habit that was as normal as eating breakfast, and just something that I did. From here, I was able to work out for an hour, shower, listen to an informative podcast or an inspirational audiobook and still be in the office before everyone else at 8am. This put me ahead of the game again and I was able to crush my most important tasks in the peaceful surroundings of an empty office.

There are significant benefits to getting up early, and a simple shift in your daily routine like this can actually give you more energy. This is what I have found. By getting up early instead of angrily trying to get more sleep, and focusing on the right and important things like gratitude, and the health of my body and mind, I have built a solid foundation which gives me a strong base. So, no matter what the day throws at me, I know I can and I will get through this. I will figure it out.

I cannot stress how important this is when you begin to optimise your life and incorporate habits that set you up for success in your life.

CHAPTER 14

DO LESS, ACHIEVE MORE

"There is nothing so useless as doing efficiently that which
should not be done at all."

Peter Drucker

Consistency is key

IT MIGHT SOUND strange, but doing less and achieving more is
made possible if you focus on consistency rather than intensity.
This chapter is all about building consistent habits. It will explore
ways that you can tweak your habits to achieve more.

To explain this further, let's use the analogy of going to the gym.
Imagine if your goal is to get a 6 pack overnight. Unfortunately,
it's not going to happen, even if you pumped iron in there all night
long. But if you were to first adopt and then stick to a regular
high-intensity workout routine for just 20 minutes every day,
you'd get the majority of the way there. Well, at least 80%.

> We often focus on the result when we should be more interested
> in the path towards the result, and the behaviours and habits that
> are performed consistently overtime to allow the individual to
> achieve and sustain high levels of success.

Who we become on the adventure to reaching our goal is the real
treasure. For example, changing your diet to cut down on sugar
and consistently eat more greens will give you better long-term
results than ignoring your diet completely or adopting fad diets
that only work for a few weeks. Small tweaks applied consistently
provide serious results over a lifetime, but they seem less attractive

to the untrained eye because the outcomes aren't instant and may potentially take years before the payoff is visible.

Of course, we can be sure there be times when huge intensity is required and you must pull working all-nighters to develop your side hustle, or fly 22 hours across the globe to attend a Facebook interview panel – no biggy – or make triple the amount of calls, posts and submissions to get your story covered by that influential magazine editor you admire, who could help you grow your business exponentially. But those are exceptions.

80/20 efficiency

You may have heard of the 80/20 rule before (also called the Pareto rule). The concept is that 20% of your efforts produce 80% of your results, or another example would be 20% of your clients generate 80% of your profits.

This phenomenon can be seen in multiple areas of life, from business to health and relationships, and you will make massive headway against your competition if you can figure out the correct drivers that correlate to results.

Life shows us that the 80/20 rule is about figuring out what is generating the most impact and mastering the principle of consistent action, whereby the rituals that we often carry out and repeat over time produces the biggest results.

By figuring out which strategies and actions create 80% of our successful outcomes, we can streamline success. Success leaves clues! By recognising the patterns of success, we can optimise the formula to generate even bigger results. There is less wastage, as once we've identified the activities that produce only a minimal improvement in results, we can stop repeating them and concentrate on repeating those activities with better results.

Spotting which patterns to repeat and which to get rid of is simple. So when you next have a win, make a sale, get a job offer, have a breakthrough, get shit done, or generally feel awesome, take a moment to analyse what it was that brought you to this point. Once you start to analyse the behaviours, tactics and activities that are bringing you the most successful outcomes, i.e. making prospecting phone calls right after lunch or a cold email template that provokes a response 90% of the time, you can piece together the themes and identify the patterns for success. By linking certain tactics together, the power and efficiency of strategies are multiplied, and the result will start to snowball. Because you are aware that success leaves clues, you start to recognise patterns frequently and they will begin to stand out more prominently in other areas of your life, like your relationships, work, and side hustles. It is the recognition of patterns and having the courage to trust your observations that will see you multiply the results.

Identifying where you could apply the 80/20 principle comes back to tracking and measuring your current activities against your definitions for success. For example, if you are required to have 5 client meetings per week (as a measure of success within your organisation for your role) then you'll need to look at how much time it is currently taking you to achieve that and what specifically you are doing to obtain the desired result. If you find that it is taking you way too long to secure these meetings, or you're burning the candle at both ends doing 25 emails, 2 calls and 2 hours of preparation to lock in one meeting, this is a sign that the 80/20 rule could be applied. But the only way you will know this is if you start tracking what you're doing on a daily basis.

One way I found I could use this principle to maximise my efficiency was to look at how I was spending my time relative to output across 4 key areas.

- **Email** - I found I am more productive between 6am-8am than 9am-11am. With people filing into the office, asking questions, getting breakfast, it's harder to focus on producing quality work and easier to procrastinate. If I come in earlier when no one is around, I can fly through my emails and get ahead of the game.

- **Calls** – patterns and habits that rely on email form easily. Once this type of behaviour becomes the norm within an organisation, it can be hard to remember other alternatives. By switching from emails to calls, I often got quicker responses and higher quality information because I was able to ask my clients questions, saving the back and forth over email and numerous days of waiting.

- **Presentations** – I was able to give more presentations and uncover increased opportunities by using a series of 3 or 4 different decks to mix and match by vertical and industry rather than creating from scratch and tailoring everything each time. I found that slides often got ignored anyway and success was more about how you told the story and the questions you ask.

- **Internal Meetings** (cancel them) – many meetings are a grand old waste of time. There's the preparation, the waiting around for everyone to show up, the social graces and chitter chatter that drags these suckers on for hours! Reject anything longer than 20 minutes and claim back the time in your schedule.

In each of these 4 areas (all very common in the workplace), I was able to make minor adjustments that had a gigantic effect. Each person and workplace is slightly different, so make sure that you do what's right for you personally. The point I am making is that it's often micro shifts, rather than major shifts, that cause productivity and efficiency to go through the roof. Track how long you are spending on each activity and what you are getting back in terms of success (e.g. responses, decisions made, sales, pitches, clients) and don't be afraid to mix things up if you find that you're not getting a return for your effort. The 80/20 rule is a neat little trick that you can apply at will to any area of your life.

Percentage of Time Spent
Per Day

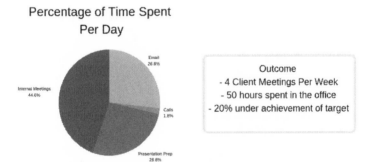

Before applying the 80/20 principle

Percentage of Time Spent Per Day

Networking 20%
Email 15%
Calls 15%
Sourcing Qualified Leads 20%
Presentation Prep 10%
Internal Meetings 20%

Outcome
- 6 Client Meetings Per Week
- 35 hours spent in the office
- 20% over achievement of target

After applying the 80/20 principle

As you'll see from the two diagrams above, the results produced are vastly different. By streamlining the time spent on certain non-outcome-oriented procrastination hungry activities (like internal meetings) a surplus of time is created that can be directed towards the 20% (e.g. sourcing qualified leads and networking) that drives 80% of the results. A simple shift in how you decide to spend your time, including when, where and with who, can lead to amazing results.

Which area of your life would you like to improve where this 80/20 rule could be applied? What are you doing currently that you could focus purely on the 20% of effort and drive 80% of the results?

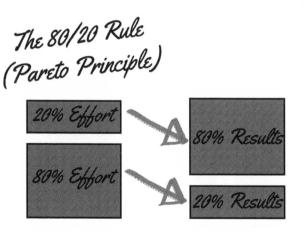

The 80/20 Rule
(Pareto Principle)

20% Effort → 80% Results

80% Effort → 20% Results

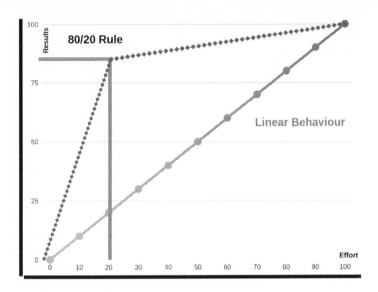

20/80 burnout

The opposite of the 80/20 rule is 20/80, also known as burnout, whereby you run yourself ragged for 80% of the time to get only 20% of the results. Knowing what to avoid helps us to stay closer to the behaviours of the mega-successful.

Avoid burnout like the plague.

Burnout can manifest itself in many forms and is lurking behind the rituals and habits that we choose not to prioritise or give up.

This can happen in the workplace. Organisational cultures are so influential, it is important to work for a business that aligns with your own approach to health and well-being as well as your blueprint for successful living.

Burnout can hide itself is in the culture of an organisation. For example, let's say you start a new job and notice straight away, in week one, that people seem to be constantly all over the place, running themselves ragged, jumping from call to call at all hours of the day and night, flying from one place to another and not prioritising their own long-term health.

When you're new to the company, this chaotic state and frenzied approach to business stands out, but over time, as your responsibilities shift and the cultural norm seeps into your life, it becomes harder to differentiate the company's culture from your own.

Being ambitious folk, we often want to do our best, and we can mistakenly compromise our own standards in pursuit of company or career success. On the surface, and to the boss, you may look totally busy, but you're actually on cruise control. This is where burnout can jump out and surprise you.

I've seen this happen. You enter an organisation and its norms start to be adopted by the masses (this is the power of culture and influence of expectations). Your own preferences and expectations become gradually tainted by this and so a new normal is formed for the individual.

What people will and won't accept into their lives is now based on the standards tolerated by the group. What was once surprising to the individual (in terms of workload, lack of sleep, days not taken off, family events missed) now becomes a badge of honour, or worse still, is not recognised due to a complete misalignment.

This is why having clear strategies and being strategic about how we achieve our goals is paramount to success, so regularly check in and revisit your own goals on a daily, weekly and monthly basis.

Are you in a company culture that is incongruent to your own beliefs and values? Do you regularly feel compelled to continue working even though you are not fulfilled?

The reason I ask these questions is not to cast doubt or cause you to make rash decisions. What I am doing is providing a platform for a deeper connection with what is true for you. Deep down you'll know instinctively whether you feel trapped in a cycle that's bringing you down or taking you up. There may be elements or time periods when this fluctuates due to seasonal trends or market activity, but generally, its best practise to keep a check on how you are feeling about an organisation's alignment with your life goals and vision of the future.

Act as if

One way to quickly change your habits, or at least accelerate your ability to move on from a situation where you're stuck in 80/20 burnout (this is not only applicable to work, it could also be a relationship or any project you put effort into) is to 'act as if' – start living the way you want your life to be. This is Napoleon Hill's mantra.

If you want to be healthy, do what healthy people do. If you want to live like a millionaire, think about what it is you think they would do and then do it. If it's sleep more, then invest in a quality pillow and go to bed earlier. If you want to be the person that's there for your family, start leaving work at an acceptable time and going to football training or those swimming classes with your kids. 'We get what we tolerate.' (Another Tonyism.)

Our habits define us, and by raising our standards and acting as if we already have what we seek, we will think and act like someone who already has that thing.

A tried and test strategy to kick-starting that process is to emulate those that have gone before us and are still succeeding today by adopting their principles and behaviours. In doing so, you draw into your life all the goodness associated with those types of decisions. Really, it comes down to a mindset shift and being able to distinguish what we will or won't accept in our lives. Sometimes, this requires you to take back control of areas of your life that you didn't even know you'd given up, like taking a lunch break or allowing yourself to go on holiday.

The cool thing is, if these actions are performed consistently over time, they will become more familiar and engrained at a deeper level and successful habits will take shape before you know it. In time, these habits will become part of your persona, what makes you you. This will shape the quality of the decisions you make and the process you go through to make these decisions.

Changing our thinking patterns means that we are less reactive – life is not happening to us, so we feel free to choose our response.

Absorb the habits of others

Mastin Kipp offers some incredible insights at his *Claim Your Power Live* event or on his podcast *The Power and Purpose Podcast* about how to play a bigger game. Mastin suggests that in order to improve any area of our life, we must first hang out with those who are already doing it and producing the results you want. This means that if you want to get fit you should go hang out with 5 personal trainers for 6 months, not just a few guys from the office that are semi-fit and will ditch the gym to go get a doughnut if pushed.

Mastin explains that hanging out with people who are getting results to live an 'aha moment life' and not just experience those inspiring 'aha moments' that quickly disappear is not enough. We must also become deeply immersed in a mentor who can help us with what to focus on and where to allocate our time and energy.

Let's look at your inner circle of friends and the people you regularly hang out with. Friends are an incredibly necessary part of life. Lions, in fact, hunt as a group. They are a pack animal because they know they can achieve more together than as individuals How often do you meet anyone new? Is it the same faces and the same conversations? The goal here is to be aware that by carefully selecting who you spend time with, you are prioritising your need for growth and development. If you habitually hang around with people who moan or criticise, it will drain you. Whereas if you hang around with people who are positive and encouraging, you will feel rejuvenated by being in their company. You may learn directly or indirectly from these people, through tips, their encouragement to improve or a certain habit that is working well for them. This is not about replacing friends that make your life better and encourage your dreams, it's about letting go of those you have outgrown, don't encourage you or leave you feeling down and deflated.

The aim of the game here is to ensure that you are always open to expanding your friendships and connections in the direction of your own intuition. The universe can bring the exact right person or people into your life for a reason, at the right time. Maybe you're toying with the idea of starting a business but need someone to give you a push, or you've moved to a new company and feel out of place. Or you're just hungry to meet other ambitious individuals with similar passions and thoughts about life.

I recall moving to a new apartment and making friends with a guy who lived in the block next door. I'd always wanted to take up boxing, but for some reason, it had never been the right time. It wasn't until he suggested going boxing did I take action and it has become a regular activity for me, even though I could have taken it up at any point over the last 20 years. Often, it's the people that come into our lives for a reason that show us the way. If you look at what opportunities you have right now to expand your circle of friends, you might see that a new world of fun is patiently waiting for you to say yes! Following your interests and passions is a brilliant way to start this process, and saying yes more is the first step to busting through our automatic routines as it shifts our lives in a positive direction.

If you feel drawn to go and speak to a particular person, then pluck up the courage to introduce yourself. Part of being the lion is cultivating your ability to be bold and push yourself into new situations in the pursuit of living large and in charge.

This means it should be a well-practised habit to seek out new and interesting people that inspire you. It might seem crude to think of this as upgrading your friends, but the reality is that you're not so much upgrading, as potentially outgrowing or moving on, which is natural. Think of it as expanding the circle and making room for new possibilities.

From now on, I want you to make it a priority to always remain open to opportunities to meet new people. It should be part of your routine to want to connect with others.

The right people have a strange way of entering your life at exactly the right moment, the key is not to be afraid of this change but to embrace it and learn from them.

Surrounding yourself with people who are ambitious, curious about life and driven to improve their personal well-being will take you in all sorts of directions and add value to your life in a way that only the company and friendship of another human being can.

CHAPTER 15

SHIFT YOUR PERSPECTIVE TO ATTRACT ABUNDANCE

"When I'm connected to my joyful presence, I attract
support from the Universe."

Gabrielle Bernstein, *The Universe Has Your Back*

How are you seeing things?

N O ONE CAN change your life but YOU!

We all have days when things suck, we don't feel like putting in
the work, hitting the gym, we miss the bus, we are late for work,
or can't be bothered doing the new meditation class we just signed
up for. On the flip side, we all have days when we are elated, life
could not be better, and we are on top of the world.

In reality, both days are the same, the difference is how we perceive
the world and our state. It's also whether we believe that we can
find the hunger and drive within us to get where we want to be and
the story that we repeatedly tell ourselves about this. This chapter
will explore the mechanics behind this and show you how you can
force yourself into a more positive mindset. This will improve your
productivity and happiness, and make it easier to maintain a positive
mindset. It's a win-win.

What story are you telling yourself?

I learned a big lesson about this when I was working in a job that
no longer fulfilled me and left me uninspired. My work suffered

and I suffered; it was a bleak and stressful time as the cycle went round and round.

The underlying problem was that I had expected the job to be different to my previous one. I had accepted it at a lower rate than I felt I was worth, which left me feeling resentful. So, there was a difference between how I thought I should feel and how I actually felt every day. This gap led to an out of sync feeling that left me feeling pissed off. Why couldn't I have a job that I loved?

In all honesty, I couldn't stop comparing myself to my peers. Why did they get jobs they adored in companies that loved them? I became obsessed with the notion that I was somehow falling behind, and this became my story.

This story, if I indulged in it, rewarded me by making me feel justified whenever I was angry and stressed. It also made me feel like my situation was unique in and I could, therefore, take time off to wallow in self-pity.

The problem was I was focused on everything else, competing with the outside when I should have been trying to outperform within my area of strength.

The truth is, there was an abundance of opportunities around me and I was learning a phenomenal amount from the experience of this job, even though sucked the life right out of me at times.

To change this pattern, I needed to remember what Tony says about gratitude and sharing joy. I needed to find the joy in the day.

I also needed to refocus on the bigger picture and change how I saw each day going forward. I needed to shift my perspective and change the story I was telling myself, and then take action and use my resourcefulness to amplify the opportunities for a new job.

The question wasn't what annoying about this job; it was what am I learning? What can I take from this experience that will empower me and drive me forward with greater strength, focus and determination? What am I learning about myself through the experience? And can I learn to face difficult situations head-on with courage and pursue my worth in spite of a work environment that is draining, stressful and disruptive?

Don't be the victim

Does this resonate with you in some way? Can you relate to it? Are you prone to a victim mentality when the sh*t hits the fan?

I think, in some contexts, we all have our 'please feel sorry for me' moments; after all, we are human.

The difficulty is when this becomes our default response to less than ideal outcomes. If being in victim mode is 'the norm' and it becomes our way of viewing the world then that's a pretty sad story we are telling ourselves, and you know what, stories matter.

Right now, I want you to commit to ditching the victim mentality.

The next time a situation doesn't work out the way you thought it would, channel your inner strength with all your might, summon the presence of calm and reframe the story you tell yourself to one of gratitude and positivity – what gems can you take from the situation? Challenge yourself.

Now, what I'm asking you to do is insanely hard. When plans don't turn out the way we thought they would, when we want something with everything we've got and it just doesn't happen, it is tough! I get it, I've been there, trust me. Flying off the handle and having a rant gives us momentary relief. But it does not help us to connect with our higher good; instead, it will only keep us trapped in the story.

> To be the lion, you must master your emotions, especially in times of struggle, and practise letting go of the defeatist's story.

Laugh out loud in the face of your crappy situations; do whatever it takes, but heaven forbid, don't allow yourself to go back into victim mode.

It's true that we have the ability to create absolutely anything we want in this life, but we can't do it from a position of lack, weakness, fear, guilt, negativity and hostility. Thinking like a victim makes progress impossible.

'Just because your mind tells you that something is awful or evil or unplanned or otherwise negative doesn't mean that you have to agree.'

Ryan Holiday,
The Obstacle is the Way

Cultivate a growth mindset

Cultivating a growth mindset, rather than a victim mentality when things don't go your way, will set you apart and ensure you come up fighting every time. You have to dig deep and find the passion and fire within you and be the lion. You must channel your desire for what you are capable of, and who you want to become, not how you currently live your life when you decide to live big and on purpose.

You must walk forward and push past obstacles, defy the normal and exceed in what you first thought was impossible.

It's a new dimension of thinking and a new energy that flows out from your core and expands. Let it engulf your mind and body with determination, commitment and resilience.

Breathe into it, and really feel it circulating, pulsating and coursing around your body, through your veins, and into your brain. Feel the expansion, the success, the freedom and the liberation from mediocre, the fire that burns inside of you to do more, to succeed, to create your vision and have life on your terms, to not be a victim of circumstance, but a warrior. That's when you are really living. When you view the world in terms of what could happen (in a phenomenal way), you don't give into fear, doubt or self-criticism. Instead, you strive for greatness.

This communication you have with yourself is vital to 10x, 100x or even a 1000x your success. To create a life at that level requires you to have a different ongoing conversation with yourself. It demands that you think of life in abundant terms.

Case study: my defeatist mindset

To give you an example that may help, when bitcoin got going a few years ago, one of my long-time good friends decided to buy a few, not as a get rich strategy, but or the novelty.

I took an interest and tracked the price up and down over the next few months. I tried unsuccessfully a couple of times to get an account. I was living in Sydney at the time and the US exchange I was trying to sign up did not want to take my credit card for payment.

Anyhow, as time went on the price dropped from $1,000 a coin to $200 a coin. This represented an opportunity as I had a few thousand dollars ready to invest.

I harboured a half-hearted mindset towards cryptocurrency at the time, after being burned badly by Aussie stocks in the same year. In the cautious, lazy-ish mindset that I was in at the time (I say ish because I did bother to research it and notice that it was down, but I didn't act fully enough on the opportunity) I gave up. I tried one last time to transfer funds into my account but the US-based exchange wasn't making it easy for me to deposit some cash, so I gave up.

Pure and simple, I did the maths. I remember looking at previous trends on my laptop and reasoning that the price could only go up 5 or 6 times and that if I did get the exchange to accept my payment it would only let me buy 6 coins at a time. Well, that was all too hard for moi.

Fast-forward a few years, and well, you all know what happened. The market for bitcoin and cryptocurrency rallied and prices shot up by over US$20,000 a coin. Even if I had been bothered to call the exchange and figure out how to put $1200 into an account and get six coins, they'd have been worth $120,000 at that time.

And that figure would have been much higher if I'd sent all the money I actually wanted to invest to my friend for him to invest on my behalf (remember he was a really good friend, not the kind that would steal my millions and disappear without a trace), or if

I had spent the time to find another exchange to use that accepted Australian Dollars.

There are plenty of ways I could have achieved this result, but the issue was to do with my mindset. I didn't believe that situation had the potential to rocket more than 600%, let alone 10,000%, or that I had the capacity to make me half a million dollars in the process through simply following my intuition.

The truth is my *desire* wasn't great enough, and as a result, my resourcefulness to seek out other methods of obtaining the goal was catastrophically lacking. It's like I was driving in first gear down the highway looking for ways to exit because I just didn't believe that the potential for expansion was there. But as history proves time and time again, opportunities for expansion are all around us.

The other error I made was to rationalise the level of expansion I thought that was possible, based on what had come before. By focusing on the history of the bitcoin trends and prices I locked myself into believing that only a small expansion was possible, yet as the universe proves, growth can exceed our wildest dreams.

Do I beat myself up about it? Hell no, because I know the *truth* of the matter, I didn't believe or want it enough. But I do find it an interesting example of how limiting beliefs about what is possible can stop us from getting big results.

There are literally thousands of situations like this going on around us every day, opportunities for huge accelerated growth, and we can spot them by engaging with an open 'anything is possible, limitless, abundance filled, grateful' mindset.

Think of the palm tree, have you ever wondered about its growth? The next time you see one stop and look at the rungs of on the trunk that represent a year of growth. See how it stretches up, multiplying in huge quantities, both under the surface and up towards the sky. The nature of the universe and life is expansion. And so, the next time you spot an opportunity, I want you to question its potential for greatness and expand your belief about what is really truly possible in this world of wonder. Let go of biases of past behaviour and focus on expansive potential.

Positivity invites abundance in

When we seek to move mountains in a big way, we have bought in fully with all our heart, mind and soul to the idea that it is possible, and it will happen for us. We know it is on its way to us, and we go about making it happen in ways that are powerful, constructive and strong.

By behaving in this way, we attract the very thing we want to us, and by changing the story we start to shift our own internal beliefs, so that we can manifest it in the outer world.

Deep down it begins with our energy, and once we understand how energy and the laws of abundance work, we see that the Universe is trying to provide for us all that we seek by opening us up to a series of opportunities, ideas, creative thoughts, chance meetings, etc.

When we act from a place of lack and are being defeatist, we are inadvertently rejecting the Universe's signals for abundance and become closed off to receiving the messages. It's like putting your phone on silent and still expecting to hear the phone call that will change your life.

We must put ourselves in the prime position for success and to do that we have to take responsibility for our own journey, happiness and feelings. We can then start to think differently and draw into our lives things that help us to move towards our higher purpose.

This shift in thinking from a place of 'the world sucks/it's never going to get any better' mentality to a place of 'anything is possible if I am open to it' is a game-changer.

Like a magnet, we draw what we want to us. The door then begins to open and we experience accelerated growth and more success. This, in turn, encourages us to act with more confidence and greater abundance instead of thinking that the world is out to get us.

The way you interpret the world around you and what is happening on a daily basis will have a direct impact on the way you experience life and the doors that will open for you. When you move from a lack mentality to an abundant mentality you are literally saying yes to life – yes, I can do this, bring it on. Let's go!

This is the vibration that you need to embody, and you can support this energy shift with the story that you tell yourself. For example, two people can experience the same situation yet have radically different points of view and interpretations about the outcome.

What you focus on you create more of. Therefore, if you are vibrating in an abundantly joyful way bring the joy you see and be the joy in the situation, as the way you show up changes the possibility of the situation.

I categorically believe that when you take action in this way, do the work and go after big goals, the Universe will support you. And the way you do this is to put a story out to the world that will push you beyond anything you thought you were capable of. It will lift you up and become your rock.

> "Give up the story that limits you."
>
> Tony Robbins

Tony's law of attraction

Tony says there are three stages to life when you're considering the law of attraction, i.e. the ability to attract into our lives whatever we wish to focus on and invite in. (By the way, I'm aware this is becoming a bit of a Tony fest right now, but stick with it, this chapter is crucial if you wish to attract the things you want into your life).

3. The strategy (the least important)

2. The story we tell ourselves

1. The state (the most important)

By using this three-step process (which is in reverse order, with the least important first), Tony shows how you can have the right strategy but the wrong story (i.e. if you're telling yourself you can't do it or this kind of life is not meant for you), which means you'll get nada.

Alternatively, you can have the wrong strategy and try for years with the right story but fail nevertheless. What you really want to do is leverage the combined power of all three stages, especially managing your state. If you have the right state, it will influence the kind of story that you tell yourself and also keep you open to receiving the strategies you need to hear.

The strategy

His advice is to seek out people in the know, listen to those with more experience than you about the strategy your desire, and get an outstanding coach. The right coach can save you years of effort trying to figure out the right strategy by seeing where you are going wrong a mile off.

The story

Next, focus on telling yourself the right story. Rather repeatedly reiterating to yourself all of the things that have gone wrong and what weren't right, you must shift to a story that will empower and uplift you by transport you to a place of joy.

In this regard, it is important to remember that you can decide how you respond at any point and choose the emotional and cognitive attention you give something.

The state

This leads us to Tony's final and all-important step, and this is state. Tony says managing your state determines how you think and feel. The key here is to think about state as the key to unlocking the door. If you're in an amazing state, the story you tell yourself about what happened is drastically improved and you will come up with phenomenal strategies. These then lead you to take actions that align with both your mission and vision.

In this space, radical shifts can take place, doors that didn't exist previously can open at exactly the time that you need them, the right people can present themselves at the optimum moment to take your business to the next level, and synchronistic opportunities take place.

Ultimately, this is the plain that lions want to be on, acting from a place abundance, in a high vibration state, with empowering stories that evoke superb strategies and draw the Universe to make it happen one way or another. This is the law of the Universe and it will support anyone who opens up their mind and heart to operating in this way.

Cultivate a high-performance state

Now let's think about how we can boost your state to that of a lion. Do you find that at certain times and in certain circumstances you are more up for it and ready to go? If so, you need to ask yourself, how can I tap into that and what can you do to get yourself into that kind of game-changing state?

I find that when I need to push myself and have a mad half hour to get a lot done, I need to create a certain high-performance state. I do this in a number of ways. It could be through listening to an inspirational podcast or YouTube video, then high-tempo dance tunes whilst working out, followed by a quick-paced walk.

This routine ups my physiological response to the world and brings me into a high-performance state. I can tell that I have reached an optimum state because I have a desire to make things happen. I am positively primed and ready to rocket forward.

I feel my fingers tingling to send out speculative emails, my body just wants to meet people, whether over the phone or in person, and I am primed and ready to receive all the greatness that the world wants to bring my way.

By getting ourselves into a state of fist-pumping, life-loving optimism, where our bodies are open and we feel we can touch the sky, we are asking the Universe, with our arms widely spread, to bring forward all kinds of joyful experiences, lessons and possibilities.

For me, I know I work best in the morning, either surrounded by hungry individuals (hungry for their life goals, not literally starving) or aspirational environments.

I will often work from hotels like the Mandarin Oriental as this allows me to be immersed in a world that I want. By locating myself in a world that I would like to be in, I can soak in the grandeur, high level of service and the detail. It's about literally putting myself in the situation that I would like to be able to afford on a daily basis. I might order breakfast or a coffee and while I am there, so that I can embrace what it means to be there in that environment.

The other advantage is you don't know who you might meet when you are there; remember, one meeting or introduction could change your life. To me, placing yourself in the environment where you ultimately want to be goes hand in hand with thinking big, it pushes my ideas of what is possible to the next level.

I'd love to be able to stay at the Mandarin in any city in the world on a weekly basis, can I afford that yet? It's a matter of how you think about it. Right now, my bank balance might suggest no, but my mind is fully saying yes.

What I can afford to do is have a coffee and enjoy the hour or two I spend there. By transporting myself into that world, I become closer to it and I play the game at a higher level. Every now and then I might even book a room and take my family for a luxury stay. It's not about being able to afford it financially, it's what message this sends to the Universe, to myself and about where we are going.

Every now and again, we must take risks in order to grow. In a normal person's eyes, these risks may seem frivolousness, careless, or impatient but in the eyes of a lion spending and investing in ourselves, it is part of the process.

There may be a course you want to attend or a place you want to visit or a coach you want to hire. I encourage you to seize that idea and grab it with both hands, for it is that spark of the imagination that creates your future. By acting in this way, you will move towards your goals.

When you get the burning feeling that you want to create, like you can't keep it in any more, don't wait, always act on it, in the moment. Compose and send that email, sign up to that course, book that trip. You never know who you might meet, what calling you might find or the reason for being there until you go for it.

In this state, I like to see how far I can push it. At times, I might play the same song on repeat, over and over again. This keeps the state of flow going, and it allows the ideas to intensify and develop. It also means I can tune out the world in order to tune in, if that makes sense.

By switching off what is going on around me, I can get deeper into creating. The same tune on repeat is almost like a meditation and it means my state is maintained. To go deeper, you must also ignore the interruptions, intrusive WhatsApp message, phone calls and emails, and tune in instead to see what you can achieve and how far you can push your actions.

Once in this state, it is all about ACTION! The world works with action. If it stays in your head, it ain't happening, even if you speak it out loud. Until you take a step forward and produce an action, you're still riding with the safety wheels on.

Don't give others the power to ruin your state

This is very appropriate for me, like right NOW! I have just moved upstairs to the co-working space, where the office is, so I can be alone and write. If I start getting frustrated, I know I can counter this by spending 15 minutes doing something creative. I will then return feeling more fulfilled and able to give more of myself to my team (in terms of energy, enthusiasm, ideas and action).

However, as life would have it, I chose the exact same spot where two other people had decided to have rather loud communication on their mobiles, as if drawn to my desire for peace.

Pacing up and down as they talked, it was a huge distraction from my zenful quest and made me angry.

I could feel the surge of anger rise up inside me, as I thought, 'How dare you come near me at this moment? I have brought myself away to get into peak performance mode and here you are destroying that possibility.'

Then I remembered what Tony had said about state. I am responsible for my own state. If I were managing my emotions, like really managing them, then these two mobile phone moochers wouldn't be an issue. If I was in flow and connected with both my 'why' and my passion, I would not even notice these guys.

Moments later, a whole team from another start-up decided to host a full-on team meeting at the table next to me. When they started to laugh and cheer loudly, I got riled. It was time for a reality check. These people weren't the problem, I was.

I was being triggered because of my state. To move forward I needed to change my state, story and strategy. I needed to relocate to a meeting room. I needed to stop playing the victim and looking for ways that the set-up wasn't perfect.

Play until the whistle blows

I want to leave you with this final piece of wisdom. Playing sports requires many of the fundamental attributes it takes to succeed; traits like discipline, the ability to be coached, mental toughness, strength, agility, speed, playing to your strengths, working with what you are given, the list goes on.

In many professional sports, games are won during the final quarter or the final few minutes. Manchester United football team used to call this "Fergie Time".

Do you have the ability to push on, to stay in your peak state right up to the final whistle? This goes back to the story we tell ourselves, we are **in charge** of the story. Tell yourself you are bound to lose and you will tell yourself it's worth fighting until the whistle blows, and who knows what you might achieve.

CHAPTER 16

JOY

"Leaning toward joy is not our default. But the more
we practice this principle, the more natural it becomes.
You have the power to shift the energy of a tormented
relationship, change the vibe in your office, or heal your
perception of yourself with one simple choice: the choice
to lean toward joy."

Gabrielle Bernstein, *The Universe Has Your Back.*

What's joy got to do with being the lion?

I WAS DRAWN to write a section on joy because it has had a profound impact on both the way I approach sales and how I intend to live my life. I mention sales because I have spent over ten years working in the field and understand deeply the repeated rejection that sales professionals learn to face on a daily basis. I believe that finding joy and creating value in the face of challenges, setbacks and down-right failures is key to creating more success in the future. For example, if I take the time to understand why a sale fell through, I can be better prepared for this obstacle the next time it shows up. We can grow by learning to see light in the darkness, and it's not just at work where this applies.

Joy and being in a state of joy has categorically changed how I do business in a number of ways, from the type of questions I ask my clients, colleagues and myself to the level of experimentation and fun I willingly put out.

The effect of creating joy has dramatically increased both my well-being and my ability to achieve results. In this chapter, I'm going to show you a few ways to tap into your joy. Who doesn't want more joy in their life?

Simon Sinek on joy

The motivational speaker and bestselling author, Simon Sinek, talks about how you can overcome your emotions if you feel nervous or stressed out before completing a big task, commitment or taking an action. He says the way to overcome it is to reframe the feelings you experience to ones of excitement.

He tells the story of watching the Olympics one year and observing that every single reporter asked the same question to the athletes which was, 'Were you or are you nervous?'

The athlete's response was the same every time, 'No, I'm excited.'

I found this realisation deeply interesting as I had experienced this myself.

This means that we can train our brains to respond differently to stress and reframe the meaning of feelings we associate with nervousness, like sweaty palms or a racing heart, to indicate excitement for the future and joy for what's about to happen.

Gabrielle Bernstein on joy

Gabrielle Bernstein captures it with the extract below that she posted on Instagram. When I saw this message for the first time, I felt that I was meant to witness this text and to fully take it in. Honestly, it was like some sort of divine intervention. My Instagram account froze on Gabby's post for the entire day until I took real notice of it. Strangely, whilst all other apps on my phone continued to work, this one would not budge; it simply stared me in the face until I got it. Freaky right?

> "Your emotions are a direct indicator of how much you're resisting or allowing. When you are in the energy of joy, you're allowing yourself to be Super Attractor. The closer you are to the emotion of joy, the more easily what you want can flow to you."
>
> Gabrielle Bernstein

Gabby goes on to warn that jumping from negative feelings directly into joy is an impossible task, and we should take small steps to move towards the presence of joy. This could be as small as focusing your thoughts on what you are looking forward to something like, 'I feel excited about dinner tonight.' Gabby states that we must 'lovingly guide ourselves back to joy'.

So, there we have two approaches to reframing emotions and moving into joy.

> "The payoff of proactivity leaning towards joy is that you'll fully embrace the flow of the Universe. When joy becomes your priority, making decisions becomes easier, relationships become more loving and you start to trust that the Universe has your back."[2]
>
> Gabrielle Bernstein, The Universe Has Your Back.

Jack Ma on joy

Now here's a third approach, take the example of multibillionaire and champion of global e-commerce, Jack Ma. Founder of Alibaba, Jack's a living legend and overcome significant struggles in his life following his steadfast belief of bringing China to the world.

As stated by Duncan Clark in his book, *The House That Jack Built*, 'Jack has made a career out of being underestimated'. He readily admits to not understanding the technology behind his empire and plays down his smarts by saying famous lines like, *'I am a very simple guy, I am not smart. Everyone thinks that Jack is a very smart guy. I might have a smart face, but I've got very stupid brains.'*

The thing is, Jack is smart, he is amazing. This approach is not seen regularly in the world, and especially by people in Jack's position, hence why I wanted to point it out. He's a maverick.

Jacks ability to talk down his own strengths is in direct contradiction to the behaviour of most CEOs and Founders of Fortune 500 companies.

---

[2] Bernstein, G. (2016). *The Universe Has Your Back:Transform Fear to Faith*. Hay House Inc.

Jack is a showman at heart and his love of defying the rules, the stereotypes, and the way things are meant to work is what makes him so successful in business. Combine that with him being constantly underestimated and it is the ultimate competitive advantage. I love Jack for his mentality. The ability to carry himself and conduct business in this way is a spectacular feat worthy of much admiration. In a way, Jack's joy has come from overcoming the odds and rewriting the rules of what's possible whilst using his talents in joyful ways to move mountains and show the world another way of doing business successfully. Whether it's performing songs at the annual Alibaba party or encouraging his employees to do headstands in the office because it promotes well-being, Jack has found an effective balance of joy and business that we can all learn from.

Duncan elaborates on what makes Jack's speaking style so effective He says it's because Jack's message is so easy to agree with, remember and digest.

On top of this is *'Jack's ability to charm and cajole has played an important role in attracting talent and capital to the company as well as building his own fame.'*

Alibaba employees sum it up as 'Jack Magic'.

What I want you to take from this is that each of us have our own magic. It may be hidden deep, deep inside us right now, but trust me, it is there! And by making it your daily mission to move towards joy, to find the humour in the situation and awaken the superstar inside you, you will find your own magic.

Jack Ma has come a long way from his days as an English teacher to global superstar, and he's done with all the cards stacked against him and it in the face of much rejection.

It is Jack's humble nature, focus on living true to his own version of joy, and his ability to bring his Jack Magic into every situation that has enabled him to defy the odds.

Go and bring your own Jack Magic to the world. You deserve it and all the success that will follow.

CHAPTER 17

100X WHAT YOU THINK YOU CAN ACHIEVE

"Whatever the mind can conceive and believe, it can achieve."

Napoleon Hill

Raise your bar

THE KEY WORD in this chapter's title is 'Think'. In this chapter, we'll look at how we really can 100x our thinking in many different aspects of our life. I will also explain the key steps and strategies you need to activate to take your life goals to the next level. It's time to go even bigger.

Making it happen requires you to extend the endurance, the faith, the courage and the will to see it through, and to sometimes push yourself way beyond what you think you're capable of.

To achieve your vision, you will need to do things that are way outside of your comfort zone. The unknown can be daunting but travelling through this adventurous terrain is what carries you forward to the next level. Once you know you can compete at this level, it opens you up to what you are truly capable of, and who you become in the process will enable you to go on to tackle even greater challenges.

Why not go at it every day like you have nothing to lose. Why not 10x, 100x, 1000x your goals and go after them with the persistence of a warrior.

The reason I want to teach you about this is because you'll need to be resourceful to the max when you are truly going for it and so focused on the goal. Like a plate spinner, you will need to be able to sustain multiple plates, despite the hurdles and obstacles that fly your way and try to knock you off course. So, let's take a look at a few ways that you can raise the bar for yourself in terms of what is possible.

Behave like a rock star

This is about staying strong, fit and believing that you can do it. The Rolling Stones rocker Mick Jagger is in his mid-Seventies, and yet still managing to produce offspring and entertain millions on stage playing energetic, sold out stadiums across the world. In 2017, Mick welcomed child number eight. Rock stars achieve the downright ridiculous! Think of his journey from a teenage musician to international stardom. That alone is incredible, but how many stars can keep it up for over 50 years. Many musicians would be happy with just one number one single or one album, but this guy is literally unstoppable!

To keep this lifestyle up, Sir Mick is said to maintain a vigorous exercise routine off stage, as he can cover up to 10 miles on stage during a single show. It has been noted that Mick maintains a diet more fitting for a premier league football player than a world-famous rock star. His daily intake consists of wholegrain pasta, beans and fish, so once again diet and exercise is a staple ingredient for success, energy and vitality.

In this way, Jagger has 100x'd what life would be like for your typical 75-year-old. The rock star mentality has transformed his expectations of what is possible and what he expects from himself. You need to find ways that you can do this in your own life. There may be pockets of opportunity all around you, waiting for you to take an interest, activate them, and extend yourself. But if you never believe it is possible to be bigger than you currently are and live your only miraculous life on this Earth in new and courageous ways, then you are allowing mediocrity to creep in and ruin the party before its even begun.

It could be anything from finishing an Ironman 70.3 race to taking up Ju Jitsu. The point is that you are actively looking for areas in your life to optimise and expand. This mentality and proactive mindset will see you climb incredible mountains, push beyond your fears and reap rewards far greater than any life of comfort would allow.

My question for you, lion, is, what springs to mind when I ask you where the 10x, 100x, 1000x strategy could be applied?

Is it in your approach to travel, your fitness, your relationship, your job, your destructive habits or exploring the boundaries of your own capability? Where have you found comfort that needs to be uprooted? Where have you accepted a lower standard for yourself than you deserve? Where could you make a difference in your life and to those around you? What kind of example do you want to set?

These are big questions and I don't expect you to answer them right away; rather I want you to muse on them over the next few days and let the answers come to you. If the answers do appear, write them down and bring awareness to what you have found and to this particular area of focus.

This is a chance to get a clearer insight into the pathway that you are meant to follow. You might find that an idea pops out of nowhere and then keeps on appearing in your mind over the weeks that follow until you do something about it. Take note and enjoy the process of discovery, it's time to live life larger and go after it with all the greatness that God intended for you.

The first step is to consciously connect with the desire and possibility of a life bigger than your current mental map allows for. Once you've got the inspiration, the idea and the vision, you can begin to put it into inspired action and go for it wholeheartedly with a 10x, 100x, 1000x mindset to drive you.

The soul surfer's passion

I want to share with you briefly the remarkable story of Bethany Hamilton, who truly shows us how to become unstoppable. Bethany went out for a surf one morning, a usual occurrence for a pro surfer, except this time was different. At 7.30am, a 4.3m tiger shark attacked Bethany severing her left arm just below the shoulder. Due to this, she lost 60% of her blood by the time she reached the hospital and spent 3 months in recovery. But this was not going to stop Bethany from doing the sport she loved. Determined to return, she taught herself to surf with only one arm and went on to win multiple competitions. Today, Bethany is one of the most inspirational professional surfers on the face of the planet and is living proof that if you put your mind to it, it can be overcome.

> "I know life can be hard, but I've learned that we can rise above even the biggest challenges and fears. No matter where you've come from, or what you're facing, you are loved by God, and you can overcome."[3]
>
> Bethany Hamilton

The reason I share this story with you is to highlight that no matter what it is you're facing, your perspective, determination and ability to think big are all key ingredients that vital to what you get to experience in life.

What's your dawn wall?

Meet Tommy Caldwell, arguably the best big wall free climber in the world. When he set his sights on climbing up the vertical face of El Capitan, following a previously unchartered route called the Dawn Wall, people thought he was out of his mind.

He enlisted a companion, the bouldering champion Kevin Jorgeson, and together they went about working out how to scale this 3,000-foot beast of vertical granite, which has only with the smallest razor-sharp handholds to grab on to.

In January 2015, over the course of 19 days, the media and the world camped out in Yosemite National Park to watch the spectacle of climbing history unfold. Tommy Caldwell and Kevin Jorgeson did the seemingly impossible and ascended The Dawn Wall.

In big wall free climbing, you use ropes to catch yourself, so that you won't die from falling, but they are not there to assist with the actual climb. Therefore, it is considered to be one of the toughest and most challenging ways to climb.

---

[3] https://bethanyhamilton.com/

In the history of climbing, no climber had ever gone after this 3,000-foot beast from base to summit. It was considered impossible and people thought you had to be out of your mind to think about doing it, let alone actually go up there and attempt it.

Tommy became unquestionably obsessed with finding a route up the Dawn Wall, it was all he thought about. To give you some context, the handholds were so tiny they needed to be marked with white chalk just so you'd know they were there. The technical complexity of the climb combined with the sheer physical endurance required to free climb up a vertical cliff face of this nature is unbelievable and hard to imagine.

If you're interested in finding out more about this captivating feat, I recommend you watch *The Dawn Wall*[4] documentary to give you a sense of the scale of the grand vision that propelled Tommy to keep on going in pursuit of achieving his dream.

I share this example with you, not to challenge you to go and climb the nearest rock face, but because it's an excellent example of someone who was committed to seeing their vision through, even though the world told him that it was impossible, even though no one else in his profession had done it.

Tommy battled through raging storms and bad weather, cuts, pain, mental anguish and torment with Kevin and they came out the other side victorious. It was Tommy's vision and belief that made it possible, without thinking big, he would have left this monumental achievement untouched. It pushed the boundaries of what humans know to be possible and that gives all something to aspire, to hope.

Don't listen to what the world or society tells you is possible. If you have an intuition, an instinct, a passion to pursue, go for it with everything you've got, mentally, physically and emotionally. The big question here is, what's your Dawn Wall?

Filter out the negativity

You need to be absolutely focused on your mission, so much so that you ignore the person who barges into you on the street or

---
[4] https://www.dawnwall-film.com/

the rude check-out person with a bad attitude. These detours will cost you in the form of your precious time and energy and serve as dead-ends on the road to success.

> *"Drama, combat, terror, numbness, and subservience-every day these things wipe out your sacred principles, whenever your mind entertains them uncritically or lets them slip in."*
>
> Marcus Aurelius, Meditations, 10.9

Don't get caught up in other people's dramas. Focus only on where you are going and the bigger picture.

You'll find that you can turn even the most annoying and frustrating situations around with a smile. When you are in the zone and some mud gets flung your way, disrupting your flow, receive it with grace. That way you are reflecting back out to the world what you want, and funnily enough, you'll find that the path which opens up is more wholesome, rich and abundant than if you had responded with your own mud flinging.

Forgive the other person who has wronged you, forgive yourself and then let go of the situation, the emotion and the negative head space. I promise you, by making smiling and being pleasant your default natural reaction in response to pain in the asses, those idiots who don't hold the door open, and rude individuals will pave your way with golden opportunities more quickly than any other reaction.

When we go really big – I mean gigantic big, 100x big – there may be times when our stomach starts to turn, anxieties creep in and you wonder what the freak you are actually doing. Please just accept this as nothing more than a sign that you are on the right track, the track to greatness.

When you think about it, it's obvious that taking on things we have never done before will lead to new and rewarding opportunities. This is because we are increasing the energy that we put out into the world.

Doing what you've done before is routine and so requires low-frequency energy, as you don't have to think much, you are on autopilot and your energy is consistent and steady. But stepping into the unknown, well, that's a different ball game entirely. Suddenly, you are on stage speaking to hundreds at a motivational seminar, or doing a six-step at a breakdancing class, or jumping out of a plane skydiving. In the unknown, you occupy a state of heightened energy.

Dream big

Is there something you've always had a burning desire to do?

Do you dream of flying a plane, owning a business, or exploring the streets of Tokyo? Even imagining our dreams raises our energy levels and connects with our inner core, the bit that makes you you, and our heart starts to beat faster as a result.

What do you see yourself doing if you really pushed it, didn't hold yourself back or engage with those doubtful thoughts. What could you achieve? Ignore those thoughts and re-engage with the excitement and energy of the thing that has just popped up into your mind.

Now, hold that thought.

How could it be even better?

Now expand that thought.

10x it.

Now 100x it.

OK, now 1000x it.

Notice where you felt the most comfortable in this sequence, was it 10x 100x or 1000x?

You will only attract what you feel you can have.

By engaging with this visualisation process, you are putting yourself back in the driver's seat of your own life. The great thing is, once you've had the thought, there is some part of you that now believes it is possible. The more you can connect with that part of you, the more it will grow and this increase in your belief will attract what you seek towards you. Once this belief has grown into **certainty**, you will need to push yourself to do more new and interesting things. Again, don't be surprised if negative thoughts and feelings jump out. Ignore them and think back to the rock star analogy – they don't stop when you achieved your first goal, the goals just get bigger, 100x bigger!

Overthinking and doubts

In the pursuit of 10x or 100x growth, doing new things, like meeting new people, attending a seminar that piques your interest or mixing it up and trying your hand at something, causes us to overthink occasionally, to the point that we freak ourselves out and retract.

When we do this, we rob ourselves of the opportunity for expansion. This small win for fear causes us to momentarily doubt our abilities and get a little anxious. By following through with our intentions and committing to the journey of growth we learn to grow our success muscle. In doing so, we can learn to continue on in the presence of fear and still move forward. It's not about avoiding any fear, it's about doing it anyway.

> Believe me, when these little thoughts creep up on you and doubt starts to take hold, you are doing the right thing. It means you are onto something, and by pushing yourself time and time again you'll learn how to overcome greater obstacles.

All the doubts and limiting beliefs that crop up when you decide to take a big leap or have an innovative business idea will you hold back from following through on that idea and taking action on it. So don't listen to the voice in your head that says, 'it's too hard,' 'I'm too tired,' 'it won't work,' 'it's impossible,' 'I've tried,' 'I've done everything I can do' – don't give in to these thoughts, see them as a sign you need to move forward anyway.

When they appear, pause and ask yourself these simple questions:

- What haven't I thought of yet?
- If I were to do this differently, how could I do it differently?
- How badly do I want this?
- What would Tony Robbins do? (Or some variant of your own inspirational mentor.)

When you start to engage with this type of questioning and being to understand that it's not what is happening to you that's the problem, but how you respond to it, you start to get better at tackling the problems.

It's not that the situations get easier, in fact, they often get harder, it's that you start thinking in a way that is non-linear. Non-linear thought enables you to pluck bits of information from your mind at will and piece them all together information in new and meaningful ways, like Bradley Cooper in the movie *Limitless*. Your mindset is one of expansion. Remember Ryan Serhant's motto, *'expansion always, in all ways'*. This is it, baby, this is where that very mantra comes into play, as well as that consistent way of thinking and the expectation that you will live large.

Flip the switch on your thinking, quieten the voices, the doubts, the fear, and say yes to success instead. Say, 'Hello new take on anything me. I am here and I am not going anywhere.' Reflect on who you'd like to become and march solidly forward in that direction, away from your fears.

Case study: WHSmith's – no room for doubts

It doesn't take longer either. When I was self-publishing my first book, *The Art of Negotiation*, I wanted to see what I could get away with, what I could make happen.

One day I was flying out to Hong Kong on a business trip (not related to the book) and had 5 copies packed, just in case I came across an opportunity for promotion.

I'd always had this vision of getting my book into an airport bookstore. Mainly because I've always thought they have a more interesting and diverse selection of books for sale. I routinely purchase 3 or 4 books on any trip.

Whilst waiting for the flight in Singapore Changi Airport, I set myself a challenge. Before boarding the plane, I needed to convince WHSmith's to stock my book in print at their airport stores. This was not only following my vision, but tuned into my desire and will to see it happen. Challenge accepted, I asked around and located a store. Upon walking into the store, the first thing I made sure I did was to place a copy of my book in the number 1 spot in the charts. I took a photo of this and posted it on Instagram. This was an important visualisation for me, plus it was super cool to see it up there with the big guns, the titans of industry and business, and it was pretty hilarious at the same time.

As cheesy as it sounds, by doing this I was actually connecting to my higher energy moment. By doing this, I was encouraging the Universe to see what I was going after and seeing my book up there, in pride of place, after all the hard work I had put into it, was the first step to realising the next part of my dream.

My first book at no.1

The next thing I did was walk directly up to counter, get in line and then, when it was my turn, ask to speak to the manager. I explained that I was a local author and I'd like to get my book into the store, and asked, "How can we make this happen?" (This invites the other person to stop any thoughts they were going to say and, instead, think about the request and how it could be possible. The linguistic structure of this exact question is important as it influences people's decisions and what they will share with you).

I was told I needed to find the big boss located in another part of the airport, at the main WHSmith's, so off I went in search of the head honcho.

When I arrived and found the store, I had to convince the person at the counter to go get the manager. She was the gatekeeper and wasn't having much of it, but I told her it was important. I did this with confidence, as I needed to back myself and back my dream of getting my booking into WHSmith's Airport stores.

Reluctantly, off she went to find the manager at the back office. Moments later, the manager appeared and I began my pitch for the second time. Once I'd finished, I told them they could keep the book as long as it got into the hands of the right person.

I value my product and don't give it out willy-nilly but, in this case, I was happy to leave it. Actually, that was my plan all along. The manager seemed grateful and promised she would give it to her buyer to have a look at. I handed her a business card and flew to Hong Kong happy that I had managed to get my book into the right person's hands and I could potentially be on the way to achieving my dream.

In a moment of inspiration, I used the high energy created from this mini-success to see what else I could achieve and by the time I'd landed, I had sent emails to all the major bookstores in the UK, Singapore, and Australia and even received a couple of replies.

Over the course of the weeks and months that followed, this chain of events led to me getting my book into all 10 WHSmith stores in Changi Airport, as well as signing a distribution deal with a local promoter to get my book into all leading bookstores across Singapore, Malaysia and Brunei. To put it in context, the first order from WHSmith was 100 books, meaning those two in-store conversations and persistence in trying to create a deal from nothing lead to net sales of $700 and the prestige of now working with one of the biggest global retailers in the world. The opportunity that laid before me was even bigger. WHSmith's operate over 800 stores, meaning that this was only the tip of the iceberg. Not only did this deal have the potential to grow through repeat orders (which they did) but just some simple back of a napkin maths will tell you that an order of 10 books per store at $7 per book across a network of 800 stores, that's a potential profit of $56,000.

All this from a desire to make it happen and see what I could do with a copy of my book and myself.

On top of this, I did another deal to get my book printed in Singapore at 40% of the cost I was currently paying in England. This is when things really started moving in the right direction. The major bookstores in Australia and the UK came on board and did deals with me.

By localising my printing in Asia, it allowed me to make more profit on all of my book deals, which gave me more motivation to see what else I could achieve. By understanding the mechanics and tweaking certain elements of the operational process, I was able to go into business with some of the largest distributors on the planet and still make a profit, even as an independent publisher.

Being a single author versus a sea of giant publishing agents with already proven *New York Times* bestselling authors on their roster, I had to realise what an incredible golden opportunity this was to get my book front and centre in one of the world's busiest airports with 62.2 million passengers passing through each year! This introduction led to my book getting into all the major Singapore bookstores and sales started to flow through.

Receiving my first $1,000 pay cheque from my cut of the sales of my first book was an incredible feeling. Finally, I had built another revenue stream, sold my first product and was adding value to the world by developing people's negotiation skills and confidence, one book at a time. It changed something in me, I had finally crossed that bridge from dream to reality and now the wheels of motion were starting to turn. I now saw how you create passive revenue streams that work for you even whilst you are sleeping.

> Remember what I said about multiple plates spinning at once. When inspiration hits you, don't wait, just act on it in the moment and try to maintain the state of energy for as long as possible.

All it takes is a simple email making a request with specific questions like, 'who can I speak to?' 'how can we make this happen?' and then a consistent follow-up with the right energy.

As an additional side note to this story, WHSmith's got in touch almost exactly 1 year later after I took this photo, and said that they wanted to add *The Art of Negotiation* to their bestseller chart. This truly shows the power of intention and thinking big.

Case study: change up the energy

I'll give you another example of energy and being in the right place. My wife Sandra is a qualified personal trainer and nutritionist. She has built up her own very successful business from the ground up. The business is called Move Breathe Dream and is a health and well-being venture that provides coaching, courses and content to support your life goals in these areas.

Things really took off once we sat down and got the foundation of the business strategy in line and all the pipes connected ready for it to scale. It was as if the process of getting the business ready for success made it a success. But there was one thing that made all the difference which we did when times got tough, and the business nearly got binned, and that was to change our environment.

At the time Sandra and I had been living, working full-time, studying, building our side businesses and having a baby all from the comfort of a tiny studio apartment situated right off the main beach in Manly, Australia. The unit was full to the brim with stuff. It was clear that we could do with a bigger space, but the money we were saving on the rent was funding our businesses, and we had fallen in love with the convenience and character of the place after 5 years there.

That's not to say it was easy. Many a night I spent working in the bathroom on MBA projects, writing to editors and composing chapters of my first book. Sandra did the same. We worked wherever we could and whenever inspiration and our baby would allow.

Before the baby, we would sometimes go all weekend barely saying a word to each other just reading and working, hustling to get our side-businesses off the ground. We were both just so tuned into what we were doing and felt completely amazing working all weekend on projects that we loved. We both had a 'let's see what we can achieve' mentality.

But one day, after many struggles with time and space, the mood in the apartment changed and what was once hub of aspiration, inspiration and growth transformed to a place of repression and lack. Sandra had been hustling to get her first product launched for a few weeks, sometimes working until 3am to craft her message and ensure she fully believed in the content she was creating. She put her heart and soul into this project and got it over the line in time for her launch deadline.

The next day, she launched her first course to the world and waited for the sales to roll in. As hours went by, she started to realise how she really felt. The weight of carrying out the task was lifted, and she let herself feel for the first time in days. In this moment, it dawned on her that the sprint was now over, she might feel a bit down and it could be an anticlimax.

We realised that if we got caught up in our day-to-day tasks too much and focus on external recognition as a metric for success then we could lose sight of what matters.

We had a chat and decided we needed to get out. Get out of Manly, somewhere that she could create fresh content and re-engage with the purpose of building Move Breathe Dream. We booked flights that morning, packed a bag and headed off for five days in the Whitsunday Islands for a Move Breathe Dream strategy session. We changed the scenery and rented a large 2-bed villa overlooking some of the most incredible landscape we had ever seen.

Much like big businesses, if you want your small business to take off then you need to treat it like it is a real business, and this means getting into the nitty-gritty of the detail around your exact business structure, what your goals are, and how you will measure success. We realised she had been jumping from one project to the next without considering the business strategy. By taking this break from the hamster wheel she had created, we noticed that the business had stopped being a hub of innovation and life and this had started to hold us back.

She needed to reshape the business and define its vision, mission and core objectives. Who was this business really for? Who did she want to help, deep down? We completed a full Business Model Canvas (a strategic management and lean start-up template designed to capture new and existing business models, which forces you to think about your business' mission statement, value proposition and customers, among other things) and over the course of 5 days came up with revenue forecasts, social media strategy, marketing plans and had many, many brainstorms.

We got creative and covered the villa in A3 flipchart paper with diagrams and words that helped to design the future of the business. By treating it like a successful business it became one, and by spending and investing the time to make sure she knew exactly where she was going, we were able to figure out how she was going to get there.

Out of these strategy days in our Whitsundays retreat came change. Sandra realised that the course she had taken for months hadn't yet reached her full potential and realised her vision, so she set about developing the next iteration. She was more accepting with her time constraints and the tools that we found on the trip allowed her to become more efficient.

The results were phenomenal, sales started to come in, her social media followers grew, and word of mouth spread. Slowing down and changing the energy had allowed her to recreate the business stronger.

So if you are ever at a point where you want to throw in the towel on your vision, maybe it's time for a change of scenery. There was a point to why we chose the Whitsundays as a destination and booked a large villa. It certainly wasn't that we had the cash to blow. It was because we wanted to strike out of our pattern. By being in a larger a space and giving ourselves the room to think in a space larger than our apartment, it allowed us to find the path forward. We needed a radical change, somewhere that would allow us to drop our natural habits of trying to fix the problem and get super creative instead. Sandra understood this at exactly the right time, and she crafted a business that was stronger, with both the foundations and strategy to be a long-term successful enterprise and, most importantly, had her gunning for it.

Sometimes to 10x it, we need to step away from our current environment and replace it with an even bigger one.

Something that makes us say, 'I want to afford this in real life, or I want to do this again'. Give yourself the freedom to have this in your life. We get one time on this beautiful planet, and a brief reprieve from the grindstone means we can step up and come back with more vigour and ingenuity than ever before. It's about breaking the habits to enhance the direction and then resetting the habits. By stepping away, it allows us the space to play big.

CHAPTER 18

MAINTAIN A MISSION-DRIVEN MINDSET

"The successful warrior is the average man with
laser-like focus."

Bruce Lee

JUST LIKE BRUCE Lee said, a mission-driven mindset is about having laser-like focus on where it is you're going. This does not mean you have a fixed mindset, there is a difference. It's about being able to stay focused on the bigger picture of where you're headed and managing all the day-to-day distractions that try to throw you off course or take you away from your mission.

In society today, the demands on our attention are somewhat overwhelming. So, if you aren't careful, it can take a phenomenally long time to get anything at all done, not to mention achieve the success you desire in your chosen calling.

From the crazy number of WhatsApp messages that interrupt your train of thought, to the non-urgent, non-important Skype messages that ping across your desktop and the notifications that bombard your mobile, there are many irritating detours in your journey to living your purpose.

It's safe to say there are a plethora of pitfalls to avoid when you are trying to create a new or improved life for yourself. The moment you decide to change your life or do something big for yourself, like start a business or write a book, people, situations and distractions seem to come out of the woodwork to try and derail your very good intentions. If this is happening to you right now, don't panic. It's actually a good thing. Take it as a sign that you're on the right track and things in your life are starting to shift.

Now we need to streamline your mindset for success so that you can stay on the fast-track mission-driven superhighway.

Being mission-driven means that you don't give in or give up when times get tough or when you experience setback after setback, challenging times or adversity. Lions are built to weather the storm and you, my friend, are well on your way right now to becoming a fully-fledged lion.

Why is a mission driven mindset important?

If you are mission-driven, then nothing and no one can stop you from getting to your goal. It doesn't matter how long it takes, or how many obstacles you have to overcome, you will make it to your destination.

Adopting this mindset when you are overcoming challenges is important because it allows you to stay on track. Imagine this type of mindset as your map. If you've ever done orientation exercises or attended Scouts, then you'll know just how important map reading is when it you're out in the field. Now imagine that your map gets covered in mud and ripped up because everyone in your group is tugging on it. It becomes super hard to read, let alone orientate yourself to your goal when you have to read it through the dirt and the rain, while fighting other people's wants and wishes. These elements can even destroy or alter the map, which makes it much harder to effectively utilise, leaving you lost and wondering how you got there.

I am speaking morphically here, of course, but you get the idea. If you let other people throw you off course or make their problems, situations and decisions more important than your own needs, or allow distractions to change where you are headed, then you'll end up going round in circles and spending your life wondering where you are meant to be going.

Being mission-driven doesn't mean that you're stubborn in not taking on other perspectives or considering other points of view; it means that you're are stubborn in the pursuit of your goal and yet open-minded and flexible about the numerous possible routes to get there.

What's your next play?

The inspirational CEO of LinkedIn, Jeff Weiner, has been at the company's helm since 2008, growing the company from 368 people to now way over 12,000 in the space of ten years. On top of this incredible achievement, he has navigated the company through major growth phases, including listing the company on the New York Stock Exchange in 2011 and its acquisition by Microsoft in 2017.

You've got to wonder how each of these growth hurdles and achievements didn't knock the company off its vision, which is to create economic opportunity for the world's global work force. How did it stay focused and not get blinded by the bright lights of success or shrink away and disappear in the hard times? What allowed it to stay the course?

I believe it came down to a philosophy called '*Next play*' that Jeff has ensured is ingrained deeply at the core of the business. This comes from a technique he picked up from Coach K (Duke Universities Men's Basketball Head Coach since 1980).

In Jeff's own words, Coach K's mantra goes like this:

'Every time his team goes up and down the court, completing sequences and switching from offense to defence and back again, Coach K yells out, "Next play!"

He repeats this over and over throughout the course of the games because he wants his players to be focusing on the next play ahead of them, not on what just happened.

> He doesn't want them to excessively celebrate hitting a big shot or to get down about an ill-timed turnover. Whatever's just happened – good or bad – is in the past.

This is not to say that Coach K doesn't encourage his players to take a moment to reflect on what just happened. Rather, his point is that you should not linger too long on it. Briefly reflect and move on to the next play. This is key.

And you see this time and time again when you look at other successful entrepreneurs and business titans.

When Elon Musk sold his company Zip 2 for $309m, banking a tidy $22m for himself at the age of 28, he didn't stop to retire on a dessert island (he did buy a Maclaren F1 though, which he was well known for driving around the Bay Area) and was off again, within a couple of months, starting a new company that would later be known as PayPal.

Within two years of founding PayPal, he sold it to eBay for $1.5 Billion, that's Billion with a B! Not done yet, he took major risks by directing all the funds he had at his disposal into 3 new ventures – Solar City, Space X and Tesla.

Each of these companies went through tough times during the recession, especially Tesla. Elon had to back these businesses with his last remaining funds because no investors would support an electric car company.

The lesson is that Elon goes all in when he believes in an idea without stopping to dwell for too long on the past. He's willing to make the hard decisions, and much like Jeff, he's going after a bigger vision.

The 'Next play' philosophy means you do not to get too wrapped up in what just happened and focus instead on where you are going as a whole in the bigger picture of your life.

Mistakes are inevitable, if you are going to grow then mistakes are the fastest way forward. This is how informed decisions are born, from previous misinformed decisions and life experience.

Ultimately, being able to learn from your mistakes and then apply the lesson so that you are able to make higher quality decisions at speed is how you can achieve new levels of success.

The benefits of not focussing on what just happened for too long are apparent and it is a mentality that I try to adopt where possible. I'm not perfect at it, but when I get it right, I can clearly see how it has allowed me to focus on where I am headed and not stay wedded to what's happened in the past.

There are countless examples of how adopting a mission driven mindset can allow you to achieve incredible feats and overcome all manner of obstacles.

Moving swiftly on from successes is a core element of how the successful stay successful; after all, growth comes from both challenge and friction, so it stands to reason that the secret to continual expansion is not dwelling on achievement for too long and getting on with the next big challenge or adventure. It works both ways, moving on to the next play after successes and the failures is the way to consistently reach your goals, expand your horizons and traverse new levels of performance.

Keep moving forward when times get tough

This is also true in times of incredible adversity. Sheryl Sandberg, the bestselling author, Chief Operating Officer of Facebook and Mark Zuckerberg's right-hand woman, wrote a marvellous book on overcoming adversity. She crafted *Option B: Facing Adversity, Building Resilience and Finding Joy* together with Adam Grant, Organizational Psychologist at Wharton and also a bestselling author. This is a brilliant read on how to move through unexpected challenges and still get the most out of life.

The book is unquestionably a gift sent to change our planet's approach to handling grief and what it means to lose a loved one.

In a moment of darkness, Sandberg reached out to Grant, who jumped on the next plane to explain that a person has 'no fixed amount' of resilience; it is a muscle that can be built, so the question is how could she develop her resilience?

The main focus the book is to provide a guide to building resilience in times of unthinkable sadness, but the message rings true for any challenge. Its creation was prompted by the sudden death of Sheryl's beloved husband, Dave Goldberg, and is born out of her experience of continuing on in life, raising her two kids on her own and facing the road ahead. Sheryl forged Option B and its subsequent community.

Option B was largely built out of Sheryl's copious notes which she wrote diligently every day in the years following the tragedy. Sheryl is determined to bring the value to the world and to make sense of a happening that does not make sense. She is fully resolved to do this in any way she can, and to help others develop their own resilience muscle, so that they can make the best of Option B when Option A is taken from you.

> "Option A is not available, so let's just kick the shit out of Option B."
>
> *Sheryl Sandberg*

Dealing with overwhelm

At one point in my life, I had an awful lot on my plate. I lay there in bed, sweating profusely, my mind panicked with thoughts about the day ahead. There was everything I needed to complete, and all the things that could go wrong, and *oh shit* my worsening and ever-expanding financial situation. My head felt as if it might explode and I just wanted everything to STOP!

Sound familiar?

We all have times in our lives when it just seems too much. Maybe it's work, maybe it's people, maybe it's your finances – overwhelm can crop up anywhere.

Then we find can ourselves looking back at past circumstances with rose-tinted glasses, like previous jobs or old relationships. We may view these now as heavenly compared to our current scenario, when in reality, there were very good reasons those things ended.

Deep down, I believe that overwhelm is connected to our need to control the situation and our desire to reduce the unknown.

The hard truth is that dealing with the unknown is unavoidable because the future is unavoidable. When the balance of unknown elements in our lives tips out of sync with what we are comfortable with, i.e. it extends past our comfort zone and there are multiple areas in our life that are unknown (When will I find a great job?

How can I afford to eat this month? What if I get fired? What if I get dumped? When will I be financially free? Do they love me? Why am I not loveable?) all screaming for attention at once, then overwhelm has well and truly got its claws in.

The feeling of overwhelm creeps up on us from behind, like a suffocating weight that can feel quite scary. If this happens to you and you find yourself lying there, with these thoughts whizzing around your head, hoping that you will eventually fall asleep, pull yourself out of bed and follow these tips to dealing with overwhelm.

Activities to help reduce overwhelm

These activities break the overwhelm feedback loop by getting you to do something different. It is often said you cannot solve a problem with our current thinking because that is the thinking which got us there in the first place. Cue Albert Eisenstein: *"No problem can be solved with the same level of consciousness that created it."*

1. **Proactively seek fun** – Play table tennis, go rollerblading or swimming in the ocean. All of these types of activities help to reduce the onset and build-up of overwhelm as they get you out of your head and engage your playful side. This includes anything that gets your body moving in quick explosive bursts in reaction to an unpredictable environment, like your opponent's terrifyingly rapid serve in table tennis, which comes at you spinning in all its glory and begging you to return it. These activities promote feelings of fun, mental relaxation, and creativity, which brings me to my next point.

2. **Get creative** – Painting, drawing, photography, writing, vlogging, or anything else that will change your focus from your immediate state of overwhelm to a state of possibility. Being creative will unwind the knot of tension in your brain, activate a different part and awaken a bit of freedom. Creativity changes your focus and therefore your perspective. After 20 minutes of creativity, you

often forget about the problem you were trying to solve. By letting go of what was overwhelming, temporarily gives your mind the flexibility to be able to perform at its best. When you return to the problem, you are then able to look at it from alternative angles and see different patterns that you weren't able to spot before. This is all because you have freed your mind and become flexible and agile again.

3. **Open your heart** - Give your problem to the Universe. Surrender to the problem instead of trying to control it. The mission here is to hand your problem over to a power greater than you. If that sounds crazy, what you're aiming to do here is to let it go. It's easy to think about, but harder to execute. Why do we wait until the beginning of a new year to forgive and start again, to begin new habits and let go? When I am overwhelmed and the above is not working, I try to let it go, even if it's by only a small amount. Remaining stressed and fixated on a problem will not help you solve it. When I find myself getting wound up by a problem, I put on my headphones and listen to the Yoga and Meditation playlist on Spotify (don't try to control the order of the songs, just start at the beginning of the playlist and let your mind wander), or get out into nature, somewhere with trees, rivers and fields if possible, and focus on noticing the beauty of the world. The leaf as it falls from the tree and the butterfly as it flutters by.

Spending an hour like this, noticing how graceful the world is can teach us lessons: patience, grace, love and of the cycle of life and death. It normally minimises my problem and gives me perspective. Nature has a lot to show us if we are open to it. This helps you to let go of your resentments, pressures and built-up tension. Instead, you can become at one with the environment. Let the breeze flow through your hair and the powerful force of nature can take over. Give yourself this gift. It's not something you have to force. Just begin the process and after a few minutes you should notice your mind start to quieten and your focus reframe as your intuition connects to your surroundings and helps you to see again. Don't be alarmed if you notice more than you normally would, this is good, and it means you are letting go, switching off and seeing the present moment. In this state, the colours may seem more vivid.

Depending on how overwhelmed I am, it could take longer than a few minutes to reach this state. That is why I try to make this practise a part of my everyday routine, letting my mind drift and detach from unhelpful thoughts. This decreases the potential for overwhelm and connects with a bigger force than myself through nature. Try it for yourself and release the burden of overwhelm you think you must carry. Try something new.

4. **Help Somebody Else** – by helping others, we help ourselves. Not only is this an excellent practise, as it takes your focus away from you and your life and your problems, it also gives you an opportunity to serve others and be your best self. It opens your mind up again to new perspectives, experiences, and solutions.

5. **Take charge and take responsibility** – what was your part and your contribution to how you ended up in this overwhelming state? What could you have done differently? What do you need to take responsibly for? What can you learn from this for the future? What is the worst that can happen?

By taking ownership and responsibility for your part in the situation, you shift from the victim to the leader and you are able to make better decisions. If there is anyone you need to apologise to, then do it. When we are overwhelmed and stressed it's easy to make rash decisions, say things we didn't mean and hurt other's emotions. This compounds the situation and makes it harder to resolve. By acting from a place of love and understanding, you are better able to transform the situation and get the result you desire. Open a note pad and make a list of whatever is buzzing around in your mind. Break down the situation into bite size pieces. Rather than this gigantic thing that needs to be solved, look at each problem individually. Is there anything you can solve easily?

These activities are tried and tested strategies for shaking you out of that mental funk (the consciousness that created the problem) and transforming your mind into a clearer, more positive state. Only once you have achieved that level of consciousness should you delve back into the problem or situation that is worrying you.

For me, I find that if I am woken up within the first 10 minutes after falling asleep (say, for example, my wife comes into the bedroom and decides that she must tell me then and there, who won *The Batchelor* – this actually happened!) then I find it incredibly difficult to go back to sleep again (not because of the result, but because of the interruption) and I am usually in for a night of broken sleep.

I am one of those people that is classed as a "light sleeper". I wake up very easily and quickly, and as soon as I do, my mind starts going and the ideas start to flow. In this state, some of my most creative and beautiful thoughts can manifest.

I love this state in the early morning, at 5am, but at 12.05am, my mind typically starts dragging in all the crap I just want to shut out, like why am I still doing this job? Or how could I have handled that situation in the meeting today better? Or should I be working out for longer or writing this book more? It goes and on and on; you get the picture.

If this happens, I have trained myself to get up. I then make the best of the situation rather than marinate in a state of increasing overwhelm in the hope that it will end, or that I will fall back to sleep.

Now I get myself up out of bed and go do something completely different to take my mind of all these awfully confusing random musings that ping about out like cooked popcorn from a hot pan.

I will then begin to write a blog post or get stuck into something creative, as per the examples above. Don't be afraid to do something different, something outside of your normal patterns of behaviour. There have been times when I've been wide awake and decided to go to the 24-hour gym to work out or I catch a late-night movie. I find that the more I lean towards the creative, like composing a cold email to enhance my business, crafting a birthday card for someone on Moonpig or even buying them a thoughtful gift, my mind begins to shift from the impossible to the possible, and the world starts to become a place of Zen. As I let go of the thoughts about money and mistakes, they start to have less of an effect on my mental state. Slowly, I return to becoming resourceful again and suddenly my eyes are opened to the massive abundance and possibility that is all around me, I then remember there are multiple solutions to my musings of only minutes ago. For example, I could apply for a new job, better yet I could brainstorm 10 companies that I would like to work for and approach them proactively now.

I could also take a course to develop my skills in a certain area and make some new friends, design an online education course about a topic that I am passionate about and then sell it online to create an alternative source of passive income.

> When you free the mind from its cage of overwhelm, it's possible to become the person you need to be to solve the problem and attain new levels of success.

By shifting away from overwhelm towards creativity, you reduce the need to control that has built up in you and become open again to possibility. I also fully believe that creativity gets the juices flowing and brings with it the joy and passion of having fun.

Overwhelm is associated with the belief that things have to go a certain way for them to be right, acceptable, or meet our standards. Whereas fun can walk into many situations and make them infinitely more inspiring.

Fun and creativity go hand in hand. When I am ready, I turn fun back on those problems I have been conjuring up in my mind.

How could I have more fun in my current work? What could I bring to this job that would make the day more enjoyable for me and those around me? What could I bring to the role?

What could I do if money way not an issue? What would I do if I had all the money that I needed? Shifting my thinking on into this dimension forces me to come up with answers that are different to the fearful ones that have been playing on repeat and I, instead, apply a less permanent approach to the circumstance.

By reducing the circumstance's power over us and reframing it as temporary, we can now manifest a deeper sense of love in the situation. This means we transition from a place of self-loathing and guilt to a place of love and abundance.

We can instead begin to pat ourselves on the back for how we have handled ourselves in the meeting today – considering all that was going on and how it could have gone down – rather than beating ourselves up over one minor point.

The shift toward self-love and self-belief starts to build once again and, in the process, we are freed from the repetitive nature of the negative thought pattern.

Once we are in this state of joy, we can look at what was overwhelming us in the first place (I'll give you a clue, it usually has more to do with us than the other person).

By looking objectively and fearlessly owning whatever comes up for us, we can surrender the truth of the matter to our higher power, to the Universe. By connecting again with source energy that is a million times more powerful than us, we give the situation over to our higher power, in whatever form this shows up for you. In my case, this is God.

Once this connection is made, we hand it over and surrender the problem up, no matter how big it may seem to us, because compared to the power of the Universe, it is tiny.

By realising and connecting to the universal power, we realise that we are not alone and we can tackle anything that comes in our path as long as we remain open. As humans we try in vain to control things that are happening to us, when we will get that promotion or fall in love. Or when the whole world will recognise our brilliance.

We are controllers, but by handing our situations over, we become so much more aligned to the brilliance and force of the Universe and can relax in the knowledge that everything we are going through is there to teach us something, and that it will come to us at the exact right time for us.

This leads me to my next point. At this stage, with our problems handed over, we are now free again to go and push the edges of what we can achieve.

I normally have a few burning ideas about what I would love to do, like sit down and interview Tony Robbins. So, I write a list and get to work trying to make it happen. I send tweets, letters, emails, tag them in Instagram posts, whatever it takes, and whatever I *think* I can get away with.

On top of this, I compose another list, my "What I would do right now if I had all the money, I needed list". I write down whatever comes to mind, then I do it. It could be a small indulgence, like ordering a tub of chocolate fudge ice cream to my house or something bigger like booking flights to India.

Interestingly, it's not usually the money that's the stopper; instead, it's not having the thought in the first place. When do we actually take time out in our daily lives to think about what we would do right now if money was no object? I like to ask myself, what would I be doing here if money was no issue? How would I be handling this situation? It's an important question to investigate because it requires thought on a new level, that of absolute possibility. It also allows us to recognise that sometimes all it takes to move in the direction of our goals is to take the first step, which doesn't have to be all that expensive. By repeating this over time, we then find that we have learned to expand the parameter of what we think is possible by taking action (even if it is only small steps) and proving that it can be done.

To condition the mind to spot opportunity, you need to repeatedly set aside the time to explore questions such as this and allow the brain to expand its horizons and break away from normal thought patterns.

> When we live a life of abundance, the things we deem to be out of our grasp are not too many steps away, if we really think about it.

This is a place of action, a place for less deep thinking and more living.

I find that money, the desire for more wealth and the activation of abundance really comes down to freedom. This shows up in the connections, relationships and options that I have, the way I allow myself to be each day, and the degree to which I can relax into the feeling of knowing that *it will happen for me*.

For example, when I talk about abundance, I am speaking about the financial gain that allows me and my family to experience new places, travel to exotic locations and pursue projects we are interested in. But I am also referring to life on a more passionate level – the amount of love we experience in our relationship, the freedom we have to explore our wildest hopes and dreams, the abundance of giving, the flow of opportunities and the abundance of worthiness, joy and compassion.

There is no greater feeling that when you are connected to the Universe, sure in the knowledge that you are one and you can live in the loving presence of life itself and be truly yourself in all that you do. My greatest desire is to be able to help anyone I chose to – and on some level – I already can, as long as I remember that both the level of abundance that is available to me and how freely I give is dependent on how I am thinking and showing up in each moment.

PART 3

CERTAINTY
(SELF-BELIEF STRATEGIES)

INTRODUCTION TO PART 3

"Our deepest fear is not that we are inadequate. Our deepest fear is that we are powerful beyond measure. It is our light, not our darkness, that most frightens us. We ask ourselves, 'Who am I to be brilliant, gorgeous, talented, fabulous? Actually, who are you not to be?"

Marianne Williamson

Now we have reached the part in the book that I know some of you will have looked forward to the most – how to build self-confidence and self-belief. We will look at all the ways that we can stop ourselves from achieving our full potential and do away with them. Personally, I am always looking for self-confidence hacks. I could never quite figure out why I was holding myself back, or why I let other people take the lead in certain situations and not others. It baffled me for years. I would feel the drive and the fight inside but my self-belief (or lack thereof) would hold me back at times from reaching my full potential, such as when I thought it wasn't meant for me or when I was being humble and letting someone else have the limelight.

In this part, I am going to show you how to engage your *fight* inside and feel a level of unwavering, go-getter, all-encompassing, rock-solid, *nothing can stop me* level of **certainty** about your right to go out there and make something of yourself. This will enable you to believe in yourself wholeheartedly. The right that it *is* yours and you *do* deserve it; in fact, it was meant for you. All you have to do is own it. Give yourself permission to own your **certainty**. It is vital to your overall success because the more you can be *you*, the more you free yourself of what you feel you should be. You learn to ditch the haters (your inner critic and other people) and focus on being all that you were born to be. Give yourself permission to be yourself.

Be proud of who you are and what you have accomplished. Be proud of the fact that you are willing to try and attain new levels of success and be proud of who you are becoming. This is your time to shine! It is time to build the next level of yourself, the you that you already are.

A lion is certain, it's king of the jungle, a lion knows who it is and what it's about. Think of all the quotes about this, like *'a lion doesn't concern itself with the opinions of the sheep'*, as it's true a lion, it doesn't give a f*ck! What this quote means is that a lion has detached its sense of self-worth from others, so it doesn't get its self-belief or self-worth from anyone else. It's not looking outside itself for that source of recognition and approval and, as such, it is free to act accordingly. That is why I love the lion analogy so much and why I decided to title this book *Be The Lion* because it is the embodiment of the 4Cs and does so without knowing it; that's just who it's meant to be.

And the same goes for us human. When we are little kids born into the world, we don't concern ourselves with anything other than living life to the full.

Then we are shamed, self-doubt appears and we start to question our sense of self. *Who am I? Am I really worthy?* We compare ourselves and our achievements to others, then our self-worth starts to deplete, and we lose our way. It's not hard to see how the world, and we as the human race, have gone so far off track.

I am here to tell you that you were born a lion, you started with your self-worth intact and it is possible to get back to that point once again. You have a purpose, everyone does. We each have unique talents and gifts that we were born to share with the world. We are more confident in what we are doing if we are authentic, if we are truly connecting with what we are good at and our purpose.

If a lion believes something is true, it is. If it believes it can do something, it goes for it with an absolute level of **certainty** that delivers the goods and a persistence that means it never gives up, whatever the setback.

There is an old Chinese proverb that describes this perfectly: "Tension is who you think you should be. Relaxation is who you are."- *Chinese proverb*

When we operate as our true self, our natural gifts and abilities shine through. Having **certainty** is directly related to how much self-love you have. Not in a narcissistic or *Instagram – everything I ever did because I'm the best* – kind of way, but as a result of a deeper knowing of who you are and what you have to offer.

You were born to be a lion, to be great and to shine. Don't let anyone, and I mean anyone, tell you otherwise. Don't give them the power to hold you back from your greatest achievements or playing big. It can be done. It will be done. You can do it. It takes all your muscles and all your might, but if you keep working it, keep fighting, you will improve and you will make it.

Behold the part of the book where we get real; we will open you up and build your inner strength like never before. By the end of this part, you will have unleashed the lion on the world and the world had better watch out because a new, more confident, more in-tune and more certain you is on the way!

CHAPTER 19

SELF-BELIEF

"Everything you've ever wanted is
on the other side of fear."

George Addair

Pump it

I feel self-belief is misunderstood. People often say, 'I could never do that' or 'that's just not me' or 'I don't know how you did it'. The thing is it's not a case of *can* you do it, you can do it, no questions asked. It's just are you willing to relax into yourself so that you can allow yourself to do it. Self-belief is awesome. When you start making decisions from a place of awesomeness, greatness happens. To be the lion, you need unwavering self-belief. However, it isn't always easy to cultivate. Lack of self-belief will really stop you from achieving your potential, so it's an important thing to get on top of. However, improving your self-belief (like anything worth doing) takes commitment, and in my experience, this is the part that takes practice. In this chapter, I will share some ways to start building up your self-belief, so that you can confidently stride forward with whatever you want to do.

For years, I held back on presenting my best self for fear of being rejected. I didn't want to be 'too good' for fear of standing out. It wasn't until I believed in myself and didn't give a f*ck what anyone else thought, just like the lion, that things changed. I still have to work at this and there are times when it can feel harder to stand in your own light, but trust me, it is way better than being a mouse when you are born to be a lion.

I shied away from challenges at work, like pitching to a big client or leading a large team. Now I have stepped up my self-confidence, I eat that shit for breakfast, but it wasn't easy and it took me years of sticking with it. The more you believe you can do it, the more you actually do it and the better you get at it. It's an ironic truth but if I'd never mustered the belief to do those big pitches, I would not be as good at them as I am today. I would have held myself back and let another colleague step up to the challenge and get all the praise. It helped when I found a tribe of people that I could relate to (the Sydney MBA and various people in my chosen career), This helped me recognise that there was more to life than boozing or just getting by and that it was okay to invest in things that *I* found interesting, even if no one else thought it was cool.

Once I tapped into my lion spirit, I could not go back. There were various moments along the way that made me so determined, so focused and so filled with rage that I refused to ever go back to the way I had been living previously.

Where in your life do you want more self-belief? Which area?

My framework for improving self-belief is simple, once you're committed and you've told yourself that enough is enough, you will no longer operate in the shadows. You are ready to begin.

How to improve your baseline level of self-belief

Some days I wake up raring to go. I am pumped with self-belief. *Goals, I am coming for you! Life, I am coming for you!* Nothing can stop me. It changes the way I walk, communicate, hold myself. It influences the way I perceive the world and the way I give back. It isn't always easy to be pumped up with self-belief, and just like life, it will go up and down. The goal is to get your baseline of self-belief higher overall by giving yourself the best opportunity to do so.

Here are my 12 core components to improve self-belief

1. Workout daily (run, power walk, gym, class, swim, boxing, weights, cardio etc. Do some form of physical exercise.)

2. Meditate for 20 minutes every day (find somewhere quiet and calm and make it your space)

3. Take time for yourself, ideally 30 minutes each day (have a bath, research a trip you want to take etc. or listen to an audiobook you like. Taking time for yourself is a way to show yourself self-love.)

4. Read interesting stuff (books, papers, magazines, articles, blog posts)

5. Get people that empower you into your life (friends, mentors, coaches)

6. Know what you won't tolerate (in your job, relationship, home, family, self)

7. Don't eat crap (limit the junk. You know what I am talking about, that sneaky McDonalds, that bag of chips or bar of chocolate in the fridge that is calling your name)

8. Don't drink crap (cut down on the soda, alcohol, and fatty drinks)

9. Don't consume anything that will alter your mood (stick to natural highs)

10. Book a massage (go for them regularly, every 1-2 weeks)

11. Leave inspirational, affirmation notes around the house to remind you how awesome you are! You are a go-getter, a lion, a lady boss/a man boss. You can do anything you put your mind to, so surround yourself with this ethos and own your greatness

12. Sleep (get a mandatory solid 7 hours per night, make it a priority)

When you need a self-belief boost

When you feel your levels flagging, here are a few things you can do to get back on track.

1.Focus on what you can give

To get into pumping-it territory, you need to focus not on what you can get, but on what you can give. This way you are in tune with the Universe. For example, if you are presenting to a large group and trying to sell them something, focus on the fact that you have an opportunity to share value with them, instead of focusing on the sale. You are gifting them information. This simple change moves you to giving territory. Trust me, the audience will open up more when they see that your intention is to empower them.

There are various other ways you can give that help you to improve your own levels of self-belief. You can give through a smile. I've said it before and I'll say it again, amazing things happen when you live life at this vibration. The people you meet will change, offer up solutions, be more likely to support your mission and you are generally helping to raise the vibration of the world.

Smiling is like a mirror, what you give out comes back to you. It might sound airy-fairy or like something out of a *My Little Pony* show, but in all honesty, I want to give you strategies that work, and this works.

When you're feeling depressed, cut off from the world or just tuned out, smiling works. When you feel like crap it can be really hard to smile. I've been there. When you're angry, sad or facing a big challenge, it is the last thing you feel like doing, but smiling is the way forward. It will help you to open doors. Think of smiling as being like energy, and this energy is flowing from you to the world. It is supporting both your vision and mission, and rebuilding you at the same time. Inside, it will top up your self-belief.

2. Don't waste time in negative debate

Another way to stay in this zone is by making sure you do not waste too much time on people that annoy you. The simplest way to reduce their impact is to just agree with them and move on (note: you don't actually have to agree with them, just pretend that you do). Some people will just annoy you. It's a fact of life. They will say things that you didn't expect or disagree with you just to get under your skin because it gives them pleasure. When this happens don't engage with it, not for a second, just agree with them and move on. When you agree with them, it disarms their power. When you rise up and fight you weaken yourself from getting to your own goals because you are spending your precious time having a pointless argument.

There is a key difference though, I am not talking about not standing up for your values, principles or matters of importance. This should not be confused. I am talking about people who don't fit into your world, who are there just to pick a fight or be obnoxious. Just agree with them and move on. You'll find they get bored and move on and you'll find you have more time to focus on where you are headed (probably away from them).

For example, if everyone at work won't stop talking about the fact that you're on a diet, like it's the biggest news ever and you wish they would just get over it already. Just relax. Instead of engaging in it, taking it on or being annoyed, just let it ride on by, like a thought cloud floating out of the window and up into the sky.

Like Winston Churchill famously said, *"You will never reach your destination if you stop and throw stones at every dog that barks."*

You must also ditch the need to be right. Do you always find yourself getting caught in a contest of proving that you are right? For example, when your boss completely ignores the truth and tells you how an event or conversation went down word for word as if it were fact, even though you know that he is completely and utterly incorrect. Do you waste your time trying to prove that you're right and he is grossly incorrect or do you let it go, leaving yourself free to get on with going after your life goals?

As difficult as it is to let it go (and believe me, I understand how hard it when you know the information is being presented in a certain light to make you feel small). However, you must let it go if you want to have time, energy and clarity to focus on what matters. This is what it means to pick your battles.

Proving that you were right doesn't achieve anything. The chances are your boss will still choose to think he was right, and you are wrong, even if you prove it, or worst still, he'll make your life more difficult for showing him up as a fool. Just detach from this potential energy suck and let it disappear on by into the ether.

3. Listen to your intuition

Your intuition is a powerful voice and it is talking to you. You must learn to tune into it and trust what it is saying.

> Self-belief is increased when we learn to trust ourselves and follow through on things that our intuition is signalling we should do.

For example, at times, I'll have a vision of what I need to do, like an epiphany. I'll see a café by a river and know that if I walk in and sit down for one hour I would get straight into creative mode (action) and produce more than in that time than I could in 24 because I'm switched on, totally engaged and ready to maximise. My intuition has told me that it is time to act and I listened to it.

Getting mentally and physically prepared for performing

Everyone gets a bit nervous before something important, like a big pitch, presentation or interview. This is exactly when you need to draw on your self-belief and relax. Aside from knowing the material and a solid understanding of the audience and their needs, I need self-belief if I'm really going to nail it. I have to get my mind up to a state where it's 100% confident and ready to go. I want to share with you what I do to pump myself up so that my mind and body are primed to perform at their best, and I can relax in the presentation room and enjoy the process.

1. **Movement**. To begin with, about half an hour before the presentation, I get my mind conditioned and ready for the task ahead. To do this, I start by moving my arms in a circular motion, round and round. This might sound strange or cause you concern if you're afraid of looking like a lunatic, but this gets the blood pumping, the body warm and it feels fantastic. By swinging my arms around and making myself bigger in size, I activate endorphins and channel any anxiety I might be feeling into positive energy.

2. **Posture**. Next, I stand up tall and straight. This simple change in posture raises my testosterone levels (this happens in both women and men) and it helps to feel more assertive, confident and powerful. Studies have found that this simple but effective act can produce an increase of around 20% more testosterone in only a few minutes. The body is phenomenal when it comes to responding to the signals that you give it and a lion knows how to maximise this. This is especially important to remember if you're going into an interview or meeting someone confrontational or taking on a really big scary challenge that you feel worried about. Changing your posture is a quick way to gain huge results, so stand tall and really go for it! You've got this!

3. **Face**. If you didn't want to look like a lunatic, it's going to be tough now. This process helps me to warm up my vocal cords and prime myself for speaking in a range of tones, tempos, volumes and pitches. I rotate my jaw, round and round, side to side. I stretch my cheeks by filling them with air and I flick my tongue up and down. I cough forcefully and make sure I clear my airways. It's a warm-up for the whole body, especially the mouth. After all, my mouth is going to be doing a lot of the work, so I need it on form and ready to work. You wouldn't go for a marathon without stretching and so you shouldn't go into a pitch without first giving your mouth what it needs.

4. **Affirmations**. Once I'm sufficiently pumped in the body, I need to pump the mind. I tell myself out loud core affirmations, depending on the task at hand and repeat statements, such as

'I can do this,' 'I will do this,' 'I am going to do this,' and 'this is going to be awesome.' This changes my mindset from fear-based to becoming more optimistic and open.

5. **Remember to enjoy it.** I then focus on reminding myself that life is to be enjoyed. Whatever I am about to do, it will probably make a good story if it goes wrong and it's the sign of a life well lived. Either way, the outcome is of little consequence in the grand scheme of things and I should just enjoy the ride. This helps me to give me perspective and gather my thoughts in the moment. I find that when I focus too much on myself during a presentation pitch (e.g. how does my voice sound, am I saying the right things, am I talking too slowly?), I analyse myself too much. This causes me to forget my patter and actually hinders my performance. However, when I focus on telling the story and what the audience needs to hear, based on who they are and what they have told me, I add way more value and the pitch is in flow. I also feel relaxed, which leads to a better overall performance, as I enjoy the event and can relate to the audience by tailoring the content to their needs because I am focused on them and not me.

6. **Remember to be yourself.** People also try to copy other people's styles, especially when presenting, which can sometimes make it harder because you're trying to be someone you're not, as well as attempting to recall the content and look awesome. You will be much better if you are authentic, genuine and yourself so don't complicate things by trying to adopt someone else's way of doing things. I would encourage you to focus on your own style, what makes you relaxed, and your own way of delivering the content. The reason I say this is because every single person has their own style. Some might be alike but they all different, and there is no way that is better style for you than your own. By embracing who you are and bringing that to the table, you can own it and I promise you the feeling of satisfaction of being your true self and performing at a high level is out of this world. So don't

short-change yourself by missing out on this feeling in your life. Next time you face a challenge and go through the pump-it steps, take a new approach and be yourself. If all else fails, just remember it's only a pitch (or whatever the particular challenge is that you're facing).

Courage

> "He who is not courageous enough to take risks will accomplish nothing in life."
>
> Muhammad Ali

Part of encouraging the growth of your own self-belief – that you can do a certain thing or put a plan of your choosing into action – is about maintaining a continuous commitment to nurturing courage. It takes a commitment because courage needs to be cultivated and maintained. You need to practise disciplined behaviours in order to attain a certain level of this self-efficacy. Acting with courage takes practise, but once you master the basics it becomes more natural and easier and easier to execute.

The way to increase your courageousness is to practise it daily. I want to throw down the gauntlet and challenge you to do one thing each day that pushes your boundaries, just to see what you can get away with.

If you apply this mentality to your daily life, you will not only strengthen your courageousness muscle, but also reinforce, through experiential learning, the miracles and wonders that come to life when you fully go for it. Even if you thought the outcome was impossible or unlikely at first, you will naturally open up and experience more self-belief and courage by applying this perception and lens to your life.

Lions are a symbol of courage and, over time, this continuous commitment to being courageous, if practised with discipline, will become your default response. The key is not to plateau if you find yourself wondering where your self-belief went. It's important, instead, to look at how you operate your life on a daily basis. Is your lack of self-belief keeping you stuck, are you repeating the same patterns, telling yourself the same old stories and basically not kicking ass?

If this is you, I want you to make a commitment to yourself and to someone you admire that you are ready for change, and that you will bring your A game to the cause of addressing your own self-belief levels.

Once you have identified that you need increased levels of self-belief (which goes for a lot of people) the key is to take courageous action every single day, forever! There are no off days when it comes to developing your self-belief muscle. Situations that enable you to foster self-belief will show up daily in the unlikeliest of events. The question is, will you rise to the challenge and do what it takes to lead a bold and courageous life?

If there's an interview for a job you want, an audition for a part in a play you'd love, or a hot guy you want to ask out on a date, send the message out. Now is the time to make that change and put your own self-worth first.

I find that affirmations play a big part in solidifying self-belief. As Henry Ford said, 'Whether you think you can, or you think you can't, you're right.' You must start believing in your own greatness. This is important, it's not vain or self-indulgent. You need to get over this idea and realise that we aren't talking about narcissistic behaviour where you fall in love with yourself and are blind to the rest of the world. Instead, this is about promoting thought processes that allow you to flourish into the very best person that you are capable of being.

Here is a list of affirmations to help you build your self-belief in abundance. Repeat any or all of the statements from this list daily, and do this for the next 30 days.

1. I am great.
2. I am lovable.
3. I own my greatness and seek to put good into the world.
4. The only thing stopping me is me.
5. I am worth it.

6. I value myself and believe that I am capable.

7. My gifts are abundant, overflowing and I recognise them daily.

8. I am thankful for the gifts that I have been given.

9. I am skilful, talented and capable of everything I put my mind to.

10. I was put on this Earth to give my gift to the world.

11. I love myself and value my thoughts, feelings, hopes and dreams.

12. I take pride in how far I have come

13. I set an example for those who are struggling.

14. I am courageous, even when I don't feel like I am.

15. Courage pumps through my veins, I am a lion

16. There are no limitations to what is possible for me.

17. I see new opportunities all around me, daily.

18. The opportunities for me are endless.

19. I am surrounded by love and love the world.

20. I give love to the world.

21. I chose to see love.

22. I give love freely and in abundance.

23. My life is a journey and I partake fully.

24. I throw myself into each new day.

25. I commit to being courageous on a daily basis.

26. I can do it.

27. I will do it.

28. I am capable of greatness.

29. I am dedicated, hungry for more and can't wait to overcome the challenge.

30. I am not defined by my past.

CHAPTER 20

FIND YOUR INFLUENCERS AND MENTORS

"Give yourself permission to dream big and be inspired.
Magic happens when you are inspired."

Carrie Green, *She Means Business*

IN THIS CHAPTER, I want to really spend some time looking at how you go about choosing the right mentor and why that's important. I will drive home the message and we'll be having words if, by the end of it, if you haven't got yourself the most incredible mentor, or at least thought of someone to ask, learn from or model yourself on.

Having a mentor is like getting the inside scoop on how to raise your game, avoid the pitfalls and streamline your plan. Anyone who's anyone has a mentor. Tony Robbins had Jim Rohn, Gabrielle Bernstein had Dr Wayne Dyer, Oprah Winfrey had Maya Angelou. The list is endless. What's important to understand here is that getting a mentor is not a sign of weakness, it's part of the process to success. Not only will a mentor be able to help you shape your plan and define it, they will also manoeuvre you through the maze of life's ups and downs give you the real deal. They'll keep you accountable, honest and push you to overcome your greatest fears. A mentor is someone who you admire and you see qualities in that resonate with you; and the beauty of having a mentor is it can be anyone.

Bring on the inspiration

What you feed your mind you become. So make sure you feed it constantly with podcasts, blogs, articles and quotes that fuel your fire and strengthen its intensity. Surround yourself and your life with greatness to push yourself to the next level. On the flip side, you need to stay away from trashy news or anything that brings up negative or fearful thoughts.

> Your mind is like a garden that needs tending. The quality of the stuff you put in will reflect in the ideas and creativity that you put out, and how possible you imagine something to be.

What you feed your mind, you become

When I was younger, my influences were the X Games sports stars and Skateboarding Pros, like Tony Hawk. Then, I moved into my punk rock phase and it was all about bands like Blink 182, Green Day and The Offspring.

Now, my life is consumed with the likes of Tony Robbins, Jack Ma, Gabrielle Bernstein, Richard Branson, Ray Dalio, Sheryl Sandberg and other masters of growth and abundance who live deeply connected to their purpose.

I feed my mind with their content daily, this is my garden's nutrition. I lap it up, each and every day, and make sure that at least an hour a day is spent consuming inspirational, thought-provoking, life-enhancing material.

It's funny because I know every song from the computer games, like Tony Hawk's Pro Skater (the first version) and all the 00's punk rock albums from the genre, I've seen all my favourite bands perform in concert, multiple times in multiple venues across the world. I was obsessive about their content and their lifestyle, and I now have this level of obsession and drive to know more, hear more and understand more about our desire and journey for success. And by success, what I really mean is growth, growth to become more each day and to expand into our true selves so that we can give back in abundance.

Surround yourself with people that push you

I never really understood the phrase, "You are the average of the 5 people that you hang out with most." It bugged me for years, until one day I was listening to a podcast and it clicked. Now, this may be obvious to you, but indulge me while I explain what I find out.

The principle here is that if we are around people who force us to raise our game, we naturally have to impose **higher standards** on ourselves, as this consistent call to ask more of ourselves pushes us to improve.

Think about table tennis in the office, if you play against a work colleague who's incredibly talented, you have to work harder to stay in the game (and this goes for friends as well, as you improve).

Who you spend time with influences your thought patterns, your outlook, how you approach problems and the standards you expect of yourself.

When you reach a point where you are willing to complete with yourself rather than look outward to compete against others, that's when you become unstoppable. This shift from competing with others to competing with what you yourself are capable of is incredibly powerful.

Persistence

It's also the persistence and belief in something bigger that we need to take to make it happen.

I remember my Dad driving me and 3 of my friends down to London's Wembley Stadium to see a Green Day gig. He waited until 2am outside in the stadium car park until I had managed to go backstage and get Tré Cool's (the Green Day drummer's) autograph.

What a legend my dad is! Who would do that? Firstly, driving my friends and me some 300 miles down to London from Nottinghamshire and back and then waiting around for his teenage punk rocker of a son to meet the drummer of the famous band he loved. He even had work in the morning! That's one pretty awesome Dad.

> If you can think it and form an idea in your mind, that is the start of making it happen. Possibility comes from having the thought, focusing on it, and then acting on it.

The forest

My dad was a mentor for me when I was growing up. He taught me to how to care for an array of animals, construct gigantic wooden forts on top of the hill in the garden, and even built a concrete half pipe in the garden for us to skate on.

When visiting family in the North of England we would also go for long walks together in the Lake District for hours at a time. I remember us waking up at the crack of dawn and creeping out of the house whilst the rest of the family was asleep. The blast of crisp Lake District air hit me in the face as I stepped out into the frosty winter morning.

Over the course of the walk, we trekked through miles of fields, deep dark woods and across meandering rivers. One time my dad caught a rainbow trout with his bare hands and lifted it out of the water to show me. He seemed to notice everything. He would spot an owl sitting in the hedgerow and call me over to peer in at it or show me a deer grazing in the fields in the valley below.

What I loved about this was Dad allowed me to experience life on the edge of my comfort zone. He would bring the world alive for me and reveal an unexpected surprise through the beauty of nature or by teaching me how to understand the laws of the world.

I always felt safe with Dad, even in the deepest, darkest forests. I had absolute faith that he knew the way out. On my own, the forest could be a scary place, especially with the noises and claustrophobic nature of the pine trees that blocked out all the sunlight, but I knew I was fine when my Dad was there.

This belief that we would be OK also extended to me believing that he would know what to do if we ever got into trouble. It was the unwavering **certainty** that whatever we came across, he would get us through it.

Sometimes our lives are like the dark forest and we get stuck in the middle going around and around. It can be hard to block out that little voice that fills our head with fearful, anxious, and irrational stories.

Walking through life with a mentor helps you to steer clear of the pitfalls, gain confidence in your own abilities and streamline your progress.

Having a trusted advisor and guide, whose wealth of personal experience and knowledge can enrich your own progress, is a must if you are to grow to your full potential.

I learnt from an early age about the importance of mentors. My Dad was my first, and through him, I learned to overcome my fears and practise things that I would normally think were impossible.

His mentorship showed me a new and improved way to do something. For example, my initial reaction to crossing a deep river was to plunge straight into it without checking the stability of the rocks I was stepping on to, which meant the ice cold water spilt over the top of my wellies whilst we were still several miles from home.

It made for a long and uncomfortable walk home. On the next walk, Dad showed me how to find the best place to cross the river and use the river's strength against it, as support to help us across.

There was another time when I sat on top of a pile of recently felled pine trees, neatly stacked on top of each other to form a pyramid. The whole pile collapsed and rolled over my body and head, leaving me with mild concussion and a nasty bruise. I never sat on a pile of logs again, but knew deep down that this test and learn approach, with Dad by my side, meant it would all be fine.

Dad taught me about life through the great outdoors, the creativity of our building projects and the joys of growing our own produce and rearing livestock.

The planning that went into designing and constructing a new chicken coop to house the two chicks that were about to hatch in 21 days' time taught me the importance of having the right tools for the job, the accuracy of measurement, forward planning, innovation in the use of materials and the creativity involved in design.

I now take these methods of thinking and apply the same philosophies and patterns of understanding of the laws of nature to business.

Timothy Why-Why-What-What Castle

Growing up I wanted to be an explorer. I wanted to travel the world to far off places and meet other races and see things that no one had seen before. I was in awe of explorers on the BBC, like Michael Palin and Sir David Attenborough, as they scoured the globe for sacred ruins and long-lost jungle tribes. I was deeply engaged in the pursuit of curiosity, the experimentation of discovery, and infatuated with the thought of possibility. The 'what if', and 'why not' that these two explorers wielded in every book or documentary.

These experiences taught to me by my mentors and influencers laid the foundation for a life of pushing the boundaries, questioning the norm and challenging the status quo. Why couldn't we do this too? What would happen if we did? In fact, when I was younger, my grandpa nicknamed me 'Timothy Why-Why-What-What Castle'. I'm not sure if that was a compliment or a dig at my insistent questions. I'm inclined to think the latter!

Mentors

Get a freakin' mentor already! Find someone who is doing what you want and then spend as much time as you can with them, learning why they are so successful at what they do.

Think back to your own experiences, who was a direct influence and mentor in your early childhood and how did this help you to form the habits that you still may harbour today?

Now think about the kind of mentor that you would like to have in your life today. What would they help you to focus on or improve? Where could you find such a mentor? Who is doing what you want to be doing?

Got a mentor in mind? There is no time like the present, go and get your mentor! Be The Lion!

Mentors can come from anywhere. Typically, they are someone who's further down the path than you are, they've got experience in the area that you want to develop in, and is open to work with you on this. The trick is to be open to spot a mentor, this could be someone at your work that you could approach, or your church, school, university, theatre, sports club or gym. It doesn't really matter where they appear (be open to them popping up anywhere), just make the effort to ask them to mentor you in that particular area. Choose someone you admire and try not to put them on too much of a pedestal.

Mentorship is one of the fastest and most thorough ways to improve in any area, as it can save you years and stop you from making some big but not obvious mistakes. Choose wisely and put in the work.

Tips for working with a mentor

1. **Be clear on your time commitments.** To make sure that you're mentoring runs smoothly, it's a good idea to set expectations as to how many hours a month you can both commit to the process (e.g. it could be a 30-minute phone call or a coffee once a week; some mentors will be able to give more time, others less). If they are busy or forget a session understand that they are only human but respect your boundaries.

2. **Be specific about what you need help with**. For example, rather than saying I need help with public speaking, drill down a bit deep and give your mentor the best possible chance to help you develop (e.g. I need help with both designing an engaging an informative talk that lasts 45

minutes and staying calm when I get flustered). Specifics give you the best chance of getting help with what you want and making progress.

3. **Keep a journal.** Note down your insights whilst under the guidance of your mentor so that you can track progress. Journals are a valuable way of capturing your insights and ideas whilst they're fresh in your mind. It's easy to think you'll remember how you were feeling and the lessons you have learnt, and then have problems recalling the specifics a couple of days later. Notetaking can be a valuable skill for years to come, and it may be you'll be facing a particular problem or situation a decade from now and you'll find exactly what you need by flicking through your notebook.

Set your own standards

The lesson here is to stop judging where you are by comparing yourself to others. When the big man Tony Robbins interviewed Michael Jordan at the peak of his career, he was unquestionably the world's greatest basketball player to have ever lived.

Tony asked him what made him so successful and his answer was profound, *'Really it's my standards. Every day, I demand more from myself than anybody else could humanly expect. I'm not competing with somebody else. I'm competing with what I am capable of.'*[1]

In other words, he is competing with himself. He wasn't concerned about what others were doing or how well they were performing. Michael was only focused on outperforming himself and what he was willing to do to make it to the top.

Jordan learned this at an early age, when the high school coach wouldn't allow him on to the team. 'But I'm the best player' he exclaimed, shocked and dumbfounded as to why he hadn't made the team. 'You may have talent, you may have skill, but you don't have heart and dedication,' the coach responded, 'therefore you're

[1] https://www.inc.com/marissa-levin/tony-robbins-and-michael-jordan-attribute-their-su.html

not on my team.' In the end, they came to an agreement. If Jordan came early to practise every day before school, the coach would train him one on one for a year. If Jordan showed up and dedicated himself to really learning the sport, then he'd be in the running to join the team. For the next 365 days, Michael showed up to training every day. He put in the work and raised his standards. When the time came for team selection the next year, the coach honoured their agreement and put him through.

Tony Robbins is also the same when it comes to setting the bar high and demanding more from himself.

> "Every event has to be better. Talk to anyone who has been to our events for 5, 10 years, some of our trainers. They'll say, 'I don't know how he does it. He always finds a way to make it better.' That's not an ego thing, that's a standard in me. I have to find the way,"
>
> Tony Robbins

Being a lion, you are not afraid to ask more from yourself, or go harder on yourself in pursuit of your goals and dreams because you're worth it. The deeper you go on your journey, the more your measure of success matters, not anyone else's. You will set your own standard that keeps you true, accountable and aligned to your values. As you go about your daily life, notice where you could be doing more to go harder at your dreams, where you could inject some extra resourcefulness, energy and passion to boost the outcome. Find the hunger within yourself and use it to keep going through the tough days and elevate your mindset around what is possible for you. I've thrown down the gauntlet and I know in my heart of hearts that you're ready to pick it up and run with it. This is a race against yourself, a race to improve steadily, day by day, and I just know you're going to win! Use #bethelion #iamready to share your stories of mentorship and give a shout out to those who've encouraged, helped and supported you to level up and tell the community how you've raised your standards.

CHAPTER 21

MY STORY: TIM VS. THE MOUNTAIN (YOU CAN ALWAYS FIND A WAY!)

"I believe it's our decisions, not the conditions of our lives, that determine our destiny."

Tony Robbins

I'M SHARING THIS deeply personal story with you because it is about one of the most real times in my life. This is the tale of how I found myself on the edge of a cliff staring down into the rocky abyss below and what it taught me about decision making.

This is my story. One that changed my life forever, taught me some great lessons about self-belief that I still use today and transformed how I approach decision making.

When you are on the very precipice of life and the beyond, it's a strange dimension. I have been there, on the edge, quite literally walking the line between life and death. In this chapter, I will share with you how to find **certainty** when the situation looks dire and the outcome is unknown. I also aim to unpack the spiritual connection that I experienced from my near-death experience and the art of decision making at times of critical importance under extreme pressure, knowing that your next move could be your last. When every step you take could signal the end of your life, and you and only you alone are responsible. So, let's get into it.

When I was 19, I was lucky enough to join my mum on a physiotherapy course/skiing holiday in Verbier, Switzerland.

I tagged along for the snowboarding, après ski and copious amounts of cheese fondue. Verbier is one of those incredibly impressive ski resorts that's packed with all kinds of exclusive restaurants and bars, and an array of terrain suitable for all skiing abilities.

It is known as being a haven for the rich and famous and a packed alpine celebrity hangout. Richard Branson even owns a chalet there!

It was a trip that I will always remember for a number of reasons, but mainly because it was the last one I ever took with my mum before she sadly passed away due to a malignant, rapid form of cancer. I treasure this time with her in my heart.

It was also one of the closest times I have ever come to death. After venturing off-piste and making a wrong turn I slipped and fell flat on my back. In an instant, I began hurtling at an ever-increasing pace down a steep mountain slope towards the edge of an icy cliff with only blue skies and a sheer 200-foot vertical drop ahead of me.

It was early in the morning on day three of the trip and I was already up on the mountain raring to go and ready to explore. The air was fresh and crisp, and the morning sky was royal blue with a dazzling sun already out, penetrating the glacial landscape and making it shine like a winter wonderland. It was clearly going to be one of those magnificent days on the slopes where you not only get an enviable tan but feel on top of the world.

I had already done a blue level ski run about three times and was getting more adventurous and increasingly curious with each go. On my fourth time around, I decided to explore and venture off-piste. As an accomplished snowboarder this was something I had done multiple times before, however this time was different.

As I made my way up over the crest of the mountainside and down the back of the slope, I suddenly hit sheet ice. The steep gradient of the slope meant I was instantly put flat on my back and began picking up speed fast.

At first, I didn't think too much of it. I was shocked from the initial fall but reasoned that I would eventually come to a standstill, but as I gathered my senses, I realised I was not only getting faster, but I was starting to spin.

I reached out and tried frantically to stop myself, but it was no use. The friction from the rough compacted ice and the speed I was travelling burnt holes through my gloves.

This is when I knew I was in real trouble.

In a single moment, I made a decision that would save my life. I leaned forward, stretched out both arms and unclipped my snowboard, to release my legs. This was the first decision that saved my life. No sooner had I done this, I launched myself at the nearest rock. This was the second lifesaving decision.

It all happened in an instant. My board sailed off, falling into the blue abyss below, and I span around as my legs went off the side of the cliff.

I clung on with the full weight of my chest on this big rock and looked down below.

What I saw changed my whole life.

Below I watched my snowboard still falling through the air, one second, two seconds, time stood still as my board smashed into the rocks below and then kept on going through the powder.

There was no way I could have survived a fall like that; it was at least 200 feet.

As I clung onto the rock and contemplated what to do, a sensation of calm came over me. I knew that this was it, any decision I made going forwards would either lead to my very quick death or my survival.

When you get this close to the edge of life, you get great mental clarity. It's the clearest and most focused I have ever been. There was no margin for error just, black and white, life or death.

I said out loud to myself, "Tim, do not mess this up." I was giving myself the pep talk of my life.

After a few moments, I shifted my weight and centralised my body on the rock, and then pulled myself up slowly. Adrenalin was coursing through my body; I felt strong but knew that any wrong decision could cost me my life at any second. I was acutely aware of the possibility of this becoming a reality.

I had only two options. The first was to wait on the rock, hoping that I didn't get tired, cold or slip off the edge whilst I waited in hope that someone somewhere would find me. This was before the days of smartphones and GPS. No one knew where I was for the day, the rest of the crew were in lectures at this stage, so I anticipated that it would be at least a few hours, if not nightfall, before my disappearance was apparent.

The other option was to try and make it over to the left side of the cliff where there was a huge pile of scattered boulders cascading down the side of the mountain. From where I was, it looked like these boulders were most likely the result of a landslide, I had no idea if they would be stable, but it looked to me like it could be my route to safety if I could climb them.

I made the decision that this was the way forward. Sitting on the rock left me in too much danger. At least if I could make it across the mouth of the cliff and over the pile of rocks I could decrease the risk of immense danger.

As I stood up and began to tread carefully, I knew the next few minutes were critical. Strangely enough, after coming this close to death and not going over the edge, I was elated in my decision to take off the snowboard. At the same time, however, my mind was crystal clear about what I needed to do with the mission at hand.

All my energy was consumed by establishing each step safely before putting my full weight down. Each step took me closer to my next goal, get to the other side. With every step, I made sure to balance myself correctly, carefully measuring the pressure and weight distribution so that I could be sure I wasn't going to topple over.

After a number of minutes, maybe ten, I made the final few steps off the mouth of the cliff.

I don't remember celebrating but I do remember a deep sense of calmness and understanding at how dire the situation was. The stakes were the highest I had ever encountered. I had not experienced life in this form before. Every decision needed to be cross-referenced, checked and acted upon.

I was well aware of how quickly conditions could change in the mountains. Now I was out of immediate danger, I still had to deal with the thought of spending the night on the mountain in sub-zero temperatures, with no food, shelter or warmth. This is where my mindset was key to keeping me focused on the goal at hand.

As there looked to be no alternative option, I decided again to try to get off the mountain whilst I still had energy and it was still light with good, sunny conditions.

Looking around me, all I could see where mountains. I knew that I wasn't too far away from the main town, maybe a few miles off the track. If I could just make it out of this predicament on the side of the cliff, I knew I would be able to walk to safety and reach the main piste again, which would lead me home. The more I explored the boulders, the bigger I realised they were. They were too steep for me to climb on top of. If I did, I would risk sliding down the whole structure and falling into the abyss, like my snowboard. It was too risky, and I knew that one false move or strong gust of wind and I'd be plunging to my death.

As I clambered up and over a few of the rocks and explored the cliff side I noticed that the rocks and boulders descended into a big black cave; large enough, I thought, for me to jump down into.

The cave in front of me was pitch black, I could only see a few metres inside and I had no idea where it led.

My biggest concern now was making sure that whatever I did, I could still get back to this point. I wasn't sure how stable it was, not to mention what was lying ahead of me or if the whole structure would collapse at any moment, trapping me inside or worse.

I determined that I should explore the cave anyway. It was worth the risk if it took me down the cliff and give me a chance to get back to the main resort before the cold night swept in and dashed my hopes. The only way off the mountain was to scale the cliff myself and venture down into the cave. It looked to be as good a way as any. **This was where I stepped into the unknown and trusted my gut instinct.**

With each stage of the descent, I made sure that I could get back up by testing out the route as I went. I went one or two steps down, then four steps back up, rehearsing the route.

At some of the more challenging sections, I had to get down on my hands and knees and crawl under and through gaps to progress forward.

Through all of this, I felt clear-headed and positive about the possibilities of where the cliff path might lead. This growth mindset kept me scanning the landscape for opportunities.

Mentally, I was weighing up every eventuality in my head. Options seemed to appear out of nowhere and suddenly, as if by magic, I would find a way up and over an obstacle or around it, something that didn't seem possible previously. To make progress, I needed to get creative.

After three hours of my descent into the cave, I finally saw it. A bright white shining hole in the darkness. It was like a beacon calling me forward. As I got closer, I saw the rays of light led to a small gap. I prayed that I could fit through the gap in the wall. As I crawled out into almost blinding sunlight, I realised I had done it. It was snow. It was the outside world. I had reached the base of the cliff. I stood up and immediately sank a meter or so into fresh, deep untouched snow. As I made my way around the side of the cliff to face my nemesis, trudging through the powder, each step required an insane amount of effort. I then walked around the base of the landslide of rocks to look back at the scale of the cliff I had just climbed down, which and had so nearly taken my life. I realised it was much bigger than I had originally thought.

There was absolutely no way I would have survived the fall. It led directly on to rocks and then snow. It must have been a 400-foot drop with no second chances.

I didn't pause for long to contemplate this as I was keen to keep going and reach civilisation again, but that image and experience has stayed with me forever.

As I followed the tracks that my snowboard had made in the untouched snow, I found it further down the mountain with a few large cracks to show for the tale.

What I learnt from battling the mountain

This experience showed me that, even in the most intense and hostile situations, it is possible to get increased clarity, and this, combined with a calm mind, can lead to outstanding results.

I have learned to apply the lessons from this experience to the way I approach the unknown in life, and also to business.

I learned that we are all just one decision away from success, but what keeps us stuck on the rock is the story that we tell ourselves. We must have faith in something greater, in a vision for the future, so that we can keep going, seeking out the opportunities and reprioritising, based on the new information we receive.

If I had not made the decision to take my snowboard off or to focus on not spinning around so that I could see what was coming, I would not have been here today. Information is changing all the time and so the ability to make critical decisions about what is of the most importance is essential.

This experience taught me to have faith in myself and to trust that the path exists. In order to get off the mountain safely, I needed to believe that it was possible in the first place. If I had given in to the thought that getting off the mountain was an impossibility, then I may well not have had the courage or strength to search out new options, or even made it across the face of the cliff.

I had absolute certainty and clarity that I would do everything in my power to make it out of this situation alive by using creativity, determination and my mindset. Managing my emotions played a big part in maintaining a mindset that filled me with hope, kept me open to opportunity, and enabled me to test and implement strategies that got down the cliff in one piece.

Being mentally strong in the face of big challenges and believing with all of our heart that there is a way forward is paramount to traversing the unknown, and it proved to be the difference between life and death in my case.

CHAPTER 22

MY STORY: CLIMBING THE STAIRWAY TO HEAVEN

"Take a chance. It's the best way to test yourself. Have fun and push the boundaries."

Richard Branson

Now I want to share another personal story with you that showed me the power of pushing myself, taking risks and also asking for help. This story really encapsulates the theme of Part 3 of self-belief and pulls in many of the topics that we have been discussing, like pushing through fear boundaries, going way outside of my comfort zone and knowing when to call on others for strength, guidance and love. This is another experience that had lion traits running through it all the way, so hold on to your hearts and don't let go, we're are about to go up, way up!

Sandra and I are keen travellers, and always on the lookout for novel tours, points of interest and exciting adventures and challenges. The day after I got engaged to the love of my life, we decided to go on an adventure. As if flying to Hawaii to get down on one knee at sunset wasn't enough adrenalin pumping action for one trip!

Just engaged!

I ditched the 'proposal on a helicopter' idea at the last minute in favour of a small pavilion overlooking Turtle Bay at sunset. (This was due to a Google search that put the actual helicopter proposal into perspective. I mean how was I going to get down on one knee in a helicopter? What about the noise? What if she couldn't hear me when I popped the question?) I hadn't flown all this way to have complications!

After what seemed like an age, and a lot of convincing to come on a walk to 'look for turtles', I found the perfect proposal spot, a beautiful white pavilion overlooking the ocean. I had to go into sales mode to persuade her to leave her lounger with its perfect view. We were walking along the beach to a place full of rocks where the sea was crashing against the surface intensely, when I realised that I had made a mistake. I had gone the wrong way. I was starting to get nervous. Where was the pavilion? And why was the ring bulging out of my board shorts pocket so noticeably, I was sure she would spot it. As I gathered myself, I admitted we had gone the wrong way. We marched over to the other side of the resort and I saw a sign that said 'pavilion'. I felt better but now I was starting to get nervous about the proposal. As we walked around the corner, the sun was setting in front of the pavilion. This was it, the big moment.

I had written a book entitled *50 Reasons I Love You*, and on each page was a statement that explained why I loved her.

What I hadn't anticipated was that Sandra would want to read every single page of the 50-page book I had written aloud before I was going to propose (which she didn't know yet).

Time was ticking and with every page the sunset was getting closer to reaching the pinnacle of maximum beauty as it neared the glistening Pacific Ocean in the horizon.

As we moved into the home straight, and Sandra turned to page 49 and then 50, I readied myself and got down on one knee.

It was just as magical as I could have hoped. What they don't tell you on Google, and I'm sure all the guys can relate to this part, is just how nervous you are when you propose. Everything has been building to this one moment and you want it to be just right. Even if you know that your spouse-to-be is going to say yes, the nerves are there. It's such a strange sensation to be nervous in front of your best friend. I mean you spend every day with this person, you see them all the time.

Then out of the blue, just as I was about to go down on one knee, I had to shoo two fellow tourists away who had inadvertently wandered into my proposal scene with glee, seconds before I was about to pop the question.

It is such an overwhelming experience, but I managed to push through anyway and persevere. I popped the question and, after what seemed like an almighty pause, my beautiful bride-to-be said yes.

It was really quite special.

So, we thought, what better way to celebrate your love and engagement than to climb up a 4,000-step ladder called The Stairway to Heaven and an illegal, abandoned hike? It was getting dark by now, so this idea would have to wait until tomorrow. After browsing Instagram, we were hooked and it was a done deal. We'd get up and hike tomorrow.

We went out for dinner to celebrate and called our parents and various family members to tell them the exciting news that we were getting married. Now I had proposed I could relax a bit; Up to this point, I had been solely focused on getting to this stage without Sandra guessing that a proposal was coming.

The next day we were still totally up for it. Our adventure senses were high and we looked into climbing The Stairway to Heaven, or the Haiku Stairs as it is also known.

At first, we weren't sure if it was a mythical spot, but pictures on Instagram revealed it was indeed real and like something straight out of an *Indiana Jones* movie.

To get to the Haiku Stairs is a mission. In fact, I would say unless you go with someone who's been before it's fairly impossible to find. Not to mention the security guard with the police on speed dial who you need to slip by without being seen to gain access to the fenced off and padlocked Stairway to Heaven. We read that some of the residents had got fed up with all the hikers coming to climb the stairway and that was why it was shut down a number of years prior. We had to be careful not to draw attention to ourselves and not look like we were trying to find the way into this hidden gem or they would call the cops and it would all be over before it had begun.

When we pulled up to the spot that all the intrepid climbers had mentioned on Google, it was a peaceful residential estate at the foot of a huge mountain range, with a massive American-sized highway overhead, which wrapped around the side.

As luck and good fortune would have it, we bumped into a family of five who would become our new friends and tour guides for this trip. We asked in hushed tones, 'Are you here to climb the stairs?' 'Yes' the kids replied jumping around. 'Our dad's been before, you should come with us.' And off we set off at quite a pace.

Finding the stairs

Seconds after passing the menacing "NO TRESPASSING" sign and walking down a dirt track, their dad jumped into the undergrowth. Worried he'd spotted the guard coming, we all followed suit and piled into the bushes.

It didn't take long to realise that he had not sprung into a fun hiding place; this was, in fact, the way. What unfolded over the next hour was a series of connected tunnels carved through a maze of trees. The thing with this dad was he liked to move fast, there was no time for questions.

This was the kind of father who liked to push his kids in an almost commander-like style, sometimes too far. He was the hero and a gym junkie. You got the sense that you didn't question his decisions. Well, there was no time for debate, he had gone already and we wanted to find the stairway, so we followed on at lightning pace.

After doing a semi-run for a good few hundred meters, dodging and driving through branches, trees and Hawaiian shrubbery, the dad's hand came up abruptly, signalling for us all to halt. We knew this was an order from the front to stop dead in our tracks and remain silent.

The dad popped his head out and scanned the territory for guards. We had reached the final frontier. The noise of the traffic on the highway overhead was loud and added to the suspense of it all. We got the all-clear signal and jumped out from the labyrinth of forest tunnels and on to another dusty main track.

All the time, the kids were putting their fingers to their lips, showing us to be quiet – *don't say a word*. We were close to the entrance and also the guard's hideout.

No sooner had our feet touched the track, and we were off again, up the other side of a large bank and into the woodland. The bank was so big (about 5 foot) that it was tough even for me to navigate. One of the little kids was so small they couldn't even reach the top; the dad was gone, so we reached back down to hoist him up. We had made it, unseen and unscathed.

You've got to imagine all of this happening in what looked like the scenery from *Jurassic Park*, well, because it was.

I thought this would be it for running, I was wrong. Now we faced another big challenge, we had to run uphill, a rather steep hill. It was hot and sweaty, and the dad had taken his shirt off to reveal a full body covered in black hair with sweat glistening in the sunlight. You can't make this stuff up. But we had come this far, and we weren't turning back yet, despite the sights that were unfolding.

A steep climb

So off we went, onwards and upwards, the gradient of the hill was treacherous. If you lost your footing or a branch of a brush that you were using to pull yourself up snapped, you would be sent flying 10-20 metres back down.

It was tough and I was concerned about the kids. There was a mum as well by the way, where did she come from? This family was just so excited to be on the adventure, they were happy to follow their dad to the ends of the Earth, quite literally.

As we neared the top of the hill, we reached a point where we could see, across a small valley, the fenced off start of the Haiku stairs. The only problem was: how did we get there?

On no, the dad had it figured out. We ran down the valley and across a small stream and then climbed up the other side. This was intense stuff, it was a like Tough Mudder, only he was making it up as he went along.

After getting way too intimate for my liking with the dad's hairy back, we were pushed up and up. One fall and it's safe to say that a nasty trip to the hospital would have ensued, most likely aided by the not-so-friendly guards who were 50 metres down the track at this point (and had still not spotted us!). Having sweaty back hair in the face was worth it, if it meant that we had finally reached our destination: the start of the Haiku Stairs.

As we emerged one by one from the side of the valley and onto the track, I saw the little guards' hut to the left of the stairway, and then beyond the fence, and to my right, was the staircase, stretching up into the skies as far as my eyes could see. It looked like a metal runway that stretched directly up into the ether along the spine of the mountain. It looked monstrous, like we were going to climb Everest or something.

As soon as "Hairy Back" had made it on to the track, he was encouraging us to move forward. As guests on the trip, I was chosen to lead. I kinda wanted to catch my breath for a few more leisurely moments, but all good, let's do this. With Army Dad shouting orders to his kids from the rear, I had no choice but lead onwards and, oh boy, upward.

This was way tougher than I had anticipated it would be. These stairs were at stages vertical. This was a climb not a hike. The hiking route had been abandoned and made illegal for good reason. There were parts that had been smashed by a landslide and were hanging off thousands of feet up in the sky.

To put this in context, if I'd let go or slipped, I would have fallen all the way down, and probably taken out a few family members on the way. My palms were sweaty, but there was no way back, I was leading! On the stairway, there's no room for anyone else to pass. If you meet someone else coming the other way as we did, they must hang off the side while you climb on by. It was a delicate manoeuvre.

There was one section about a thousand stairs up, where the gravity of the situation (pardon the pun) really got to me mentally. Physically everything was burning, I was focused on stepping each step and making sure I had a firm hold of the handrail. Physically, I thought I might be able to continue (maybe); mentality I was ready to give up. I looked back and saw Sandra who was behind me. Anyone who's met Sandra knows she's a fitness expert and gym fanatic. She wasn't having as much difficulty as me, there she was smiling away, loving it.

She could see it in my eyes that I was struggling and just looking back at her gave me the strength to know that I could do this.

She told me not to focus on all of the stairs ahead or feeling sick, and said, "Just put one step in front of the other, that's the only thing you need to focus on." And it worked!

It was one of those truly special moments (like getting engaged) when you know you are meant to be together. Her love gave me the strength to carry on. I was determined, no matter how much it hurt, no matter how much my brain was telling me this was INSANE – and difficult and what if I fell? – that I would keep going.

Step by step, I made it through the vertical section, passed the landslide where there were limited railings to hold onto and kept going upwards. After another 10 or so minutes we arrived at Base Camp 1.

I had thought that was it, we were at the top. It had to be. It certainly seemed high enough. From here the view was magnificent. Up here, it felt like we could see all of Oahu. We met some other folk who were coming the other way and started talking to them about their own trek to get here. Turns out that we were lucky, they had got up at 2am and begun hiking in the dark across another mountain range to get here because they didn't want to chance it with the guard. It was now 2pm, meaning they had been going for 12 hours. We had only begun two hours earlier. Suddenly, I felt uplifted knowing that we had saved 10 hours thanks to the kids' kind offer to join their family.

Just keep going

Anything is possible

At the top of Base Camp 1

The view of the mountains

It wasn't long before Army Dad had rallied the troops and we were off again on the ascent to the summit of Base Camp 2. This time I wasn't leading, I think Army Dad thought I was too slow and wanted to up the pace to really got on a sweat. One of the kids decided they couldn't go any further and was left at Base Camp 1. Looking back now (and being a father), it was a very odd experience to leave the kid behind, but it was also a monumental climb from Base Camp 1 to Base Camp 2 and a few thousand stairs stood between us to bridge this gap. I really wasn't sure I could stomach it, but not wanting to let Sandra down, I persevered. I could feel lactic acid starting to build up in my calves and thighs. I felt heavy and sweaty, it was clear now that we hadn't brought enough water, so the kid gave me some of his.

As we carried on, I started to enjoy the climb, the hike to Base Camp 2, which thankfully involved less vertical sections as we were traversing the relatively flat ridge. On either side of the staircase there was still a vertical drop, but it felt more stable, now that we weren't hanging off the side of a mountain with our bare hands and a family of 5 behind us and a few guards watching on.

Celebrating the wins together

The road continues

At Base Camp 2, we stopped briefly to rehydrate and then pushed on to Base Camp 3, the summit. Base Camp 3 stood perched on the crest of the mountaintop and had been beckoning reassuringly to us since we reached Base Camp 1, and now it was only about 100 metres of staircase away. Base Camp 3 had given me something to aim at. After the initial shock of the vertical incline on the way up to Base Camp 1, I was feeling calmer. Reaching Base Camp 1 had been a big achievement. The significance of having goals to aim at – in this case Base Camp 1, then Base Camp 2 and now Base Camp 3 – was not lost on me, and I recall waiting to retain this lesson and apply it in my daily life. It stood out to me that getting to Base Camp 1 was a big deal, and I overcame my mental fear, moved my body, arms and legs, and worked to align my mind. This had given me enough of a chance to refuel my drive and set my sights on the next stage of the ascent.

Now that we were on track to reach the summit of the climb, I felt relaxed, and I could properly take in the beauty of the surroundings as the whole of Oahu was laid out in front of is. It went on for miles, as far as my eyes could see, and there was more to be discovered.

It dawned on me that this climb was like life. I could be only a few more overhanging vertical steps away from achievement in other areas of my life, and as daunting and fear stimulating as they were, what I needed to do was dig in, hold on tight and push through the fear. It was as if this climb was a representation of overcoming all manner of challenges. There was the moment I wanted to quit, when it seemed impossible, when my mind started doubting my body. Then there was my support system (Sandra) who got me back on track, then further along, there was fatigue, more doubts about a change in the weather, and finally, there was success.

What this climb taught me was that all it takes is an idea to reach the top of an impossible mountain, but along the way, we will need guidance. It will test our logic, mental strength and inner determination but if you stick with it, and follow your instinct, you will succeed in reaching the top.

At the top of Base Camp 3, there was an old, abandoned lookout building with a large semicircular satellite dish perched on top (which we later found out was used to by the US Army communicate across the Pacific during the Second World War, hence the need for the staircase).

Now that the mission was complete, Sandra and I both felt a deep sense of gratitude for one another. We had done it together! We were elated to have not only found the Stairway to Heaven but to also have made it to the top. Reading stories prior to coming up, we had wondered if we'd even manage to get to the staircase let alone scale the thing.

I was impressed by who we had met along the way. To me, this was one of the craziest and intense things we had ever done, but to some of the people we met, this was just regular fitness training. This gave me a whole new perspective. It's all subjective, what is scary for you is just a regular activity for someone else, and what you deem as a big achievement, might be just getting started to someone else. This insight has given me the fortitude to keep on trying and pushing myself – in the gym, in work, in my career and entrepreneurial pursuits – and if some people are willing to play the game at a higher, more improved level then why can't I?

It has taught me to always try and do my best, regardless of what is possible for others.

We met a guy who ran the stairs every day in his lunch break, for fun! I mean he must have been a Navy Seal or something because he was hauling ass! This guy was flying down the stairs, without fear or hesitation. It showed me that experience combined with perception brings confidence in one's own ability. Talk about self-belief.

At the top of the summit, Army Dad and his oldest son jumped over the fence and continued to explore the ridge. Either side of them was a 2000-ft drop, one slip and they would have been gone, but they were having fun. This again showed me that what I considered to be the end of the road was just a checkpoint for others. Their self-belief and pursuit of their goals carried them over the boundary of the fence and onwards to explore. I'm not condoning reckless behaviour, but I am in support of questioning your own path to success; what might be the end of the road to someone else might only be a checkpoint and it's important to remember to check in with yourself once in a while to see if you can push further or if, in fact, there's more to be done.

For me though, I was satisfied. This was the mission completed and we turned back around to head back down the 4,000 steps we had just come. This is also just as important, knowing when you're done!

The way down was, thankfully, a lot easier. Gravity played its part, so all I had to do was focus on not slipping and I'd move forward. Army Family was a hundred meters or so ahead, gallivanting, and we were happy to make our own pace for a while.

We figured out that it was best to face forward, so we knew what was coming and there were still some incredible hairy sections like the part where the stairway had been broken off and the stairs were just hanging in mid-air a thousand metres up. Step by step we made our descent together. All in all, it was faster coming down. I'm not sure if it was because our muscles had got used to the required movements or the satisfaction of reaching our goal that made each step just a bit more streamlined. What I do know was that on the way up, we were stepping into the unknown, but on the way back down, we had been there before, it felt familiar. This works for self-belief because the more you push yourself out of your comfort zone, the more the territory becomes familiar and the easier you can traverse it.

Whereas on the way up I was focused on not falling off, going down I was focused on not rushing. It was tempting to run ahead or go faster because I knew the way and the movement of stepping down and forward was more like a reflex than a thoughtful action. I had to constantly tell myself to take it easy and slow down my movements so that I could ensure the pathway ahead was safe. This shift in focus enabled me to remain on the right side of pushing my comfort zone, the side that would allow me to successfully complete the stairway and explore, yet not suffer the fatal consequences of a fall.

Your focus and particularly what you allow your mind to dwell on, the emotions you allow to take priority and the veracity with which you do so either guide you towards increased self-confidence or away from it. Be careful to notice what you focus on and where your attention goes when you are up against it. If your mind is telling you to give in or to quit, do you indulge this thought, do you act on it? The answer to that question will tell you what your tendency is when it comes to unpleasant or non-supportive thoughts. If you identify yourself as someone who normally gives in easily or doesn't push through when things get hard, painful or challenging, this is the time to recognise this pattern within yourself. The way to overcome it is to catch yourself the next time a situation, event or circumstance arises, and you find yourself pulling away from it and question the validity of your response in contrast to your desire to live big and make it happen. If during this introspection you feel that there is any possibility of a way forward, I want you to commit to trying.

It is in the midst of uncertainty and friction that we grow. Many of the inspirational leaders you read about in this book and online, in magazines or watch on YouTube, all reveal that periods of extreme adversity, hardship and difficulty contributed to both an increase their self-belief and in their understanding of what it means to live fully.

Experiencing adversity doesn't mean that you are destined for a life of failure, far from it; it means instead you have been gifted an experience that you can use to help others overcome their own struggles, trials and attributions.

Your unique perspective can help the world become a more supportive, open and loving place. Don't let your one life that you have slip away unnoticed, soon you'll be in a grave with no more chances in your earthly body to have a go left. What if this challenge is all that's stopping you from achieving your goals and dreams and all you have to do is keep going forward instead of retreating?

Don't look down, mind over matter

When we finally reached the bottom, we walked past the guards' hut and on to the track. We were so exhausted and elated we hoped they wouldn't spot us and give us a big fine. We had heard that they were there to stop people going up not down but didn't want to chance it.

Luckily, they had gone, so we found our way back through the maze of jungle and undergrowth and back to the main track. We were nearly safe. At which point, Sandra tripped on a pebble and fell flat on her face. I mean completely. There were a few tears, but we had to laugh at the hilarity of the situation. We had done all that and now, out of sheer exhaustion, a pebble was the thing that got in our way.

We got in our car and drove straight to McDonald's. We needed carbs! And lots of them. Climbing 4,000 stairs with my fiancé was an experience I will never forget and one that I will look back on when we are grey and old, and I'll be so glad that we did.

What I learnt about taking risks climbing the stairway to heaven

1. **risk is subjective.** When taking a risk, everybody has a different perspective. What might be considered risky to you might be rather mundane to someone else. The other thing about risk is, once you've done it and climbed the stairway, your perspective shifts because you are more informed. Therefore, our view of risk is subjective.

2. **Risks can help you grow.** When I thought I could go no further, the sheer height and the fear of falling got to me. However, with the support of my fiancé and the strategy of controlling my thoughts, I was able to persevere. In business, your team can be your support and sometimes all you need is the right words from the right person to give you the mental fortitude to carry on. Look for these people that give you a growth mindset and build you up. The other aspect is growth from managing the unknown. Risks are often perceived to be dangerous because they contain some element of uncertainty. Learning to operate in these conditions can help to build your reliance and adaptability as the weather conditions, obstacles and people change.

3. **Risk can have a big payoff.** There was always a plethora of ways the climb could have turned out. The payoff, in this case, was that we achieved a challenge together and built memories that could last a lifetime. We grew together, we experienced and, as a result, our bond grew.

What I learnt about business from climbing the stairway to heaven

1. **Progress is made by putting one foot in front of the other** and taking small steps to what it is that you want. Whatever you do don't stop moving, even the smallest step keeps you progressing in the right direction.

2. **Seek help from those who have been where you want to go** – this was a big one. Had we not found Hairy Army Dad, I can safely say we wouldn't have got to the stairs let alone scaled the entire thing in a few hours. By getting help, we were able to streamline the process, saving heaps of time and possibly a fine from the guard.

3. **Endurance, Enthusiasm and Empathy** – The Three Es (Taken from Ryan Serhant's book *Sell It Like Serhant*). Climbing the four thousand stairs up into the sky was much like sales. You need endurance to keep going, and just when you think you are about to close the deal, another stairway appears with a new set of challenges. Endurance to keep going and play the long game gets you to the best results and to the top. A "never give up" attitude and winning spirit also counts.

4. **Look For Support** – Sandra's loving guidance and encouragement at my time of need gave me the boost I needed to keep going and to get my mindset right

5. **Take The Risk** – Everything you want is on the other side of fear. Taking the risk and completing the hike was so worth it. It goes for anything that you want to do, take the risk.

Bonus tip: Finally, if you are considering climbing a four thousand step staircase then please make sure you do the following:

Bring More Water – by this I mean come prepared. The journey was longer than I had anticipated or prepared for mentality and physically. The same applies to overcoming some challenges, they can stretch on longer than you first thought. Make sure you have all the resources available or are on the lookout for them in order to make sure you can complete the journey no matter how long it takes.

CHAPTER 23

DO SOMETHING THAT MAKES YOU ROAR!

"I would like to die on Mars. Just not on impact."

Elon Musk

What makes you roar?

The key to being the lion is doing something that makes you roar. And by roar I mean really roar, that feeling you get when you're so fist-pumpingly excited about doing something – taking the next gigantic step, opening up that store, upping your game, taking it to the next level, embracing who you were put on this planet to be, and being in tune with life, your goals and your vision. I want you to recall a time that you were so excited about life you could let out a gut-wrenching, deeply passionate roar. What were you doing? Who were you with? What was it about this time that made you so excited to be alive?

As you do this, notice how your body shifts, how you feel inside and the way you feel unstoppable. This is the self-belief within you talking. It's there and it's alive and kicking, waiting for you to do something that makes it want to ROAR!

When you find and connect with something that makes you roar, there is no plan B. There's no need for cheat codes and you certainly don't make excuses. Think of Arnold Schwarzenegger's ambition to become Mr Universe or a successful Hollywood movie star, or Elon Musk and his vision to colonise Mars. These are examples of people who have found what makes them roar! These lions roar with passion as they put in 18-hour days and do the hard yards. They go at it 24/7 until their burning desire is forged in the history books as fact.

In this chapter, I am going to share the techniques that will get you roaring again because when you tap into your deepest inner strength, your why, you can fully embrace being the lion and cover more ground, deflect all manner of obstacles thrown in your path and foster the resilience to keep on going, no matter how badly you want to quit.

When you are in this "roaring" space you operate from a place of love, not fear. You are comfortable for the most part with who you are, remain focused on being the best version of you that you can be and operate at higher and higher levels.

To achieve the impossible, visualisation on its own is not substantial enough; the contribution you must make to push past your fears comes from within. It's a ferocious vibration of energy that could, if you so wished, be let out in the form of a roar.

When Gareth Southgate's England team beat Sweden to make it into the 2018 World Cup semi-finals, he individually thanked each player, walked right out onto the pitch, in front of 32 million jubilant fans watching on TVs across the nation, and he let out one hell of a roar, fist pumping the sky as he did it.

Lions are motivated by hunger

There are many variables that make up success, but hunger is key. Hunger is what keeps people driving forward, working on their businesses late into the night, and doing what no one else does so that they may get to places no one else gets to.

When you want it badly enough, you will do the work necessary to change the bad habits that take you further away from your goals. You'll say, 'You know what, I'm sick of these old patterns holding me back and keeping me stuck, this time I am going to make changes that support my growth for the long-term. I am hungry, and I am ready, I commit to being the best version on myself that I can possibly be.'

When you break through your fear, it empowers you and you will see changes in your life beyond what you previously conceived to be possible. It's as if the Universe comes to meet those who overcome big challenges by pushing beyond the boundaries of their innermost fears by willing to play ball.

Once you've done it and had that experience, you can't 'unhave it'. You have achieved it and expanded your ideas to the point where they transform from ideas into a physical reality. You have broken through the shackles that were keeping you bound to old patterns that no longer supported you, and now you are free to repeat this process at will. The experience of pushing through your fear and exploring what lies beyond is where your self-confidence will expand, your determination and resolve will strengthen, and you will feel different about your life and what is now possible for you.

Tony put it best when he said:

> "Belief is a poor substitute for experience."
>
> Tony Robbins

I believe that everything happens for a reason, and also think that the most challenging experiences are there in order to help us grow and put things into perspective. Failure can help motivate and tell us what we want. It's in the moments of struggle that we learn the most about success. Let's be honest, if we get an easy win but we don't earn it then it doesn't feel that awesome, like when you were in high school playing computer games and you used the cheat codes to move to the next level. It feels great for a second but deep down, you feel a little bummed out because you didn't make it there by virtue of your own skill, practice and determination. The victory doesn't feel so sweet because deep down you know it wasn't earned. Real victory comes after giving it your all for every single moment of the race.

CHAPTER 24

MY SON, THE LITTLE LION

"However desperate the situation and circumstances,
don't despair. When there is everything to fear,
be unafraid. When surrounded by dangers, fear
none of them. When without resources, depend
on resourcefulness."

Sun Tzu

IN THIS CHAPTER, I am going to share with you a true story about my son Levi and how an unexpected turn of events pushed us to be more resourceful than ever before and fight like hell. This was a time when our backs were truly against the wall and we couldn't catch a break. It felt like we were in the boxing ring with Muhammad Ali, and no matter how much we ducked, dived and weaved, the punches kept coming, raining down on us, trying to pummel us into submission. The event that followed changed me and made me expect more from myself. It pushed me to go bigger, harder, faster and longer than ever before. It gave me a reason to roar! I vowed never to be in this position again for my family and for myself. I made a commitment that I would not give up. It was done. I am on the path and I still work with this burning fire inside fuelling me every single day.

We were $60,000 in debt (the most we have ever owed) and living on one salary for nearly 16 months while my wife looked after our son, and trying with all our might to get some upward momentum in our lives to take us to a place of financial freedom, not just make ends meet.

We had been waiting for our big break when we would finally be able to claw our way out of this dark and depressing place of balance transfers, automated minimum payments and the ominous day that the interest-free period on one of the six cards ran out.

The aim was to play the game at a higher level, to really launch and get some momentum behind our side businesses so that we could step away from our day jobs, but this was proving a tough cookie to crack. It felt like we'd finally get over one hurdle only to be slapped in the face with another bigger obstacle almost as quickly as the first was overcome. We wanted more than ever to be financially independent, to not live day to day on our pay cheques. So we were looking to get our financial house in order, but every time we got close a big bill or problem would come along.

For example, no sooner had we trusted our intuition and relocated to Singapore did our old landlord in Australia take us to court for a small stain on the carpet in our old flat. This meant that even though our lives had moved on, we were stuck sorting out petty legal issues from our previous tenancy.

The first we heard of it was when the real estate agent emailed to inform us that we had missed the court hearing and a claim had been filed against us! To say that we were shocked was an understatement, but what compounded the intensity of the situation was frustration.

The long and the short of this surprising turn of events was that we felt, in our gut, we were being taken advantage as we weren't in the country and so were easy targets. The cost of a flight back plus the time off work would take a large chunk of the money we'd recoup if we won the claim by flying back to Sydney to represent ourselves. Above all, the situation just didn't feel right. So we mailed in our plea along with detailed photographic evidence and hoped that on the day the right thing would be done.

In effect, the right thing was, partly, done by the courts, and we managed to recover a very small amount of the deposit, but we felt we had won in our hearts by standing up for what was right. We hoped that the larger ripple effect of this would have an impact on the estate agent, as the eyes of the legal system would now be on them, and through our very candid explanation of the events, we had potentially safeguarded future tenants from having the same experience. Either way, it felt like a victory.

Sometimes events happen to us in life for the greater good and although we had been taken advantage of, the knock-on repercussions of us making a seemingly small but important stand against the big players and challenging the normal pattern, e.g. just stumping up the cash (which I believe they fully intended us to do) may have made the world a bit better for someone else. Not getting the full amount of a few thousand dollars back for the deposit was a financial blow that we hadn't anticipated or accounted for.

Our $60k debt wasn't amassed through either irresponsibility or neglect of our finances; far from it, in fact. We had ended up here through a combination of careful and strategic investment in our own learning, training and development, calculated investment in our own entrepreneurial ventures and online businesses, and covering the general living costs of a family of three who are living in an expensive city like Sydney.

To be frank, we were living on credit, six credit cards in fact. Each week involved a hectic movement of money to pay off the card with the highest interest and then funnelling money back through balance transfers to take advantage of any zero per cent interest deals elsewhere. The thing I resented most was the loss of time that this process took. It was mentally draining to keep track of our money movement. This made me even more determined to never feel the stress of money again.

The beauty of the struggle was that we were slowly creeping our way out of debt with each week that passed, and by applying the principles of George Clason's timeless classic *The Richest Man in Babylon* we had been paying ourselves first, creating a nice little savings pot that had been building for over a year. Clason's rule is to understand that 10% of all you earn is yours to keep, and you must pay yourself first by putting this into a savings account before paying anyone else. This might involve delaying payments for bills, or securing other revenue streams, but the golden rule is you always put away 10% of anything that you earn into your savings, no matter what you owe. To be clear, this process is about valuing yourself. The goal is to put 10% of whatever you make away into savings. This is not to be touched, no matter what, even if you've got bills that need paying. You must then do whatever it takes to find the money (if required) to pay your bills. This could be taking on more shifts at work, negotiating a new bonus structure, extending the payment terms on your bills or living more frugally. By saving 10% of all you earn, you train yourself to pay yourself money. It's a habit that if established firmly will see you gradually build your wealth and value money.

This savings pot had been invested in products that steadily tracked the S&P 500 and some select investments to provide us with wealth for the long term. In truth, even though we were gradually beginning to make progress, our debt levels kept me up most nights. The way we ensured our debt would reduce was to allocate any windfalls (bonuses, birthday money, payments for extra jobs, selling unused items) directly to the debt that was most risky (e.g. about to transition to a higher interest rate due to the promotion running out). We also had to keep up with all minimum payments on all credit cards so that we got to retain the benefits of the promotional terms. The only reason we could afford to take on this amount of debt was because the majority of it was secured on either 12-24-month interest-free credit terms. Of course, once these periods ran out, then it was a case of doing more research, finding an appropriate offer with a competing bank and transferring the remaining balance over to the new bank to begin the process all over again. As long as you're able to make the minimum payments this process works during times of financial hardship and allows you to continue to do what it takes to invest in yourself and your ideas, and go out into the world to try and create a business that can support you in the long term. However, I want to be crystal clear, this strategy takes careful management and requires that you can afford to take on the level of debt as it increases. So be extremely careful before considering this. The risk here is that you lose your job or ability to make the minimum repayments, which means goodbye to the cheap promotional terms and hello to higher interest rates due to a defaulted payment. Things can escalate quickly. I am consciousness when it comes to money and made sure, the best I could, that both my job and the level of debt never got too high. Although, to be honest, we were starting to approach unchartered territory.

It's never fun to worry about money. I hadn't experienced this for a while, where the debt wakes you up, making it hard to go back to sleep. Your heart and mind pounding, searching for ways to get out of it.

I was determined to increase our financial prosperity and apply the knowledge that I had built up by investing in education over the previous months. I had been devouring all the content, books, podcasts I could find on obtaining financial freedom and how to accelerate the process.

And, you know what? It was working. Money kept appearing right when we needed it. We were on our way; slowly but surely we were making progress, one breath at a time. One example was when I posted a photograph I had taken on Instagram of the balcony at a villa we had stayed at in Thailand overlooking the ocean. As luck would have it, the finances fairy was watching over us. I used the hashtag #roomwithaview and various others, a normal process when posting on social media. What I didn't know was that this was also the hashtag for *Condé Nast Traveller*'s prestigious Room With A View[2] competition. It turns out that every month *Conde Nast Traveller US* pick a photo that best represents a room with a view and use it on a full page on the last page of the magazine and on their website.

It wasn't until a few days later that I received an email from a person purporting to be from the magazine requesting me to send over any other shots I might have from the stay in Thailand that showcased the view. They revealed the magazine would pay $500 for any full-page spread and write up that was successful.

It was 5am when this email came through, but my entrepreneurial instinct was alive and raring to go. I was stunned to have gotten an email from the most well-known travel magazine in the world, but I was game.

I searched through our photos from the trip, praying that I had taken more of view from our room. Luckily, I had. I soon found a photo that stood out head and shoulders above the rest on every level. It captured the romance, the privacy and luxury, the

---

[2] Check it out here: https://www.cntraveler.com/gallery/room-with-a-view

ambience and the sheer beauty of this magnificent hotel in all its glory. This was the one. I fired back an email and didn't think too much of it, still wondering if this was a scam or whether it would come off and I would get to see my photography in print all over the globe.

Moments later, I received a response. This was starting to feel more real now. The person loved the photo and asked me to send over everything I had. This made me feel uncomfortable because it felt like I was handing them the photos they wanted before the payment was settled and I was certain they were legit. But I decided to go with it; after all, if it was a scam, what could they do with a bunch of sunset balcony pictures? If it was an authentic request; well, this could be the start of something very exciting. So, I hit send and waited with anticipation. It was 2am in New York so I didn't hear back until the next morning, which was a Friday.

I opened up the email and, to my relief, it was good news. They promised to show my photograph to the editorial team first thing on Monday for approval. This was sounding promising. They said they'd be in touch and might need me to have a phone call with the editor to get more detail for the article.

Monday rolled along and there was no email, nothing. I figured that I should just be patient. If this was legit then I had nothing to worry about plus a few days earlier I hadn't even had this option on the table.

Tuesday arrived, and with it brought the news that the editors had selected my photographs to be featured in the December issue of the magazine. I couldn't believe it, not only was this an unexpected financial windfall of $500 but even better, my photography (a creative skill that I have always been passionate about) was going to be printed in a highly credible magazine that would be seen all across the world. Not only could this open up more opportunities for sales, but it could advance my side-career as a photographer. I was overjoyed.

What this taught me was that if you say yes to opportunity and the moments of randomness, in spite of feeling uncomfortable, it can lead to incredibly advantageous places and benefit everyone. If I had not unwittingly used the competition hashtag, I wouldn't have been on their radar, but more importantly, had I not pushed forward, weighed up the pros and cons and gone for it, my photography would not have featured in a globally renowned magazine for all to see.

As I mentioned before, the money just kept appearing in various forms, but appearing nonetheless. Things like (extra bonus payments, pre-selling my books in stores, producing an audiobook and it making a profit after it had only been on sale for 3 days).

My photograph in *CN Traveller*

Levi's lesson

Then out of the blue, the unthinkable happened. On the 1st July 2018, our 14-month old son Levi had a huge seizure. It was Sunday afternoon around 3pm and we'd all decided to take a little rest as a family. I was in the living room on the sofa and Sandra and Levi were sleeping on the bed in the master bedroom. Moments later I heard Sandra shouting, *"Tim, Tim come here now!"* As I ran into the bedroom, startled by the screaming and slightly dazed from waking up so abruptly, I wasn't prepared for what I would see.

On the bed, there was Levi, fitting, incredibly tense and writhing around. His eyes were rolled back towards the top of his head and he was struggling to breathe. He was making a small noise but other than that there was nothing.

He was having a seizure, although we weren't sure at the time that this was exactly what was happening. We didn't know if he was choking or having a heart attack.

Luckily, Sandra had been sleeping next to him on the bed and felt his body moving violently, which had woken her, meaning we could act immediately.

The wave of panic that came over us in this moment was unreal. I couldn't locate my mobile phone, so I grabbed Sandra's and she called the hospital.

I couldn't move fast enough but putting on my shorts was difficult. It felt like all my normal skills had dropped away. I moved Levi onto his side into the recovery position and it seemed to help. However, we were still unsure if this was the right thing to do. We didn't know what had caused it or why it was happening, it just was.

Sandra was on the phone to the doctor and requested an ambulance, but they said they couldn't send one. I grabbed the phone and shouted at the guy, he gave us the emergency number right away. It's not often I get angry. I'm a pretty chilled guy but I was livid and he got it. There was no time to waste. Help was on the way although I could help feeling this overwhelming sense of powerlessness. Here was my baby and I couldn't do anything to save him. Then I remembered that we weren't alone. I called our friends in another condo and told them to come over right away. It's an insane conversation to have and I am sure it's not a nice call to receive from a panicked father telling you that his son looks like he is dying and he needs help.

Levi was still struggling to breathe and his little body had been shaking now for over 15 minutes. He was fighting hard to stay conscious. When I connected to the gravity of the situation, I couldn't take it. It was like my mind wouldn't work. The emotional intensity of the circumstances made me want to explode with tears and anger at the same time. I felt the deepest, most primal instinct I have ever felt to protect my son. He was in mortal danger.

After a few more minutes, our friends arrived at the door. Just having them there was all we needed, and it gave us support. We moved Levi into the living room and continued to try and help him. Giving mouth to mouth to my 14-month-old baby was not something I'd imagined myself doing, especially after we had been playing basketball just 30 minutes earlier. We were trying everything to keep him with us.

In a blur, the paramedics burst through the door and immediately took over. They said we had done a good job and explained what they were going to do. After administering the first round of drugs and putting Levi on oxygen, nothing happened. The seizure didn't reduce in size or stop like it was supposed to. The paramedics rushed him out of the apartment and down to the ambulance. My friends and I gathered outside the front door to say a prayer, asking God to come into this situation and take care of Levi. I will be ever thankful for their grace and support during this event.

Sandra hopped in the back of the ambulance with Levi and I was in the front. I remember looking back and seeing Levi still fighting, still shaking violently, still tensing up. I called the hospital to see what drugs they had prescribed Levi (earlier in the day we had been to hospital with Levi because he had a cough that wouldn't go away).

As we raced down the highways of Singapore towards the children's hospital, I wanted us to go faster. I wanted to grab the wheel and drive us myself. When we stopped at a red light, I had to restrain myself. By this point, Sandra and I were at our wit's end. The enormity of what was happening was sinking in fast, like we were drowning in quicksand and the pressure was suffocating us. We just wanted the seizure to stop. After 20 minutes of driving, we pulled up at the ER and Levi was whisked into a private room filled with about ten different doctors and nurses. We were told to have a seat outside and they would keep us updated.

It didn't feel right, so after a minute or two we walked back into the ER and told them we wanted to be with Levi. He needed us, to hear our voices and know that he wasn't alone.

I hope that no one else will have to experience the level of heart-wrenching panic we felt that day. It was truly the most horrific and awful experience watching Levi suffer whilst trying everything we could to help him breathe. We honestly thought we were going to lose him. We tried everything we could to get the seizure to stop but it truly felt like were we in a dream watching the worst thing possible happen. When we laid next to him, watching him leave his little body, we felt powerless, overcome with emotion, stress, and pain. It's a horrendous experience and my heart goes out to anyone who has ever gone through this or worse. I truly feel for you.

The seizure was so powerful and so strong that it continued long after the ambulance had rushed us to the children's hospital. In fact, the seizure was so bad it couldn't be stopped with regular drugs and needed 3 different sets to bring it under control. It had lasted more than 60 minutes in total (typically they go on for 5-15 minutes and stop of their own accord). Our little man had been through it.

As a parent, to see Levi lying there in the emergency room, his little body struggling to breathe with his eyes rolled back in his head was OUT OF THIS WORLD SCARY. At one stage, early on, whilst we were still at home waiting for the paramedics to arrive, he turned blue and then his face went pale white. It felt like a race against time! Every moment was fraught with the most intense emotion I have ever experienced.

Thankfully, I am pleased to tell you that my little lion pulled through against remarkable odds and showed me what a fighter he really is. I am happy to say that after 5 days in intensive care, Levi was discharged and allowed to come back home with us. But for these 120 hours of pain, life had moved up a gear. Better still, since that incident, there hasn't been any repeat occurrence of the seizure. Levi has continued to grow up into the charming, cheeky chappie that embraces each new day with fun, enthusiasm and a beaming smile.

What I learnt from this trauma

This traumatic experience, although terrifying, brought home some big realisations for us about what was important and all the little stuff didn't matter. Actually, nothing at all mattered apart from our baby's health and well-being. With this experience, things became even clearer. People talk about how it puts everything in perspective when people die or traumatic unexpected things happen. This incident did just that. Our perspective was resolute. Life was now in 4K high definition and screaming for me to take action on a massive scale.

When life is dealt on these terms, it's clear. We would have done anything to help Levi and get him back to full health. **This made us ROAR**.

The hospital bill took out our life savings and the nest egg that we had been slowly building. Of course, we would have paid anything to have him well again. The experience of seeing him lying on the living room floor while convulsions overpowered his little body was horrendous.

It changed something inside of me massively. It clicked. There is power in the moments of our greatest struggle, and if we can capture them, they can become our greatest source of motivation. I didn't care how much it cost, or what we needed to do, my baby was going to get the care he needed, and I was determined to ensure that he would never be in this position again. I had found my why and the reason to roar.

In all honesty, before this incident, I didn't think I could get much more focused, goal driven or ambitious, but this event made me cutthroat. It cemented absolutely my determination to succeed and provide for my family, for Levi. It inspired me by opening up and tapping into a deeper part my being, not just mentally but spiritually, emotionally, physically and soulfully. It was like a river was flowing through me at the very core of the waterfall of emotion, and I remain steadfast in my belief and determination to do whatever it takes to provide a life for him that will give him the opportunity to get the best from his life.

I knew I never again wanted to be in that position again. On day three, while Levi was still making his recovery in hospital, I began making changes outside.

Not only did I need to find another ten thousand dollars to pay the hospital bills, I also needed to up my game again and play even bigger than before.

What I had thought was a decent amount of effort (reading books on wealth, sending my previous book to publishers, writing blogs, cold-calling influential people to try and set up meetings) was not enough. It wasn't enough to create the amount of change we needed.

I was driven by the determination to succeed for myself, for my wife and for Levi, and the fact that we had no choice, no way out; the only way was forward, with big brave steps.

Ray Dalio talks about this when he considers his stance on tough love. Ray Dalio, says '*What I want to give people, most importantly to the people I love, is the power to deal with reality to get what they want. I will often deny them what they "want" because that will give them the opportunity to struggle so that they can develop the strength to get what they want on their own.*'

What I learnt about resourcefulness

Below are my principles for resourcefulness. As you've read, we sometimes need to be at our most resourceful during our worst moments in life.

You could be reading this and be in a dead-end job, which is making you miserable, or have an unfulfilling relationship, or you could need to get out of debt.

Whatever challenge you are facing, there is a way out and it all starts by reframing what you are facing.

My principles for resourcefulness in times of trauma:

1. Go purposefully forward with a smile, open mind and decisive nature

2. Act with integrity and speed

3. If in doubt, act and believe it will be so, then hack it together

4. Start with the basics, get those big elephants sorted first

5. Tackle tasks in a focussed sequence, don't dwell or hop between multiple missions that support the overall goal

6. Take aligned action

7. Pause, refocus, recalibrate, and move

8. Try not to be rude, but do get your point across

CHAPTER 25

BE MORE RESOURCEFUL

"Every rejection we got was an invitation to keep going."

Joe Gebbia

Your resourcefulness is a true asset

I love this quote from Joe Gebbia, Co-Founder of Airbnb, as it truly captures what I mean about changing the conversation on how you view your current circumstances. Being resourceful is about finding ways to keep going even when the world keeps hurling rocks at you and you are face down in the dirt. The power to be resourceful is the internal attribute that carries us forward when the other person gets the job, or the job is lost, or you face a crisis.

Although serious life challenges can force you to be resourceful, it's important to work on being resourceful every day. It will enable you to see opportunities and solutions to problems that would have remained invisible before. In this chapter, I'm going to drill down a little deeper into the subject of resourcefulness and share some of the resourceful things I've done which may seem crazy or audacious. I hope to inspire you.

Resourcefulness is a skill that you can build. I'm not promising it will be easy. In fact, it will push you into a lot of confronting and difficult situations. If you're doing it right, you'll spend much of your time feeling uncomfortable, making calls that you don't want to or asking for something from someone who can help.

Being uncomfortable when you are being resourceful is a sign that you are moving in the right direction.

If it was easily available to everyone then you wouldn't need to be resourceful to get it. It's like air; we don't think about where our next breath of air is going to come from, we just breathe and it's there. But money, contacts, opportunities, introductions and a successful business take more work to obtain. Resourcefulness has more to do with taking action in the moment and less to do with the outcome.

By making the phone call, you find out new information which leads you to the next thing. It's about being able to handle repeated rejection and closed doors and not losing faith.

We all have emotions and it's perfectly fine to listen to them, feel them and understand them, but we have a problem when our emotions limit us or hold us back from the bigger life we were meant to live. So we must get used to acting anyway despite how we may feel.

For example, if you want to launch an online business, it is imperative in today's world of social media, connections, followers, subscribers, and influencers that you have some content and you're willing to put yourself out there. You need to share your opinion, be a thought leader, fight for your business and to have a place in the market. The audience won't come to you unless you go to the audience first. You have to give them a reason to find you, discover an affinity with your brand and buy into your story. Without these components, the business will struggle to get off the ground. This means that you might have to make those uncomfortable promotional videos or record a Vlog on YouTube that allows a potential audience to get to know you better, buy into your message and relate to you. It will require you to reach out to the local or national press, focus on PR and do things that you deem yourself to be "unqualified" to do. It will require you to be the person that calls up the local radio station and asks if they can do an interview with you or gets a speaking opportunity at a co-working space to introduce new people to your business. It requires you to get uncomfortable, push yourself into new arenas and focus less on how this is different or challenging and more on the value you are adding to others, all the while fired by your motivation to see this business come to life and flourish.

How can you learn to be resourceful?

I was once asked during an interview, 'How would you deal with repeated rejection?'

I responded with, "It comes down to shifting your perception of failure and rejection and it goes back to the mantra of 'failure is only a lesson'. It also depends on if you expected rejection. If we can learn to expect rejection from time to time, we can also learn how to move the conversation forward on a new line of questioning without becoming defeated. If we don't expect rejection, we take rejection personally and get caught up in the story."

And you know what, a similar skill is required when you're learning to be resourceful. Resourcefulness is the ability to think of new and interesting options and strategies that you can bring into play to move forward when faced with an obstacle. If you expect to have to be resourceful, you always look for new ways to do things and new opportunities. Because you expect obstacles and challenges to be there, you aren't taken by surprise when they come along, and you are able to adapt. It pays to have this flexible mentality so that you are in shape and able to adapt when the time comes. Lions stay in shape for when they need to make a big move or get creative in order to thrive.

Master the resourcefulness mindset

Being resourceful is about having a mindset of possibility and using what you have to create what you don't. Resourcefulness is about not taking no for an answer; it's about looking for alternative routes to solve problems.

What makes this mindset so powerful is that you're not waiting to land that high-paying job before you take action or consider yourself to have the right amount of influential connections to make it happen.

Being resourceful is about using what you have right now to get where you need to be going.

There are millions of people in the world who have access to all the resources that anyone could ever want and yet they still have trouble creating their best lives, fulfilling their vision or getting their ideas off the ground. This is because resources and resourcefulness are two completely different things. In one situation you can have the money, the power, the connections and still not have the skill to put it all together in a meaningful way. In another situation, you can have very little in the way of resources and all the tenacity, grit, purpose and determination to see your goals come to fruition.

Set mini-challenges

The way I train my resourcefulness muscle is to set myself mini-challenges; for example, if I wanted Alex Banayan, the author of *The Third Door,* to write the foreword to this book, I would set it as a mini challenge and figure out a way to make it happen.

Next, I go about breaking the mini challenge down into simpler tasks.

First, I need to get on this guy's radar – how can I do that?

The best way would be to add value to Alex in some way. I could do this through a thoughtful blog post promoting the merits of reading his book or supplying him with interesting information about an event or content that I know he'd be interested in reading.

> Adding value to people is the number one way to make an impact.

Other ways to get in front of him would be to attend a conference or talk show that I knew he was speaking at.

If that's not an option, then I could call his office and try and get a meeting with "the gatekeeper" by explaining the situation. There will normally be someone, whether it's a PA, an EA, or Chief of Staff that is the gatekeeper to his schedule and the diary.

If I can befriend this person and get them to support the cause I am much more likely to secure a face-to-face meeting, which is the ultimate goal here because it allows for a deeper experience (much like I did with Richard Branson's Necker Island PA, and I am still working on getting the meeting).

And if all else fails, I could try reaching out to him on email, social media or calling his company office to ask how I could arrange a meeting, call, email, letter exchange.

The key is to try all of these strategies and not just rely on one.

One common problem that I frequently hear people moan about is, "I don't have their email address." People let small issues such as this hold them back from a lifetime of opportunity. It's not going to be easy, but who said it would be.

It's better to be strategic about who you tell about your mini challenges. Some people will try to talk you out of it by telling you it's not possible. They secretly hope that you fail for being courageous and trying. Others will tell you that even if you make it through a maze of obstacles and finally make contact with the target, they won't respond. This is another example of a lack fear-based mindset.

Do not listen to it. It is not grounded in truth and clearly not based on experience. Anyone who's applied some out-of-the-box thinking to successfully contact a famous, influential or hard to reach person will not try to discourage you with such baseless small-minded thinking.

In my case, I did not have Alex's email address. This is where I need to turn part juggler, part private investigator. Juggler because I need to be able to balance multiple strategies to connect with Alex and also get his attention, and private investigator because I need to track this down.

The first port of call was his company website, which is a treasure trove of information. I scroll down and find the contact us button. I am looking for any email address to see how it is configured, e.g. name.surname@company.com or firstletter.surname@comany.com.

Remember there could be a few variations and email addresses of the founders, leaders, top dogs and head honchos are not always easy to spot. You may need to try several emails before you are successful. If you keep digging though, you will find clues to the potential configuration somewhere, or at least a configuration pattern that you can work with to build out workable options.

Secondly, once I am satisfied that I have found his email address, I need to go about crafting the cold-email. This is the fun part because you can add a little bit of flare and show how much you know about the person, so that they can tell you're not spam and you've done your research.

It important that the email doesn't get fobbed off as spam at first glance. So it should be clear from the get-go, through the language I use and the way I structure the email, that this is not spam and is worth considering. The email is my chance to go straight to source and make an impact. It is a first impression, so be as authentic as possible when writing these types of cold-emails.

If you are reaching out to a famous movie star, politician, industry leader, senior figure, or celebrity, always be polite and respectful. Remember, as much as you know them, they don't know you.

The way I structure my emails is simple.

1. Demonstration of understanding
2. Introduction
3. Context and request
4. Gratitude
5. Final one-line request
6. Best wishes

The structure and the way in which you explain succinctly what you want is important. They don't want a long story. It is likely these people are very busy and if they're not, you have about 15 seconds to make your mark and grab their attention before they press delete or get distracted.

This works in all manner of situations. For example, you can use this email structure at work, when cold-emailing new clients or prospecting new business. It works a treat and is my go-to method.

It is why I am not afraid of reaching out to anyone, because I am going to be respectful, polite and informative. I see this email as adding value, especially if it is to a potential new client in business.

This shift in mindset is part of the self-belief that you have in your work, your purpose and how you view the value you bring to the world. Once you view this email as an opportunity for them to engage with you that could lead to a multitude of mutually beneficial outcomes, (not just a one-way thing in which only you stand to gain) then you unlock the self-belief to be unstoppable.

Think of what you are giving not what you will receive, and it will transform the way you write, and you should find that you are less likely to hold yourself back when you come up against a roadblock and question if you send them a cold-email.

The way to get their attention is to be relatable and show understanding

1. **Acknowledge their time.** You want to state that you understand that they are busy. This shows them that you understand their world and the importance of their time, and you aren't here to waste it either. *"I understand you're incredibly busy and you must receive emails like this all the time, so I will keep this short and to the point."*

2. **Briefly introduce yourself.** Give details of who you are and what you do. *"My name is Tim and I am an author. I came across your work,* The Third Door, *and couldn't put it down. I read the whole book in 2 days. I felt like I could relate to all of the points and your stories, especially the one about not being able to talk to Larry King at the event. To give you some context about who I am, I am a tenacious, ambitious individual with a penchant for entrepreneurship and I am drawn to those who take risks to make their dreams come true. I work in sales, have a family and live in Singapore right now. I am a huge fan of your work."*

3. **Outline the context of the situation and make the ask.** *I am writing my second book,* Be The Lion,

and would love for you to write the foreword to it. It would be such an honour to have your words begin the journey to help people overcome big challenges, create new habits and make their visions become a reality."

4. **Be grateful**. Express your thanks and how specifically it's them that you want. Show you've done your homework *"I understand you're very busy, and even if you can't grant this request, I wanted to thank you for writing* The Third Door. *It changed how I approach situations in my own life when I am presented with moments of opportunity. I really do feel that your voice at the beginning of my book* Be The Lion *would set the tone to send readers on the right path if you could spare a few moments to write a few words."*

5. **End with a one-line short request**. *"If you find the time to read far this could you quickly just let me know if this is something you could consider?"*

6. **Round off**. If the circumstance calls for it, close with a funny, memorable, and light-hearted few words. Something that shows your character and that you're a real person, not an automated or templated message. Give your email a personalised touch. *"Here's hoping I won't need to come to your annual shareholders meeting to ask this in person like you did with Buffett."*

7. **Final thanks**. Then thank them and be on your way. *"Thanks for your consideration of this request and I would be over the moon just to hear back from you. Best Regards, Tim Castle"*

Next, it's time to practise patience. Remember these influential people have busy lives and have probably been on 4 private planes and 2 super yachts since your email landed in their inbox.

It is best to wait a few days before following up, or better still, use the email as a platform to make other inroads. For instance, the email gives you a credible reason to call their office and check the email configuration, leave a message or simply touch base to find out more information. Just don't be annoying.

Demonstrating that you understand *their* world is half the battle in getting them to come closer to you and bring you in. Once you have the initial email, don't stop there, you really should be trying all other methods as well, like getting to the gatekeeper or timing a well-planned run in by bumping into them "randomly" at a conference.

Think of it like boxing, it's a combination of punches, moves and continued intensity that wins the fight. Everyone thinks it the final punch that did all the damage, but that's just the finisher. In reality, what took the opponent down was the continual pressure mentally and physically on the body, the darting around and fast-changing pace, the fancy footwork and small, rapid punch combinations to the ribs that built up to the big opportunity for a knockout.

It's the same principles here that will lead you to victory. It takes discipline to keep going even when you think it's not making a difference, when there are no visible signs of success. You will need to employ your mental fortitude time and time again to pursue your dreams, even when it does look like it's working. Even when you get rejected and hear "no" a hundred times, you need to pick yourself up, keep going and have faith that it will all come together.

When you are being resourceful, you are pushing on all fronts. This is being resourceful. That's how you make reaching out to someone happen.

Your mobile phone is a resource to be used

Let's face it, we live in fairly privileged times. If you have access to a mobile phone or you can afford to buy this book, then you're already doing pretty damn well for yourself compared to practically any other generation in the history of the world. The mobile phone is like having an infinite sea of opportunity in your pocket. No longer are you bound by the normal rules that would keep businesses in beta mode for years. Now it is possible to launch a business in a few hours and test multiple strategies to get traction. You can reach out to your favourite inspirational gurus and ask them for help. There is a wealth of success waiting for you if you just take the next step. It's not about having it all planned out, it's about taking the next to step, seeing where it leads and responding with that new information in hand to try and take yourself closer to your goal.

Know when you need to go offline

You can have too much of a good thing and addiction to smartphones can actually clog up your resourcefulness. One thing I feel needs to be said is that when we go on Instagram, Facebook, Snapchat and Twitter, or read blogs, emails and vlogs, everyone makes it look like they have got it all figured out, all the time, like they never have a bad day. This is categorically not true. I am sure you know this as well, but after a while scrolling through Insta feeds, reading well-written inspirational posts and listening to everyone who's doing amazingly cool shit and "winning" at life, your sense of reality can start to get a little warped. It's easy to think "why is it not happening for me? "why don't I have 5 trillion likes on my page?" and "what's wrong with me".

What you don't see is the failures that these individuals face on a daily basis. Some of them may have just got lucky, others maybe buying traffic from South America to bump their numbers. Others may have just figured out, after years of trying and failing, how to make valuable content that sticks.

The point is not to compare yourself in this way. Look for inspiration, but the moment it starts to feel like a competition for love, appreciation, validation or unfair, this is where you may need to take a tech break.

In 2018, Marc Benioff, co-CEO of Salesforce.com, the world's number 1 CRM platform, knew that he needed to make some changes. He needed to take some time off, so he mailed his iPhone, and iPad to his house in Hawaii and set off for a two-week tech-free vacation around the Galapagos islands. He was only contactable by landline in emergencies. On returning from his adventure in Hawaii, he found the answer. He knew he could no longer be CEO and do the work that he was called to do (philanthropy, like lobbying for new regulations to support the homeless, or working on the future of Salesforce as a business). He quickly promoted a new co-CEO internally to share the responsibilities in a "divide and conquer" strategy. This was an unprecedented move in the tech industry that had not been seen in for decades, but the time off the grid allowed him time to unplug and see things from a new perspective.

And that's my suggestion to you. Any time you feel yourself trapped by habits that don't support you or you start comparing yourself unnecessarily or become unfairly harsh with yourself, take a tech break. Get off the grid, go into nature. Take a trip.

If a CEO worth $5.8 billion, who has built one of the most successful companies in the world (its stocks grew 34% last year outperforming the market), has decided that taking a tech break for 2 weeks is a smart thing to do, then I'm with him.

Your resourcefulness challenge

Now, I have a question for you. I'm curious, what do you have on your list of inspiring things you want to do for your business, brand or for yourself that you're deemed out of reach or never got around to doing?

You can see where I'm going, can't you?

Now is the time to do it!

Whatever that thing is, begin it now, right this second. I want you to take out your phone and get to it. This is an order from your resourcefulness personal trainer. It's like you are at the gym and your PT says, "Get down and give me 10 push-ups." I say get out there and make it happen. Send 10 emails, make 10 calls, sign up to 10 new events, add 10 new interesting people on LinkedIn and then message them for a coffee.

Step 1: Break it down

When facing a challenge, I break down resourcefulness into a series of specific questions.

Who do I know that could help me make it happen?

- Who do I know that knows someone that could help?

- Where can I find people, information, or business that could help? (If I don't know anyone personally or through introductions).

- How could I contact them? (Via email, LinkedIn InMail, Skype for Business, Twitter, a hand-written letter, Facebook, Snapchat, Instagram, by phone, in person, at an event, interview, training session, event, conference, on video call, WhatsApp).

- Who haven't I thought of yet?

- Who do I need to be on board?

What do I want to make happen?

- What does success look like?

- What are my goal(s) in order of priority?

- What do I need to occur for this to happen?

- What information do I need to know?

- If I could speak to the right person, what would I ask them?

- What are 5 ways I could make that happen? Which of the above 5 ways would I like to try first and why?

- What are my options right now?

- What haven't I thought of yet?

Why do I want it to happen?

- What will it give me?

- What is the driving force that motivates me to make this happen?

- Why do I care about this?

- Why now?

- Why am I holding myself back?

How could I make it happen?

- How will I know when it has happened?

- What is the worst thing that could happen?

- What is the ideal way it could happen?

- What are the ways it could happen?

- How am I going to be during this process?

- How will I carry myself? Mentally, physically and emotionally – what standards will I hold myself to?

Dare to ask

Resourceful people don't stop because of the rules or perceived "rules" that society has imposed, such as the accepted norms or ways of behaving. The resourceful have taught themselves to solve problems by asking for what they need and then finding ways to get around the rules, perceived or otherwise.

Sometimes we could all do with being a little **bolder**, like walking up to someone at a networking event and introducing ourselves or pushing for entry into the backstage area of a leading conference.

> Being bold at times is all that is holding you back from getting the information you need, finding the person you need to speak to and making it happen.

People drive themselves crazy doing everything under the sun, running around like headless chickens when sometimes all they need to do is to be direct and ask. By having the courage to ask for what you need, you are being resourceful. It takes balls to pluck up the courage to make a request, but that could be exactly what is required to open the doors to the next kingdom that will allow you move forward and obtain your vision.

Think differently

The game is won and lost, not by how many resources you have at your disposal, but by how resourceful you are. That's it!

Have you ever heard that wealth often skips a generation? This tendency occurs because it's not about how much money you have – with the wrong mindset you can still fail – it's about how you hustle, how you play the game. The struggle creates the need to produce, to play at your best, and to go after your goal every day. That passion and fire come from the same place inside of you as your ability to be resourceful.

The skills are learnt in times of adversity, that is when you grow, when you try different strategies, elevate your thinking.

> Focus on the tools you do have, not those which you don't. Focus on what you can control.

In 1972, when US President Richard Nixon made a visit to China, it signified the resurrection of harmonious relations between the two nations, thus leading China to open up its doors to the West. At the time a young Jack Ma (Founder of Alibaba), then 18, noticed an increase in American tourists visiting his home town of Hangzhou and he spotted an opportunity.

Jack would seek out US tourists and take groups around the city as a free tour guide and, in exchange, they would converse and teach him English. This is an example of being resourceful, you don't need money to be resourceful. Jack didn't have the money to pay for an English tutor, so he solved the problem in an innovative and sustainable way that allowed him to get as much or as little learning as he wanted, unconstrained by his lack of money.

Be flexible

Flexibility is key to overcoming challenges as things have a way of never going exactly the way that we plan. The legendary fighter Muhammad Ali was a master of this. He would often outbox his opponents by shifting his style and moving around the ring, making his challengers dizzy. By keeping his combinations flexible, it kept his opponent guessing as he kept finding new ways to solve problems and would eventually knock them out cold.

Ali is referred to as "the greatest" after he won 56 bouts, 37 by knockout. He only ever lost 5 bouts in his entire 21-year professional career. To be resourceful you must be flexible. In his early years, Ali's signature move was to pull his head straight back when his opponent punched, causing them to overreach and create an opportunity for Ali to go in with a knockout hook to the jaw. As he got older and less agile, he had to adapt his style to take more punches to the lower body and absorb the energy of the fight, tiring his opponent out and then striking.

Ali would hurl verbal insults at his opponents to throw them off guard, like "Is that all you got?!" He was playing mental games with his opponents, beating them in every way he could think of. Imagine how it must have felt chasing this 6"3' champion around the ring for 12 rounds. You land your hardest punch into his ribcage, only for him to come back at you with: "Is that all you got?!" Another famous one was and "float like a butterfly, sting like a bee. His hands can't hit what his eyes can't see. Now you see me, now you don't. George thinks he will, but I know he won't."

It was this variety of resourcefulness in and out of the boxing ring that led Ali to victory time and time again.

Leverage other people's mistakes

It's easy to complain that everyone around you is killing it in business or having more success than you but when you focus only on their successes you miss another crucial opportunity. It is more resourceful to find people, companies and competitors who have been where you are before, or are there now, and then learn from their mistakes. If you learn to look at the mistakes rather than focusing on only on where they are winning, you'll get far more information than you ever could from looking at the successes alone.

This strategy is especially effective when time is a limited resource, or you are working to a deadline. When time is scarce, the rational mind naturally looks at successful people and sees how they did it, but this is an error. It is better to focus on the mistakes of others so that you can see how to you pivot, shift strategy and save time by leveraging the lessons of others to fast-track your own success.

I first noticed this strategy during an exercise during the first weekend of my MBA. The cohort had been split into 6 teams of 8 and was tasked with building the tallest tower made from drinking straws. Twenty minutes was put on the clock and off we went, full on, into the competitive land that was a classic MBA team-building ritual. The purpose of the exercise, of course, was to highlight the benefits of effective communication in teams, but it was a lot of fun and the teams got passionately into building their straw towers.

On reflection, I noticed that not many teams delegated people to look at what other groups were doing and so ignored a vital piece of information. If we had spent more time looking around, we could have saved time by clearly seeing which strategies and designs were failing (and thus what to avoid wasting time on) and which ones were having more success (and how we could leverage the combination of information around us).

It was a pivotal penny-drop moment for me: in the heat of the moment, the passion and enthusiasm for building the tallest tower led us to ignore the valuable information around us.

We got caught up in putting one person's idea into motion, which caused us to forget that one of our biggest resources was all around us (the failed attempts of the other groups). We got so caught up in what *we* were doing and rolling out *our* idea that we were oblivious to the fact that the table only a few feet away from us could have nailed the best tower building strategy or equally worryingly, be failing with the exact same design that we were so avidly pursuing, but be ahead of us.

By looking at mistakes we can navigate around potential pitfalls and avoid costly detours that drain both our finances and time.

Ask for a sign

Will the Universe to give you what you need or point you in the right direction. The world is giving you signals, showing you the way, drawing the right people to you, into your life, for a reason.

Listen to life, don't ignore it, thinking you know better. Being resourceful is as much about hustling and creating your own opportunities as it is listening to the world around you and remaining open to receive new and valuable insights.

Ask yourself these resourcefulness questions

One of the ways I consistently challenge what I think is possible is by asking myself the following questions:

1. If you had 24 hours to get it done, how would you achieve it?
2. Who would you need to speak to?
3. What questions would you need to ask?
4. What is the biggest priority?
5. If there was a gun to your head and your life depended on it, how could you do it?

Being resourceful is also about knowing that you can be open to resources. Life doesn't have to be hard for you to be resourceful, you can stack the deck in your favour and play to your strengths. An example of this would be leveraging the power of your network and asking for introductions to people you would like to secure a job interview at a certain company. Doing this ahead of time, before you get restless in your current job, is an example of being resourceful and applying the skill.

Once you have answered and digested the questions above your mind should begin to overflow with possibility. When we give the brain a challenge by asking it questions, it goes to work. As Tony Robbins says, the quality of your life comes down to the quality of the questions you ask, '*If you want a better life, ask a better question.*'

Ways to be resourceful (in the context of securing a new and exciting job)

Going through the process of researching, application forms, interviews etc. requires a special kind of resourcefulness. Below are my top tips to get you through this. These have worked for me and supercharged my career.

1. Challenge yourself to reach out to 5 of your most interesting contacts each week, set up meetings and see what opportunities come out of doing something different. You will be surprised by the things you learn and the wealth of possibilities out there.

2. Proactivity compose and send out 10 speculative emails to the HR department and decision makers in companies that pique your interest each week.

3. Get an executive coach, someone who will challenge your current story and advance how you represent your skills, experience and grow confidence in your abilities. Getting a coach can help you to see things differently and elevate both your mindset and how you view the trajectory of your career no end.

4. Start a blog in an area that you intend to own as your brand, then post it to LinkedIn, build up an audience and you will find that, over time, you become associated with the topic that you are promoting, and even know for it. Building your brand is as much about what you say as how you share what you know.

5. Take a new course. By investing in yourself through an online or in-person course you give yourself a new lease of life and inject and refine your skills, giving you increased confidence and new networks, connections, ideas and a refreshing vitally that will transfer into your interviews. Employers love to see people who are consistently pushing themselves to grow. The course doesn't have to be related to the job you are applying for, it could be something like photography, website design or wakeboarding. What is impressive is that you aren't settling for the status quo and you have a learning mindset. The new wave of energy that you will get from learning or developing a new skill will show through, and

this is the type of energy that employers and people, in general, are drawn to. So, go out there and shine. Now is your time to invest in yourself. Plus, you never know who you'll meet or what it might lead to.

6. If it was possible, I would do (x)... One way to increase your resourcefulness around job hunting is to think in terms of possibilities (and this is also applicable in multiple life scenarios). For example, if you knew the VP of Sales for Google you would make contact with them, or if you had a million dollars you would take a sabbatical and travel for a few months to broaden your horizons whilst applying for jobs. The purpose of thinking in this way is to distance yourself from fixed mindset thinking and open up the possibilities around you. In this way, you can see what you are most attracted to and what excites you beyond your wildest dreams. It then becomes clearer which path to follow. Part of job hunting is reducing the anxiety, dread and frustration that comes with not having a job, or wanting to be in a different job. Therefore, it is your mission to stay on the positive side of that battle by focusing on the abundance of possibility around you. For instance, say you found the travel option most appealing in the example above. Perhaps then you could look into options to take out a loan to fund the trip, or research organisations and charities that would offer you accommodation and food in exchange for food. Thinking in this manner might also lead you to consider working abroad and, as such, you realise you have been searching for jobs in entirely the wrong city, country or discipline.

7. Never, never, ever, give up! When it comes to job hunting, you never know when your application is going to get picked up or which role might just miraculously be the right next move for you. Things can happen very fast when it's a fit, and just because you've applied for 150 jobs and gotten nowhere doesn't mean that the role that's meant for you isn't right around the corner.

Resourcefulness in this sense comes from finding ways to keep diligent and be accountable to your job search. This could be in the form of striking up a conversation with that friendly person at WeWork or reaching out to an old acquaintance for a referral. You never know what is possible unless you try, what is meant for you will come your way as long as you throw yourself into it.

CHAPTER 26

HOW TO CREATE MOMENTUM MOMENTS

"Perfection is finally attained not when there is no longer anything to add, but when there is no longer anything to take away."

Antoine de Saint-Exupéry

Why momentum matters

Anyone can create mountains of action but action that's not focused is just a bunch of hot air. You need to create action in the direction in which you want to go and have the discipline to maintain the consistent application of focus rather than get distracted. In this chapter, I'm going to show you how you can build on the momentum to get to your destination a lot faster, and once you start doing this, things get easier, become unstuck and problems get solved.

Momentum is everything. It's the ability to move from one failure or success to the next, either by taking the lesson and implementing the learning to improve the quality of your decisions, questions and thinking, or by building on the platform of your successes.

I found that cold calling a great way to practise momentum building and resilience when I was faced with a series of hard knocks. By picking up the phone and speaking to 1, 2, 5, 10 people in a row and moving forward, regardless of the outcome, building on either the win or the loss, was like a gym for building the momentum muscle.

I found that the more I practised, the more knockbacks I overcame, the more calls I made, the more questions I asked, the more the momentum muscle came out to play. Just like hitting the weights in the gym, the more reps I conquered the bigger my guns became, and the less afraid of heavier weights I was.

In fact, when we overcome knockbacks and failures, the story can actually turn around and we anticipate heavier weights or hard clients because we possess an increased confidence in our ability to smash it out of the park and move forward regardless.

This level of confidence, this phenomenal self-belief, is not only the result of physical change through consistent action that is driven from pushing through the pain and working out in all conditions (making the phone calls when we don't feel like it), but it also represents a mindset shift.

In this place, we are no longer bound by the limitations and biases that we once brought to the situation. This mindset shift is important because where we once saw a block in the road, we now see an opportunity to overcome a hurdle and continue on. The hurdle can be conquered in many ways. We could find alternative ways around it, we could master it and turn it into a strength, but what's paramount is how we perceive the hurdle in our mindset and the ability to continue to create momentum despite the appearance of the said blocker.

I have been talking in metaphors but, hopefully, this will help you to get the idea that what we are or aren't capable of is decided in the mind, long before the appearance of any challenge.

When you struggle to build momentum

Now we need to talk about being able to manifest momentum, because you know you can't just flip a switch and, hey presto, you become superwoman. Some days, you just don't feel it. Maybe you watched *Eat, Love, Pray* the night before and are contemplating what the hell you should be doing with your life, or you keep on getting rejected from the perfect job that you know would be awesome at, or your Instagram followers are in decline, even though you've been producing more content than ever. Whatever it is, there are times that momentum can be hard to muster.

That said, it is important that you know how to find the strength within yourself to continue so that you don't blow the big opportunities in life. It's about being able to transform yourself into your peak self at the times when you need it the most.

This could be for a big pitch for your business, a negotiation or leading a team. There are moments in life when the stakes are higher and you know that being able to perform at your best will lead to bigger rewards which will propel your life in new directions.

We must be very intentional about the person we chose to be and is showing up in that moment. For example, if you have the opportunity to present for your company at a large conference, be intentional about who is showing up on that stage so that you can get most from that experience and take full advantage of everything it offers. It is important to have a mindset that will carry you through your fear and keep you pushing with everything you have to perform at your best. You never know who will be watching and what opportunities it may lead to. Public speaking is consistently ranked in the top 5 things most people fear along with a terrorist attack, but really, what is it? It is just a conversation with people; you are relaying a story and it doesn't have to be perfect to impress. What's impressive is someone who communicates with heart, conviction and authenticity. That's what is memorable, not whether you fluffed a line up or were nervous. It's completely fine to be nervous. In fact, 85% of people report feeling nervous before speaking in public. The way to deal with these nerves is to accept it as normal, so that it doesn't get worse.

Next focus on deep slow breathing, fix your mind on something you appreciate in life and hold that thought for a few seconds. Then smile, stand up tall and visualise yourself proudly having this conversation with the people in front of you with passion, warmth and confidence.

What you'll find is that the more you are able to go through this process and recognise that feeling nervous is completely normal and fine, as long as you don't let it stop you, you'll actually start to get a buzz when you dominate on stage or in the pitch. Being comfortable talking to people can transform into an energy that gets you excited and suddenly, you find you have a strength that you never knew was there.

In an interview for Tony Robbins' podcast (which I highly recommend you subscribe to in order to get your daily injection of goodness for the soul, mind and body), Joe Gebbia, Co-Founder of Airbnb, answered a question from a woman in the audience. Her question was, 'How do you know when it's the right time to quit your day job and go full time with your business?'

Joe suggested that she find ways to step out of your comfort zone every day, to notice what made her uncomfortable, and then do it. By doing this gradually over time, you can look back at the series of challenges you have overcome, and think *oh wow, I've done all that.* You'll then find that stepping out away from your day job becomes the next natural step.

> Often the satisfaction of success comes not from beating the other person, team or winning the deal, but from overcoming the self and, more specifically, the self-limiting beliefs that have been keeping us from achieving our full potential.

Do you ever find yourself knowing that you could do more, offer more to the world and be of service in a greater order of magnitude?

Could you offer more of yourself to others and make more of yourself in this life?

Momentum pitfalls

Back in the day, Seneca, the Roman philosopher wrote a letter to Paulinus, a Roman missionary and the first Bishop of York, which contained much wisdom about the use of time.

He said, *'It is not that we have a short space of time, but that we waste so much of it. Life is long enough... Vices beset us and surround us on every side, and they do not permit us to rise anew and lift up our eyes for the discernment of truth, but they keep us down when once they have overwhelmed us and we are chained to lust. Their victims are never allowed to return to their true selves; if ever they chance to find some release, like the waters of the deep sea which continue to heave even after the storm is past, they are tossed about and no rest from their lusts abides.'*

I came across the Seneca quote one morning when browsing a blog that had one very clear objective, it was devoted to helping us make better decisions and live a better life. It's called *Farnam Street* (www.fs.blog) and I recommend you check it out.

When I first clicked on the homepage, I was presented with the tagline, '*Mastering The Best Of What Other People Have Already Figured Out,*' in bold white type, and from then, I was hooked.

I curiously scrolled through the pages and came across an intriguing post on the four misuses of time. FS argue that we routinely waste the world's most valuable resource, time, repeatedly across these four areas of our daily life. The core of the message is below:

1. **Productivity** – In our quest to become more productive, we completely miss the point about being the benefits of being efficient because we don't properly value time. The mistake is as we find ways to become more efficient, we fill our newly created time with more tasks and thus become amazing at completing tasks but not truly spending time on what matters. We fill the space with more layers of work rather than life.

2. **Learning** – With learning we tend only to 'skim the surface' because it will 'save us time' rather than getting deep into a subject and taking our time to expand our thinking. By adopting this approach to learning we again miss the point about the value of time. The results are, therefore, minimal because we have only 'skim learned' and we have not 'done the work'. We are then unable to improve the quality of the decisions we make because we haven't, in fact, learnt anything. FS reason that as the outcomes of learning are uncertain and unlike a financial investment, which is quantifiable, we rationalise that learning as fast as humanly

possible is the right and quickest way to reap the benefits. Sadly, this is not the case.

3. **Relationships** – Can you think of a time you were too busy to spend time with your parents, read the kids a story before bed, or you prioritised your work responsibilities over date night. The error with this type of habit is that we are 'too busy' to spend time with loved ones until it becomes too late, at which point we would do anything to get the time back. For example, in your late twenties and early thirties, when you are set on building an impressive career and scoring that promotion, you don't have the time to see your children grow up or you miss out on spending quality time with your partner, and so you drift apart. I have found that rising early and getting to work on projects or tackling big issues at work is best done in the early morning before anyone is awake. This has helped me to prioritise what is important in my own life and to make sure that I am there for my family as a dad, husband, brother and son. It allows me to be more efficient whilst still being able to go home in the early evening and be fully present for the moments that matter most.

4. **Meetings** – These are often poorly organised, poorly run, with no agenda. *Man, this is so true!* How many meetings do you go to in a week that have no point, no agenda and half the meeting is spent gossiping, waffling on or chatting about nothing of actual substance, all under the guise of team bonding. Meetings are a time drain. Be careful which meetings you freely give your time up for and, if you have the flexibility, make sure you review this on a monthly basis with ruthless consistency. Pointless meetings have a habit of creeping into your diary and depleting your ability to get ahead.

Another possible pitfall when you're creating momentum is patting yourself on the back for tasks that didn't need to be done. It's easy to be busy. Productivity and busy have become the buzz words of the 21st century.

I would suggest that you regularly ask yourself, what is the most important thing I can do with my time, right now, at this exact second.

Because if you spend your time in procrastination or denial, celebrating the moves you've made during the day and the tasks you ticked off your list, but none of them relates to your mission, you'll spend an awfully long time on the journey to success. It's like taking a detour or going around in circles before continuing onwards. Don't be fooled. It takes huge discipline and skill to determine what is the best use of your time, especially when the answer is not obvious.

Building momentum

So, let's talk about what you can do when you have a big win that is on point, and you're celebrating your creative, genius self for husting. I call like to call them **momentum moments**.

The way to move from a momentum moment to the next is to capture the feeling of exhilaration of success and use it to make your next decision. Take massive action at that exact point in time. Don't wait for the moment to pass, you will get distracted. Use the rush of endorphins, the boost in creativity and confidence to make your next move.

I do this all the time. When I make a large sale or win a pitch, rather than revel in the success until it passes, this is actually my peak time to make those calls that have been knocking around inside my head for weeks, or compose and send that email, or walk into a client's office and ask if they are available to meet up because my confidence and self-belief have just had a big boost.

It's actually in these momentum moments that we have an increased propensity to create more success. The next time you experience a big win, for sure, take a couple of minutes to do your dance and high-five the man sitting opposite you on the train, and then get to it, setting yourself up for your next win. It's not just what we do when we are struggling that matters, it's also how we approach the world when we are winning. Like attracts like.

I hope this is starting to give you an idea of the power of your physical body, the importance of harnessing your emotions and how you can create success in your own life. The next level of this game is the ability to tap into how you feel when you have a big win, how you act and how you carry yourself. This includes how you think and the action you will take to create that sensation as if it has happened to you so that you can operate at your peak state. This is when the world starts to open up for you even more and you will experience increased success and a stronger belief in your abilities.

Being able to operate at this level without relying on the big win to propel you there is the gift of champions. Sports is a great example of this. You see it all the time when sports players repeatedly prime themselves through visualisation, meditation, team chants etc. These tools are all used to prime the individual and transform them into their peak performance state, which increases their propensity to take life to the next level.

CHAPTER 27

MY STORY: DOUBT IS A SNEAKY MOTHERF*CKER

"Fear is the cheapest room in the house, I'd like to see you living in better conditions."

Hafiz

Doubt and self-belief

I gave you a quick note on doubt back in Part 1 of this book, but I want to revisit it here specifically to show you how it can crumble away your self-belief. There's a solid confidence that comes from knowing who you are and where you are going; it can't be moved, it can't be undone, it's powerful, instinctual and passionate. I'm sharing my story to show you just how deadly doubt can be, how it can keep you from realising your dreams and get stuck in the monotony of your own nightmare.

Looking back to my mid-twenties, I struggled with self-doubt. I doubted my capabilities to perform in business and didn't ask too much of myself in the other areas of my life, like fitness, health and well-being, finance, education and personal development. I just did whatever came along and felt good at the time.

This approach stifled my development and held me back from pushing for bigger opportunities to really stretch myself. I did what was comfortable, habitual and easy, *not* what I was passionate about or was tough, so I did not test what I was capable of. I settled for mediocre and preferred to talk about when I would have a thriving business or a property empire but never saw these ideas through to fruition fully.

On the surface, of course, I outwardly projected a different story. I was confident and outgoing. Inside, however, I was reeling with turmoil and felt alone. This was a painful and volatile time, and I truly feel for those who can relate to this and can't seem to find their way.

The simple cycle of comfort and familiarity sets in easily, especially when we are young and forming our opinions of the world, and causes poor habits to be established. It can be a hard track to get off because it's so damn easy, like hitting the snooze button when it is cold outside and you spend an extra 30 minutes in bed each day rather than getting up and working on your side hustle. It's so easy for these areas of "average" to creep into your life patterns and lead you into a spiral of self-doubt and retreat.

In my case, it took years to break out of this cycle of doubt and still takes consistent commitment to growth and learning, which has now become my favourite habit. Thank God.

The old me

Back then, I much preferred to numb my thoughts with big nights out (I enjoyed the London clubbing scene). I loved the music, the energy and the feeling of being up in the early hours, which I am sure many of you can relate to. I was on a constant quest for sensation, entertainment and feeling alive. I want to point out here that there is absolutely nothing wrong with clubbing and going out, but it was my approach to it that was wrong. I was addicted to the rush and used it as a distraction to enable me to avoid dealing with, or listening to, any thoughts or feelings that resembled doubt. When I look back, there were some needs it was serving, but it was also masking pain. What started out as fun became a repetitive loop of self-sabotage. It was a cycle that I created by constantly asking more of myself, to keep going out more and more without stopping to pause and reflect on why I didn't want to stay home.

Aligning yourself with the beat of your favourite DJ or tune provides a certain sense of freedom that when the bass is played out across the crowd into a club you can just let go, riding the beat and letting your mind relax. This was my utopia at this time. This night-time existence was where I felt safe; I felt at home, and yet I knew I could be doing more.

It was an absolutely fantastic distraction from the bigger picture of my life. I knew I expected more from myself, but I had the attitude of 'I'm young I am supposed to be having fun, one more night out won't matter, let's live for today.' Except then that this was my go-to excuse every night.

For whatever reason, I just couldn't connect to what made me excited outside of this incredible world of dance music, parties and people. I just didn't know. I had become so used to blocking out the truth with entertainment, excess and distraction that the thought of connecting to my deeper self filled me with fear.

It scared me to think of self-development. I knew there was more, but I was lost. I wanted to live the fast life and had a 'Come what may, let's live for today and f*ck tomorrow' type attitude.

At one stage, it got pretty bad and life moved so fast I feared I would join the 27 club, I repeatedly had thoughts that this club was destined for me, which is an unsettling place to be, I didn't literally want 'to party 'til I die'. I knew I had more to give but how could I give it if I wasn't taking care of myself or putting the time in to develop.

I most definitely wanted more but was looking at it from completely the wrong perspective. I wanted what I could *get*, not what I could *give*. This mentality is one of lack and ultimately put me in a spiral of doubt, self-sabotage, and low energy that created more drama, burdens and pressure rather than elevating me to my higher purpose.

In order to break through this cycle, I had to completely shift my thinking to come from a place of love rather than just blocking out the noise with more noise and destructive habits that were getting me nowhere.

The cycle kept on repeating because it was a deeply ingrained habit. It was far easier to keep drinking, keep forgetting, and keep experiencing the high of exclusive clubs night after night, rather than get serious and do the work. I needed to get a grip and come up with a solid plan for my life that I would stick no matter what.

Looking back, I was still a young man rather than a man. I just preferred to enjoy the thrill of the party, and come what may, I could let doubts rule my inner world and that was fine because I could drown it out with booze and clubs. This way I didn't have to face what I was capable of achieving because I was in a world of self-centred fun and constant distraction.

This strategy of distraction works until it doesn't, until I said enough is enough, it's time to get on. It's time to build.

I hadn't yet started the work to build my house on a solid foundation and trust that the Universe indeed had my back. That concept was alien to me, but I was open to trying it out.

In this stage of experimentation, I was dipping my toe in the water and striving to move upward, but in sporadically random directions rather than a well-designed plan, and made no valid attempts to really go for it.

For example, I'd rock up to potentially career-changing interviews for jobs I really wanted unprepared and think I could just wing it, or not even wanting to get it because that would force me to level up (a self-sabotaging strategy). My philosophy was broken and I only half-heartedly wanted change. I was easily be led back to my old energy depleting patterns – there's good tunes and a party tonight. Let's go.

I was making unfulfilling decisions rather than investing in my growth and learning. I was trying to move forward but like a boat without a rudder, sail and an oar. I was using my hands to paddle, sculling my way down the river of life with no real direction and only a faint-hearted commitment to my growth.

However, deep down, in the quiet of my own head, whenever I would my mind to go there, I always knew I was destined for more. I knew I was destined to help people. This was my deepest passion. I came alive when helping others with their problems and I relished the opportunity to help work through or resolve the deep issues of their work and their life.

Creating a shift

Once I took a step back and gave myself an opportunity to really connect with my universal gifts, I found a sense of self-assurance. It took years to build this up (and the process is still ongoing today) and realise that what I needed was within me. I had all I needed.

This assurance enabled me to begin my journey and start to mend the bridges and heal the pain that I had been lugging around like a heavy, wet sack for a long, long time.

> With the distraction over and game face on, I was ready to bring it on. The Lion had left the cub behind.

This shift meant I was able to stop resisting. I knew that by focusing inward, I could progress and allow myself to feel the love, the light and the certainty.

Gabby Bernstein has this incredible way of describing it in the introduction to her book, *Spirit Junkie*,[3] and I want to share it with you here, as there are some parallels and it brings great value.

Gabby begins (in reference to *A Course In Miracles,* which many of her teachings are based on).

'Through my interpretation of the Course's principles you'll learn that all of the safety, security and love you're seeking is not "out there," but inside yourself. Trust me: I spent more than two decades looking for happiness in all the wrong places. I thought that happiness was in a credential or a boyfriend or a new pair of shoes. I thought that if I accumulated or achieved enough, my misery, insecurity, and anxiety would somehow disappear and be replaced by joy, confidence, and light-heartedness. It never worked.

---

[3] Bernstein, G. (2018) *Spirit Junkie. A Radical Road to Self-love and Miracles*. Harmony.

Turning inward can seem like an insurmountable challenge, but by committing to the Course you'll learn that inward is the only place to go. When you truly know this, you can release the need to be saved, stop controlling, and let life flow.'

What I want you to know is that if you are stuck in a destructive cycle, habit or pattern that's slowly taking you down, destroying the seams of your life so that you unravel, then know this, **there is a way out.** It can be done, but it **takes a firm decision** and requires that you to **do the work**, but the path is there, it does exist, and you can choose in an instant to move your life in this direction.

When you engage with the hunger and drive within you, that's where you find the knowledge that there is more to life. As a first step, I recommend you ask a friend for help and read *Spirit Junkie* and the *Universe Has Your Back*[4] to begin the journey that will guide you back to love.

What I learned from my period of doubt

1. **In the moments of quiet, you know you are capable of more**. Sometimes, it takes a moment of quiet reflection to reconnect with your true self and capabilities. It's easy to drown these out with day-to-day drudgery, so it's important to give yourself these quiet moments.

   Do you ever get that niggling feeling that you were put on this Earth to do something, to be more than you currently are and to leave a legacy? If you do, then welcome to where I was. I feel your pain, and I have been where you are in one way or another. The single biggest way I found to rid myself of self-doubt and pick myself up out the rut was to face the things I was most scared of doing. For example, I had a hunger inside of me that wouldn't go away. I was hungry to leave my mark on this world and to leave it better than when I

[4] Bernstein, G. (2016). *The Universe Has Your Back:Transform Fear to Faith*. Hay House Inc.

found it. However, I had become complacent in taking the easy road. When I took a job that I was unqualified for, I forced myself to level up, to put in the hours, to trust that I could be as smart as everyone else in that company, and could deliver on what I said I was going to do. I backed myself into a corner and burned the boats. I quit my comfortable cosy nothing-ever-changes job and forced myself to deliver the results. Luckily, the company in question hired me for my aptitude and not my technical ability, which meant they were willing to give me a shot as long as I could raise my standards and put in all that I had. This meant that I had to get comfortable with being uncomfortable. I had to do things that no one else was doing and upskill and trained harder than everyone else around me because this was my time. It meant that I worked through weekends. I started at 4am in the morning on weekdays for the first few months and I took every opportunity to learn that I could. As a result, this level of dedication, commitment and perseverance, along with the initial "burn the boats" push, meant that I was able to get results that my superiors were over the moon with. I suddenly had my eyes on the prize that was greater than myself. I put my energy into an outcome that was larger than my life. It now mattered what my bosses thought, what I could do for the company and how I could build a business that was solid from the get-go. This change, this adaptation of my previous habits and patterns of behaviour opened me up in ways that I wasn't prepared for or could conceive of before I had embarked on this journey. It was through this experience that I resonated with being a leader, a leader that empowered others and took the time to listen to their ideas and values.

It wasn't about me anymore, it was about company culture, and collaboration and shared success. This removed my doubts, fears and anxiety and moved me to a place of excitement, knowledge and expansion.

To find your own turning point, you need to find a moment of quiet and step away and reflect each day. This is important even when you are grinding away. In management journals, they call this getting off the dancefloor and on to the balcony! The idea is that by looking down on the dancefloor (stepping away) you are able to spot the opportunities for strategic tactical advantage. In this time of quiet, ask yourself if you are really doing all that you are capable of. Next, identify what you are scared of, what are you running from, what keeps you stuck in these bad, destructive, mediocre, average habits and patterns of behaviour. What is it about these patterns that feels safe, what do they protect you from? Once you have got clear on what it is that you are afraid of, you can start to brainstorm what it is that you want. This can be an emotional experience because you are breaking the boundaries of your old thought patterns and allowing yourself to focus on a life without limits. From here, map out all the things you would like to do if self-doubt and old sneaky patterns weren't at play. When you get this raw with yourself, there is no hiding anymore. When you strip away the layers of excuses and finally see what is underneath, it no longer looks like the ugly monster that it was on the surface. Many times, our fears stem from our need for approval, or to be loved or to feel worthy or not judged. Now you have identified what you want to do and what is holding you back, the path should feel clear to you. The key step now is to act. I want you to take one action that will lead you in the direction of your goal, vision or dream right now, this second. No excuses. Take action today to move your life forward in a new direction. Don't let doubt be the reason why you don't become all that you could be.

2. **Balance is key** – Part of the reason why I did not want to let go of my habitual cycle was that it was so incredibly skewed towards my areas of comfort, like late-night socialising, parties and having a whale of a time. However,

it failed to incorporate any inkling of self-development or personal growth as I didn't have time for it; plus actually addressing the issues that were causing doubt had kept me firmly in place, treading water. I didn't want to do the work, no sir, I'll just keep on living life to the full on the party side of the spectrum, please. The part of me that woke up to the realisation that I should be more was alert to the possibility that getting in at 3am every morning and then up at 8am was not great for the long-term prospects of my health, and that I should really try to achieve some semblance of balance.

This was easier said than done. These patterns were so deeply ingrained in my psyche they automatically occurred without me even thinking about it. I was on autopilot, like I had been switched to set and forget. I would automatically not want the night to end or get to the after-party and be the last one to leave or get back out to lunch following the night before.

For a period of years, I tolerated the discomfort of knowing this was not the best way I could be living. I made vague attempts to keep a gym schedule and stick to a routine, but for years I never fully committed. Not where it mattered, inside. I would talk about it, and actively promote a new lifestyle to my friends and colleagues, but I didn't begin to make progress until I made major changes to how I valued myself, my time and my ability to create something from my life. To inject balance in your life, you need to be deeply committed to sticking to a schedule, no matter what. This may mean changing your environment and either moving out of your frat house type environment, or changing jobs to one that allows you to have more free time and fewer nights out. The change must be made, and it must be deep so that the patterns of behaviour are severed completely. Unless you consciously (not automatically) go out of your way to destroy your new schedule, you will be in a completely new place to being to move further away from doubt and rebuild a more confident, self-love and complete version of the balanced you.

3. **Value – know your worth.** Self-love is absolutely critical when it comes to moving through doubt. Countless friends and relatives would tell me how good I was at photography, speaking or business development but it didn't matter. I didn't seem to hear them, because the story I was telling myself was that "I'm not as good as them" or "I won't stick with it, so why bother" or "I don't feel like it so it can't be true." All these mantras kept me stuck in the same place – doubt. I was controlled by fear even though the Universe was giving me signs and signals about how I could offer value to the world, be creative and live a bigger life. To increase your sense of self-worth, it's so important that you change the story you are telling yourself on a daily basis. Switch off the autopilot and consciously listen to the words that you speak when you describe yourself and your abilities, or the possibility of something happening. For example, I walked out of my house the other day and was greeted by a neighbour. As normal, they asked, "How are you?" and I replied, "Not too bad thanks." An off the cuff, normal exchange you might think. Wrong, there are a million ways I could have described how I was that morning that didn't involve the word "bad" or have a negative association attached to it. This struck me as particularly odd as it wasn't like I was having a bad day, and for someone who is now heavily into psychology and the self-help space, I should have had a better grasp on how to describe myself. This wasn't even on a bad day, god forbid. It caught me off guard and normally I wouldn't think too much about it. But it made me realise that we can never get too comfortable with how we think we value ourselves and talk about ourselves. Bad habits can creep back in and start to pull you down, even on the days when we are doing

fine. Now when I am greeted by someone and they ask how I am I respond with, "I am good thanks, doing very well." This small but significant change has a ripple effect throughout my life and changes how I view myself. I now make a conscious effort to control the language I speak to myself in my own head and when speaking to others so that it is not off the cuff or throwaway, but said with purpose, meaning and love.

4. **Distraction doesn't feel good.** Every refresh of your Instagram feed rewards the complacent part of your brain with hits of dopamine. The problem is you need more distraction to fill the void. As you try to plug the hole, the need keeps on growing. The more you try to escape your fears, the more you need to drown out both the anxiety and self-doubt. This is a destructive cycle that you can change. It won't happen overnight; in fact, there is no quick fix or hack that will speed up the process. No one in this state wants to do the work, but those who do accelerate their lives towards greatness. Do you want to take charge of your life again and have more time on your hands to do the things you care about? If this is you, then listen up. It's a long road and I speak from experience when I say that there are many falls and stumbles along the way, but the feeling you experience of regaining that sense of control over your life and its meaning is totally worth it.

> Distraction is cheap and underneath that temporary high, it feels lonely.

By creating a schedule for your day that determines how you will spend your time, you allow yourself to become accountable for your patterns. That quick 20 minutes spent scrolling through Facebook in order to feel good happens 5 times a day and it isn't helping you to achieve your best life.

When my friend Evan lost his job unexpectedly, he had to get to it. Rather than letting the sad thoughts drag him down, ruin his confidence and make him worry about his ability to perform in a new company or wig him out about interviews, he got structured. Anxiety and doubt can creep in when we are focused on looking backwards at the past. These emotions don't have time to grow when we get busy working on our future in the present, as we no longer have the time to entertain these downright depressing soul-sucking thoughts.

Evan white boarded out his daily routine and from here, he could see all the items that were important to him.

Evan's schedule

6am-7am Gym

7.45am-8.30am Job review

8.30am-10.00am Write book

10.00am-10.30am Break

10.30am-12.30pm Content creation for website

12.30pm-1pm Lunch break

1.30pm-2.30pm Job review

2.30pm-4.30pm Gym/meeting/interview

4pm-8pm Fun/making new friends/inspiration/seminars/conferences

8pm Job Review Final check of the day

Evan chose not to focus on how he was wronged for losing his job or what he could have done differently and decided to stay present and in the moment. Instead, he focussed on what he *could* control rather than get lost in a never-ending maze of doubt, fear and loss. The schedule helped Evan to stay on track and promote a growth mindset, as he saw this as an opportunity to take on new challenges, make new friends and grow through the experience rather than be limited by it.

5. **Look at what's surrounding you, and don't copy it unless it's productive** – Sometimes you will need to up sticks and leave. As we have talked about in previous chapters, the people you surround yourself with rub off on you, and so when you consider your patterns of doubt and unhealthy self-talk, self-care and self-belief, it may be time to get a new crew. If anything about the people you hang out with is a factor in holding you back from success, or they are afraid of you taking steps to improve yourself, then it's time to find a new pack. By doing so you are able to implement changes and hold yourself to a higher standard.

For example, if you are surrounded by friends that want to go out boozing all the time rather than study, focus on self-growth or building a business, then it is likely that they will try to influence you away from doing what you need to do and pull you back into the cycle from whence you came. When you have made the decision to improve your self-belief you need to get ready to make some tough decisions, this means doing what's best for you and putting yourself first no matter what other people's excuses are. Other people may not get what you are doing and prefer "the old you" or complain that you're no fun anymore. Just let these comments wash off you like water off a duck's back. When other people don't understand you that's okay. It means that you have started to change the patterns of behaviour. The reason they get scared or worried is because it highlights their own insecurities around how they are choosing to spend their time on this planet. Trust me, this is less about you and more about them. I have experienced this so frequently to the point that it now doesn't faze me.

> I do me! Not you. I'm not judging you for the decisions you make, I am focused on competing with myself and only myself.

The competition is on and it comes down to who I am today vs. who I have the potential to be. Raise your standards and you raise your game. That is why professional boxers and sports stars go away from all distractions, influences and people a week or so before the night of a big fight or game. This is because they are solely focused on what's in front of them and not what's going on around them.

6. **Ask yourself who you want to be.** A simple way to tell if you're on the right track is to look at those in the positions above you. Do they inspire you? Would you like to be like them? Are they a supportive influence on your life? Do they push you to expect more from yourself? Are they helping and encouraging you to grow?

If you are stuck in a job right now, doubting your capabilities, look around at those further down the path than you in their careers. This could be your line manager or even the CEO. How do they spend their time? Are they someone you would like to be? Are they respected? What are their values? What drives them? Could you see yourself in their shoes? If not, it might be a warning sign that you are not on the path you're meant to be on and it's time to move because this is not your crowd. If, however, the person you chose is someone who you aspire to be, someone you would like the life of, then do more to model how they operate. Aligning yourself with a mentor (discreetly or directly) helps you to develop your sense of self-worth and find purpose, pride and value in your work and your adventure.

7. **Focus on today**. Don't try to think ahead for a year, or a month, take it one day at a time and be the best you can be for that day. When you work in this way, you are at ground zero, doing the work and accomplishing it one day at a time. They say it takes 90 days to create a habit, but sometimes the focus on the 90 days becomes too distracting, and rather than being a goal that creates a habit, it becomes a barrier to break through before you go right back to your old ways. Had I known my wife Sandra back then, she would have surely told me, *"How do you eat an elephant? Little by little, bit by bit,"* as she does now when I am trying to work through a big challenge. It's about getting the simple stuff right, the basics, doing the gym, the mediation, the gratitude journal, the work, consistently every day, so that it can expand throughout your life and you'll reap the incremental benefits over time. You're building a solid foundation for your life, relationships, family, goals and dreams to flourish upon.

CHAPTER 28

SELF-BELIEF HERO: JEN SINCERO
'YOU ARE A BADASS'

"You have to want your dreams more than you want
your drama."

Jen Sincero

Meet Jen

Jen Sincero is the ultimate self-belief guru. If you haven't heard
of her work already you need to get her into your life. By hook
or by crook, you need to be streaming her through your ear holes,
blasting her out of your car stereo or reading her each evening until
you complete both *You are a Badass: How To Stop Doubting Your
Greatness and Start Living an Awesome Life* and *You are a Badass at
Making Money*. I am prescribing you these mandatory titles as they
will inject a huge self-worth boost into your psyche, hands down.

To give you some context about why I am so passionate about
Jen's work, she is totally relatable, down to earth and brings you
along on the journey in a non-cheesy type of way. Jen is authentic
and resonates with me down to my core.

In this chapter, I will give you the low down on Jen, her work,
principles and my carefully selected Top 10 steps that you can
take to increase your self-belief and start believing fully in the
phenomenal being that is you. I will also give you the inside
scoop on the biggest lessons and takeaways I have learned from
studying Jen's teachings. Hold on to your hat because this chapter
packs a punch and if it's implemented correctly, it could see you
transforming yourself in a life-changing way.

Jen's philosophy

The backstory on Jen is she realised she was capable of more. One day, she got fed up of only just scraping together enough money each month to pay the rent, hanging out with her broke circle of friends and procrastinating about what was wrong with the world. She knew deep down that she was awesome but was struggling to get out of her old patterns of behaviour.

What I love about Jen's story is that she fearlessly pursued this quest through self-help and invested tons of money that she didn't have, tried a bunch of different things and now opens up fully to share this with the world.

Jen's story is beyond inspirational and I know you'll love her. She was broke up until her 40s (her words not mine) and living in a garage. She'd suffered through years of low-paying jobs and even tried her hand at becoming a rock star. She went all the way from making $28,000 a year to now making seven figures!

It wasn't until she started a business helping authors to write book proposals that things really started to change. It transformed her into becoming a motivational coach, author and speaker. It's fair to say that her books have done phenomenally well. They often feature in the Top 10 bestseller lists on Amazon in the wealth and self-help categories.

After pouring over self-help material, attending seminars and conferences all over the US, and making a commitment to figure out how to change her life, she went on to figure out how to triple her income in a matter of months and build sustainable sources of revenue. Jen's business coaching authors gradually built up over time to a point that afforded her the luxury of travelling the world whenever she wanted to so that she could focus on writing, speaking and doing whatever the hell she wanted. I mean, come on, isn't that the dream. Well, it is for me anyway, so who wouldn't want to read a couple of books to get the wisdom and guidance from a person that's figured it out by doing the work.

When asked about how she managed to turn her life around so radically, she describes the time she was travelling through India as a particular turning point in her life. It was the time when she decided to stop screwing around with her approach to money and her value. In her own words, she shared: *'I do recall one moment when I went to India by myself. I was paralyzed with fear to travel alone, but I had this intuitive hint that I had to do it. It was transformative and beautiful. I also saw poverty and suffering on such a massive scale. I thought I'd be so grateful to go home to my converted shit shack [the garage she was living in]. But when I went home, I realized I was so much more powerful than I had ever known, and I could do so much better. That's when I started hiring coaches and playing a lot bigger.'*[5]

Below I share with you my top ten learnings and insight from Jen. There are hundreds more, so make sure her books end up in your possession by the end of the day.

Jen's 10 steps for improving your self-belief

Step 1

All energy vibrates at a certain frequency. Which means you're vibrating at a certain frequency, and everything you desire and don't desire is also vibrating at a certain frequency. Vibration attracts like vibration.

Step 2

Watching someone else totally go for it can be incredibly upsetting to the person who's spent a lifetime building a solid case for why they themselves can't.

Step 3

It's just as easy to believe we're awesome as it is to believe were giant sucking things.

---

[5] https://www.marketwatch.com/story/how-badass-author-jen-sincero-went-from-living-in-a-garage-to-being-rich-2017-04-18

Step 4

Appreciate how special you are.

Step 5

Don't get caught up in the thunderbolt hype.

Step 6

Your brain is your bitch.

Step 7

Gratitude: the gateway drug to awesomeness.

Step 8

Faith is having the audacity to believe in the not yet seen.

Step 9

Remember that done is better than perfect.

Step 10

Money is an exchange of energy between people.

What I learned from Jen

We all need coaches and mentors throughout each stage of our growth.

It's totally fine to ask for help and outsource to create a successful team rather than go it alone.

In her books and teachings, Jen continually promotes the idea of having a coach or mentor to support your growth and help accelerate your transformation into a badass. As we've discussed already, this is someone who's been there and is doing it, someone who's made the mistakes, has money in the game and is further along the road than you. This idea that we need to do everything ourselves is a distorted projection of ego.

Jen shares, 'Olympic athletes at the top of their games have coaches. Broke people at the bottom of their games insist they can get rich without any help. Just sayin'[6].' And it's true, what makes us think that we have to go it alone or that it's the way it's done? When you look at anyone who's at the top of their game, whether that be in business, sports or family life, they've all got a support network, an advisory board or a coach to keep them in check.

Embrace badassery

You *are* a badass. One of the biggest nuggets of gold that I took away from Jen's wisdom was that being truly yourself is the best and most ultimate expression of #winning. When you just ditch the negative self-talk a whole truckload of opportunities just come rolling in. I've always been a bit of a deal maker, rebel and soul that likes to test the boundaries, but this was a mental shift that got me to test and learn on a grander scale. Armed with Jen's badass wisdom, the more I realised it was acceptable to be myself, and the more I gave myself permission to be myself and release the idea of what I thought I should be.

Over time, this new strain of confidence grew stronger, and slowly the goals got bigger and the love I found for myself grew.

Being more closely aligned to my true self gave me a sense of belonging, a sense of connection and released me from the idea that I needed to be something other than fully myself or to be a carbon copy of every other 'successful' person on the planet in order to have 'made it'.

---

[6] https://www.marketwatch.com/story/how-badass-author-jen-sincero-went-from-living-in-a-garage-to-being-rich-2017-04-18

In embracing my badass, I could take full ownership of my definition of success and it finally became incredibly fulfilling.

It's OK to like and to want money.

Jen states the number one reason why people don't have an abundance of wealth is because 'we refuse to give ourselves permission to become rich'.

Sometimes the obstacle holding us back is mental, rather than physical or a lack of opportunity. If you're starting out in business or a budding entrepreneur, your mindset towards money could be blocking the flow of money coming towards you. If you're saying things like, 'I can't afford it' or 'I don't have any money' you need to shift the story you're telling yourself to one of wealth in order for things to change.

Once you do this, your mind can start to find things that prove the statement right, rather than keep searching for evidence to prove you are indeed broke. The penny dropped for me when I read *You Are A Badass At Making Money*. It felt as if I suddenly realised I am worthy and have the ability to make it happen and get really wealthy, and I don't need to feel bad about that desire.

It is only when you give yourself permission to be rich, earn wealth and add so much value to the world that you are proportionally rewarded for it. The process of removing your money blocks begins, your mindset towards money changes and it starts to flow to you.

The same principle and mantra apply to opportunities. Once you believe you're worthy of them they will show up all over the place. This dynamic was a revelation to me and gave me the juice to really get out into the world and show it what I was made of.

You don't have to be perfect

Jen is one real, down to earth, genuinely cool chick. She owns the process and admits to her followers when things are icky, embarrassing and ridiculously 'uncool'. Attending motivational seminars, doing self-help exercises, rejigging your routines can all feel uncomfortable initially, but we've all been there. Sometimes, it's just about getting stuck in and doing the work, even if you feel like you'd die of embarrassment if your friends saw you roaring like a lion or doing jumping jacks to get your get yourself into a peak state.

In studying her work and following her community, events and meteoric rise over the past few years, she has rubbed off on me and I've given myself permission to get started on multiple projects that I wouldn't have even begun if I had waited for the perfect timing, perfect execution, perfect everything.

Now when I think of perfect with respect to launching a business, overcoming challenges and making decisions, I see that it is a falsehood, an unobtainable hinderance. It's another defence mechanism that has the capacity to keep us stuck in procrastination mode and ensure our greatness stays hidden from the world.

I'm not saying you shouldn't strive for high standards (far from it) but you don't need to wait for perfection before you can get started and this has been a distinct difference in my approach to many things, from drafting emails, writing blog posts, recording videos, understanding different business models, company structures, pitches, making contacts, and building a life supported by self-belief.

Through Jen's teachings, I have given myself permission to try, to fail and to go for everything over and over again, without having all the pieces of the puzzle before I get started.

PART 4

CONNECTION (SPIRITUAL)

INTRODUCTION TO PART 4

"I am always being guided, even
when it doesn't feel like it."

Gabrielle Bernstein, Spirit Junkie

THE SPIRITUAL ELEMENT was part of the process of overcoming challenges and making it happen that I ignored for a while, to my own detriment, I stubbornly wanted to do it all myself, until I figured it out through repeated hard lessons that it is all connected. Ignoring your spiritual side is a limitation. If you want to expand then it's important to know how to connect, in your own way, to your higher power and to learn how to give yourself to the world. This is not about being selfish but letting spirit in (and pushing your ego to the side) to help you achieve more and help more people.

The spiritual element is important because, without it, we are less than aligned to divine energy. We are not in flow or, in sporting terms "in the zone", so we are easily distracted, listen to criticism (including our own) too much and cannot focus on whatever we are trying to do, whether that be creating a piece of art, mastering a sporting technique or building a business. The spiritual connection is like turning down the noises buzzing around you so that you can be your full self. In this divine energy we are able to use our gifts, talents and strengths to help ourselves and others. Divine energy supports and maximises our creativity, conditioning and certainty. Spiritual connection pulsates across all facets of our lives and should be baked into everything we do.

Spiritual also links strongly to having courage, and courage is a major part of being a lion. Maya Angelou says, 'Courage is most important of all the virtues, because without courage you can't practise any other virtue consistently. You can practise any virtue erratically, but nothing consistently without courage.'[1] This is important because when you look at the significance of the impact that you want to make and the difference you can create in your life, either by your example for others or by the habits and patterns

---

[1] Graham, S. (2006) Diversity: Leaders Not Labels. p. 224

you change for the better, a commitment to practising courage is required.

All of the top experts in the field of self-development typically go on a journey of self-discovery and that journey usually ends up here, at living with more spirituality in their lives. The likes of Tony Robbins, Gabrielle Bernstein and Marianne Williamson all credit their connection to, and faith in, a power greater than themselves for their ability to lead the lives they do.

If you aren't willing to look more closely at this section of the book, I understand. I was like you for years. However, I would ask you to question why. In not putting your all into this final core principle of being the lion, you are limiting yourself, abandoning your path to self-improvement and throwing the towel in before the process is complete. Don't write it off and think you can go it alone.

This connection is where the internal strength and stamina to continue on in the face of pain, rejection and hurt comes in. It is the piece that binds the other three sections together and holds it in place. Connection is where you dig deep inside yourself and summon the courage to take the path that scares you most, putting all the strategies and tools that you have learnt in the book up until this point to the best use.

When you are faced with a challenge that scares the living crap out of you, or completely blindsides you and threatens to ruin life as you know it, your connection, faith and spirituality need to be at its strongest. You need to be practising the mantras, rituals and practises daily without fail, so that you can handle those challenges when they come your way.

This is your time to get centred and to connect with what you have to give, to the legacy you want to leave and to open yourself to the magnificence of your inner kindness and light. Adopting this mindset of spiritual courage will grant you the power to be anything you want, desire and need. You are worthy and you deserve to live life in the light of your best-self, shining brightly.

Like Fat Boy Slim said in *Right Here, Right Now,* you've got to tune in and connect, you courageous lion you.

CHAPTER 29

MY STORY – MAKING LIFE HARDER THAN IT NEEDED TO BE

"Do the best you can until you know better,
then when you know better, do better."

Maya Angelou

LOOKING BACK TO my formative years growing up as a teenager, there were only a few things I cared about passionately: self-expression, demonstrated by me rocking a purple Mohawk at secondary school, music, playing the drums in my band and cycling. Looking more deeply there were also subtle displays of rebellion littered throughout the years that made the road more challenging than it needed to be. For instance, choosing not to work to my full intellectual potential for some years and then dominating in exams the next. I'm going to be honest with you and share my not-so-finest qualities as a teenager, to show you how this same principle still holds adults back. I carried this same attitude towards spirituality, which cut me off from a lot of potential growth for many years. I want to be open about this so that you can see where I'm coming from. The spiritual element has been the hardest for me to grapple with because I wrongly thought it was a 'nice to have' and only relied upon it when times got tough rather than building it into a consistent daily practice.

I believe that this assumption may have come about for a number of reasons, such as I found it easier to do everything myself. Self-reliance allowed me independence, plus if I failed no one knew. Then there was the question of what if I asked God for help and he didn't answer, and if I failed, what then? I was waiting to find my own connection, which was a mistake. I was waiting rather than building a connection in this journey we call life. What's apparent is there are multiple reasons as to why I thought I could go it alone without dedicating time and energy to developing my spiritual side and erroneously thought that it didn't need any more cultivation (unless things got super bad). I am sharing this because if any of this resonates with you, I want you to know you're not alone. What's important is that you stop and recognise the significance of this section of the book with regard to your own relationship with God, faith and yourself.

Rewind to schooldays

I knew education was important, however, unless I had something to fight against, like a teacher saying I couldn't do it then I would cruse, I preferred to get by with tactical amounts of effort, thinking that this was the smart way to do things. I needed it to be a "must" in order to motivate me towards action.

The problem was the volatile rollercoaster of stellar grades followed by less than average grades took monumental amounts of effort on my part. I had to work extremely hard to turn the ship around when it finally came time to put in the work and led some teachers to believe I wasn't capable or to write me off completely. My educational career was a mountain of sporadic effort, dips and plateaus rather than the consistent formation of knowledge.

Ultimately, this put me at a disadvantage within the class when it came to gaining a quality education as, naturally, teachers choose to focus on students who were consistently trying to improve rather than me and my all or nothing approach.

The long and short of it was that by not applying myself or doing my best consistently, I gave them a reason to doubt my ability. It was like I enjoyed the thrill of proving them wrong or the thrill of the chase. Will I or won't I make the grades?

My strategy was to wait until it was a "must" and then go all out rather than gently building up a steady trickle of improvement, e.g. I must make the grades on this paper or else I won't progress versus studying hard consistently. As a strategy, it worked to get me to do the work but it came with a price and there was something missing. Had I been able to link paying more attention at school to the bigger picture or finding a motivator outside of the traditional career paths that were suggested, entrepreneurship perhaps, I would have aligned and made more of a consistent effort. I was making life way harder than it needed to be.

I remember I was told by my maths teacher on one specific occasion that I wasn't smart enough to sit the higher-level GCSE exam paper. He was trying to protect me from flunking the class and, in his mind, that was a distinct possibility. Getting below a D grade on this paper would mean failing and I would automatically be graded an F, there was no safety net. His recommendation was for me to take the lower tier paper where the maximum grade possible was a B. This was to limit the downside. If I got an E, I would still have something to show for my 5 years in secondary school.

To me, this was totally unacceptable and none of what he was talking about was ever an option. Faced with what he was telling me, I knew I had to convince him to let me take the higher paper with the opportunity to get an A grade.

I knew that I had what it took to be in the higher tier, and he was letting his perception of my attitude towards him and my appearance interfere with his judgements about my mathematical capability. The truth was I didn't care for his teaching style much and I'm pretty sure he didn't care for my learning style either.

This possibility made me more determined than ever. It created a must. I lobbied him and convinced him to submit me for the higher paper anyway, and I would take responsibility for the outcome. I knew that my grades needed to match my aspirations.

I hung with an intelligent crew. I had older friends who inspired me to raise my game. I also knew if I put my mind to it, I had what it took to smash the exam. I enjoyed maths and had been trained by my father for years, doing extra workbooks that he would create for my sister and me to complete at home after school. I wasn't about to let some sceptical teacher set the boundaries and determine the limitations of my future.

Being put on the lower paper meant accepting a lower track for myself than I was capable of. As a result, something inside of me lit up. It was almost as if I needed this friction, this challenge, and in a way, this is exactly what I had been looking for to push me harder to the work. I now had something to fight against.

I got to it. Luckily, one of my best friends Richard was a maths whiz and he took pity on me. I told him the story and he set about tutoring me. Every night for weeks we would set aside the video games and sit about on the floor of his bedroom going through equations, algebra and pure maths.

Richard would set me homework, and this taught me for the first real time the benefits of aligning yourself with others who are further ahead of you or have the skills that you want. It taught me the power of resourcefulness and seeking out those who have the capability and knowledge. It also showed me how quickly learning could accelerate when you are around true masters of their craft in a one-on-one situation. My maths ability advanced too in a matter of sessions. Richard had sat the test a year before and knew what to expect. He took the time to go through my questions with me, showing me the tricks and cross-checks that had scored him an A*. Things such as writing down your workings on the side for the examiner so that they can see your thinking when you tackle a problem. That way even if you produce an incorrect outcome, they can follow your thinking and see where you went astray.

On the day of the test, my mind felt focused, and I knew I had put all of Richard's tips to good use, like sitting at the front so not get distracted by others who left the room. As I turned over the page and saw the questions, I was excited. I wanted to dominate. I had worked hard and now it was time to show the maths teacher what he had overlooked in me and prove to myself what I already knew to be true.

After a few minutes, silence fell over the exam hall and the only sound that could be heard was the click-clack of fingers punching frantically on calculators and pens scribbling on paper. Then all of a sudden there was an almighty bang that startled everyone in the room. One of the student's desks had collapsed causing an uproar. One after another people turned around to see what was going and on and the exam hall descended into a state of disruption, but not for me, I remained completely focused on the paper in front of me. You could have thrown a rock at me and I wouldn't have moved. I was determined and in the zone.

I was putting everything I had learned into practice, skipping questions and moving on if questions stumped me for too long with the promise of returning to them later if I had time. I was flying through the paper, getting all the marks I could.

I finished with 15 minutes to spare and used this time to cross-check my workings and attempt a few of the hardest questions that I had left. The adrenalin was pumping through my body in a good way. I knew in my heart of hearts that I had done enough not to fail; even better, I knew I had done well.

The months eased by and when mid-August came around the summer holidays had got into full swing and the results season was upon England. This is the day that we had all been waiting for. We went into school to pick up the A5 envelope with your name on it that contains your grades, and see if all those months of hard work have been enough.

As I opened it up and pulled out the sheet of paper, I knew what I would see, but it was an indescribable feeling of achievement to see it in the flesh. I had a got an A. It was not just the hard work but a reward for sticking up for myself in class and using the disadvantage of a teacher not believing in me to fuel my vision, to go harder and put in the hours. When I saw Richard later that day, he was super proud of me and I felt as though I belonged.

As well as being a good example of turning disadvantages and adversity into an advantage, the point of this story is that I made things harder than they needed to be by not giving the subject the attention it deserved from the start. Had I shown more effort in class, then I wouldn't have risked being forced on to the lower grade paper and miss the opportunity to test my mathematical ability to its fullest capacity.

Sometimes, it's not always best to back yourself into a corner in order to perform. As a teenager burning the boats had been my strategy to trigger myself to perform. It was my way of saying FU,

I'm going to prove you wrong. Whilst this worked as a strategy to get me through these times growing up, it didn't work for me so much as an adult. Of course, there are times when this strategy is the perfect motivator but it's about knowing which tool to pull out of the toolbox. **What I have found is that by developing a spiritual connection I am most in alignment with the action I need to take to achieve the goal and its effects are amplified.**

Same old story

In case you thought this one scenario would be enough to teach me to change my ways, let me give you another example, a year or so later. I was in the first year of my A Levels, and taking Maths, Biology, Chemistry and Psychology. Looking at the subjects now, I can tell you they were the completely wrong choices for me. I was motivated more by how they would look on my CV and which girls were in the classes than the passion I had for the subject. Psychology was my only real choice and, as a result, I had no problem paying attention and staying motivated to perform. In fact, I enjoyed it so much I went on to take it in my undergrad. I couldn't believe there was a subject that allowed me to study patterns of human behaviour and talk about criminals, human nature and relationships. The other three subjects got the wrath of my disinterest and, as a result, I ended up being graded a U for ungraded in Maths and an E for Biology and a D for Chemistry.

Instead of dropping back a year, I wanted to progress to the second year of Psychology. So I begged the Sixth Form Principle to let me resit all of the last year's exams again whilst progressing into the second year of the sixth form. This meant I was in both sets of classes. I was doing the upper and lower sixth at the same time and resitting my first year at the same time as doing the second year, which meant the pressure was on.

What changed?

It took a lot for me to sit in the class with students a year below. Again, teachers in these classes didn't hold high hopes for me after my dismal grades and lacklustre performance the year before. But this became my ultimate advantage because I had found what I wanted to do – read Psychology at a red brick university – and to do this I needed to up my grades to As and Bs if I was to have any chance of getting in. Suddenly, I was motivated. I had a goal and I was going to achieve it.

Because the second year of the Sixth Form is a step up and much harder, I reasoned that I would need to get As in all of my first-year exams and settle for As, Bs, and Cs in the second-year exams to end up with a medley of As and Bs overall, meeting the requirements for university. This strategy allowed me to focus hard in the repeat classes and soon, with my new attitude and drive, the teachers began to upgrade their opinion of my potential. It wasn't like they thought I'd get As (and they told me so) but, in their minds, achieving C grades had become a possibility. This only fuelled me more, to prove them wrong and take out the top spot in the class. Repeating a subject requires you to be humble while not letting comments, funny looks or other people's foregone conclusions influence your mindset completely.

I was the underdog; down went the punk rock montage, downhill mountain bike racing posters and the Holly Valance calendar (an actor turned pop singer from the Aussie TV show *Neighbours*). In their place, my bedroom walls were transformed into a canvas featuring a blanket of chemical compounds, diagrams of osmosis, and the cardiovascular system. A3 sheets depicting detailed drawings of the surface area of alveoli stretched across the ceiling. I said no house parties and chose to spend time in the library at lunchtime rather than on the sports field with my friends. It was game on and I completed a 180 from the previous year, wrote hundreds of revision cards, pretended I wasn't home when friends called round unannounced and made it my obsession to improve my grades.

What I learned about making life harder

Again, going through all of this was punishing, sitting both sets of classes in a year and preparing for the exams was gruelling. It didn't need to be this hard, but this was the price for not connecting earlier to my deeper purpose.

1. **I need to be authentic to be my best self.** Had I figured out earlier that Psychology was a passion or trusted myself to select subjects I enjoyed, like Business or Geography and Art, rather than what I thought looked good on paper, I would have had an advantage. These are both times in my life that serve as examples where I had to hustle to make it happen, but had I connected earlier to my inner desires and truly listened to what the world was telling me rather than trying to cram at the last minute to get back on track, I wouldn't have chosen subjects I had no real interest in. I made life much harder than it would have been if I had chosen subjects I was more passionate about and enjoyed spending my time on. Maybe if you're in a dead-end job or studying you can relate to this?

2. **I need a purpose to stay motivated.** It wasn't until I took time to really seriously consider what I wanted in my future that I really saw with crystal clarity what I needed to make happen and how. When you're truly passionate about something, all those hours spent researching aren't painful, they're incredible.

3. **I have to clear away excuses and distractions.** I failed in my first year of the sixth form because of what I prioritised. After my success in the GCSEs, I got complacent, and the jump to A Levels was a leap I hadn't prepared for. Plus, with the introduction of cars, music and house parties, I didn't really have time for studying regression analysis, preferring to hang out and rehearse with the band I was in.

4. **I shouldn't wait until it's critical before I take action.** Waiting to take action adds to the complexity of the mountain you are trying to climb. My strategy now for accomplishing big tasks is to break them down into smaller chunks, to project manage it from end to end and to leverage my resources by asking for help from

specialist along the way. Had I learnt the lesson at GCSE stage and applied this approach during my sixth form or degree level courses, I would have built more significant relationships with tutors, professors and industry experts, which may have led to a deeper understanding of the topics and concepts at hand. Waiting is costly on your resources, not just financially, but your most valuable resource, which is, of course, your time. Cramming versus having a consistent daily practice made it difficult to cover the same ground and have that connection to the subject.

What's that got to do with spirituality?

The point is, I was making it harder for myself than it needed to be by putting off something I knew, deep down, I should be doing until it became critical. And this is similar to how I have found my relationship with spirituality. I think this is true of a lot of people. They only pay attention to the spiritual when they really need to draw on it to overcome a challenge, and will then, of course. find their levels of spiritual resources low. Whereas someone who has been constantly working on their spiritual side has rich resources whenever they need them.

It was easy for me to overlook the importance of spirituality, but now I see it as a fundamental building block of being the lion. I'm talking about being in tune with your higher purpose, surrendering your plan for God's plan and connecting to a vision that is bigger than you.

The lion is connected to its purpose, it is focused on being the biggest most badass version of itself. If a lion decided to try and be a dog it wouldn't get very far. Firstly, it would starve to death. There is a natural order in the world that works best when everything in it is striving to be uniquely them.

The other thing about connection and spirituality is that most people get confused or outright reject the concept of spiritual energy or something greater than themselves. Now I am not here to judge or to tell you what to believe in, I can only speak from my experience and tell you that I have found the greatest value in understanding, trusting and having faith in a power greater than myself.

A final note to the sceptics

I refused to embrace this as part of my life for many years. Had I course corrected sooner and allowed my mind to be more open, I would have seen everything that I needed to get out my destructive patterns was there already. The path existed, I just rejected and refused to acknowledge its presence, choosing rather to go it alone, believing that I, and only I, knew best.

This was one of my biggest mistakes. It cost me years of punishment, self-loathing, and pain. I repeated the same traits, time and time again, expecting somehow that each time would be different, but ended up treading the well-trodden path of shame and disapproval. I beat myself up internally with such force that it kept me pinned to the ground and I clung tightly to the rituals, habits and patterns, searching for some way out but only finding darkness.

Now you have come this far, for the sake of avoiding my mistakes and losing valuable time on this beautiful Earth, I would ask you to put your scepticism aside and read on consciously intending to keep an open mind for the next few pages. The change you induce might be the one you've been seeking.

CHAPTER 30

MY STORY – HITTING ROCK BOTTOM

"Something magical happens when you're in a space
where you're uncertain about what's next. There's a
feeling of letting go, which allows you to surrender
so you can receive something greater. Sometimes
you just need to pause for a moment and listen.

Allow divine guidance to enter."

Idil Ahmed

BECAUSE THAT'S WHAT it is, a journey. Part of the way through writing this book, I hit rock bottom. Everything was going fine, the words were pouring out of me like never before, the material just kept appearing right on cue and I continually remarked to my wife Sandra how the book was writing itself. I felt like *this* was the book I was meant to write. And then it happened, I hit a rock bottom. I'm sharing this with you and telling you how it really was because this is an example of what can happen when your life is unbalanced, when you are not sharing your energy equally between each of the 4Cs and you neglect Spirituality all together.

For weeks and months, I was so focused on the external achievement of hitting goals and milestones that I had totally forgotten to check in with myself and stay connected to my inner world. I was pushing forward on all fronts hard – in my work, my relationships, my family and my own personal goals, I was dead set on doing it all to the very best of my ability. On reflection, I can see that I was skewed 60% towards **Creation**, 25% towards **Conditioning**, 12% towards **Certainty** and 3% towards **Connection**. This imbalance was desperately unhealthy. It's strange that I could be writing a book about successfully overcoming challenges whilst facing one of the most difficult periods of my life.

If I look back, the signs had been there for a while that this was coming, and it was coming fast. I kept pushing myself harder, surviving on less sleep (3 hours a night) for weeks on end and still expecting more of myself with no time allocated for recuperation. I was not following my own teachings and learning the hard way that, as I described in Part 2 Conditioning, the body needs us to prioritise sleep so that it can do its best work. Of course, there are times when we need to do late nights or get less than an ideal night's kip, but this had become the norm not the exception for me.

I went out one night and completely broke down. I unravelled fast. My mind was overwhelmed, overstretched, exhausted and exasperated, and in a word, I felt beat! I was facing burnout on epic proportions. It hit me like a ton of bricks in the face. By hitting rock bottom this time (I say 'this time' as there has been another time previously) it showed me, without a shadow of a doubt, that a large part of 'making it happen' is prioritising taking care of your inner self through connection. I hadn't realised that I was so close to burnout for months, teetering on the edge after weeks of sleepless nights, working day and night on business trips across Asia, balancing the stress of trying to keep the family afloat financially, starting a new job, networking and building new relationships, and doing all the necessary hundreds of hours of research for this book (which I loved).

The combined heavy weight and stress of it all was unbelievably soul-crushing and starting to take its toll on me. That evening I was on the brink of burnout before I even went into it. I was so sleep deprived that during the day I felt like I was on another planet. As I sat at my desk, it felt as if the office was spinning. I experienced a strange sensation like I was floating in space; I was there but not really. I felt delirious. I had been pushing and pushing and pushing myself to perform day after day, week after week for months, expecting my mind and body to keep up and produce the same number of results at the same frequency despite my compounding and urgent need for a break.

I had an unbalanced, unhealthy focus on action and being in a creative mode. Due to my lack of prioritisation of the other 4Cs, I was totally oblivious to how I was feeling inside. Normally, creating momentum moments give me more energy not less, but recently I had been doing so many tasks and activities because I "had to" and not necessarily because I enjoyed them. I just wanted to get them ticked off the never-ending to-do list of things that *needed* to be done. I wasn't taking the time to give my body a break from the hectic schedule of travel, work and life. In this spinning state, I was doing everything, including the things I didn't want to do but "had to" and disastrously not letting go of the things I enjoyed. I was trying to do it all to my absolute determent. When I should have been prioritising recovery to get over the exhaustion of my gruelling work/life schedule. I needed to give myself some time to breathe instead of jumping from one thing to the other and trying to dominate at everything.

I was attempting to work on my side businesses, write this book, work incredibly hard and support a family, and over deliver in each area whilst juggling all things at once. I just wasn't feasible, but I didn't stop to listen to this. Anyone who's overworked or knows they are burning the candle at both ends, listen up. THIS is your wake-up call, it's not worth it. Put your energy into a balanced 4Cs approach and you'll see your results magnified!

> I learned through this experience of burnout that there's no point in getting to the goal if when you arrive, you seek to destroy the very thing you have been going after.

To try and understand that took something colossal, a breakdown of epic proportions. I had to breakdown so that I would physically and mentally stop and take stock of the reality I was creating. I was working hard but not smart. The breakdown forced me to look at what I wanted out of life and realise the hard truth, which was that I hadn't been practising what I preached. I'm eating humble pie as I tell you this. And the truth is it is difficult to keep yourself in balance. We all need to keep working on it and improving. I didn't have balance or structure to my life and was depleted due to my over ambition to produce on all levels.

My focus and drive can border on relentless, and I find it hard to switch off sometimes. I spot the opportunities and act on them, especially when I feel close to moving up. I hate the idea of plateauing and was determined to avoid that at all costs. As mentioned previously, operating with the '6 months to live' philosophy gave me no choice. When I needed to make a decision or an opportunity came up, these questions were answered YES and HELL YES. Go for it. I thought I could do it all. However, inside I was starting to feel empty. The momentum moments were replaced with a sensation of numbness and delirium. I had lost the rush of adrenalin when fantastic things went my way, and no longer lingered to celebrate the victories. I just moved on to the next thing on the enormous to-do list, solemnly determined to push on. The fun of the chase had disappeared, and I was no longer enjoying the journey.

Self-sabotage

I went out that night and had a few drinks. They affected me way more than usual, and I found myself getting angry about why things with work weren't the way *I* wanted them to be. I was playing the victim. I was sad about how my life had ended up here, at this point, and felt full of regret. I felt frustrated that my mum had died, and that 12 years on, I was still in this life where things kept going the wrong way. I was focused on why everything was wrong and it brought up all my old fears, doubts, and regrets. Anger is just fear in disguise. I knew this because I felt it. I broke myself down to a raw state where there was nothing left. No amount of shaming myself or beating myself up could compare to how I felt when I let the emotions go. It was like a volcano erupting, but instead of molten hot lava, I was spewing all the anxieties from years gone by, everything that had ever happened and hadn't gone my way. I felt ready to give up and I was beaten. It was still early, so I called a cab and went home, fell asleep on the sofa and lay in my pool of misery and victimhood. I'm not sure what set it off, or how it was triggered or whether it was just an accumulation of poor patterns of behaviour repeated over time combined with a hectic schedule and extreme lack of sleep.

After my night of breakdown, I woke up the next morning ready and willing to change. I realised that I had been so focused on creating external success, taking action to create the life that I wanted on the outside, I had forgotten to take action on the inside.

To become the best I can be, I had to put into practise every single step in this book. I had to put in the work.

I realised that *knowing* is not enough. I had to get on with *doing* the spiritual work, resolving the issues deep inside and healing the wounds so that I could continue on my path and receive all the greatness that the Universe had in store.

In writing this book I had been researching personal development topics and habits of success for hours on end, crafting the *Be The Lion* message, and I absolutely loved it. I was obsessed. It lit me up inside, but I hadn't been taking the time to get a deeper connection to something bigger than myself.

I realised that in order to complete this book I needed to Be The Lion in all elements of this concept, including spirituality. No excuses, this book was going to help me address the issues in my life that I had struggled with for over a decade. I needed to share even more authentically by going through the spiritual side of the process as I wrote the book.

I couldn't just focus on where I succeeded best and knew I could perform. For example, I am skilled at business development and sales, it's a strength and I love these areas of business because I am good at them, therefore I choose jobs that align with my strengths. I consistently read and surrounded myself with more and more material that expanded my knowledge in these areas and engaged in opportunities for learning and development to keep this high-performance cycle in play and keep pushing the boundaries. Makes sense, right?

Spirituality and success

But when it comes to personal growth and self-improvement, we need to tackle it on all 4 fronts, including those that we struggle with. It's a complete immersion in all four elements of **creation – conditioning, certainty** and **connection**. Neither one can be prioritised or undernourished or we become unbalanced in our development. For your inner lion to grow strong and healthy, you must achieve balance across the 4Cs. If you don't allow yourself time to recuperate and become quiet to listen to your inner voice, then you will build a lion who is unable to compete at the very top level. Going to the gym and only working certain muscle groups and ignoring all the rest leaves you weaker overall than if you adopt a balanced approach. The same is true for the 4Cs model.

I feel like I was meant to hit rock bottom during the process of writing this book so that I would include this fourth pillar into my model and framework for living a bigger life!

Originally, when I had planned out this book, I missed the spiritual element entirely. It didn't feature on my roadmap to success, which is ridiculous when you think about it. I can't tell you the amount of times that I have prayed to God for the things I have in my life today. When it really comes down to it, when it matters most, God is the first person I go to for help. Yet, for some reason, I hadn't joined the dots and made the connection to how important this was in the masterplan for overcoming big challenges, even though it was a foundational component of success and achievement.

It's funny because I grew up in a Methodist household, so I am no stranger to spirituality.

Facing the wounds

What's different here is that to develop habits that would progress me to a deeper level and allow me to take on bigger and better challenges, the actions were now to do with my inner conversation with myself and healing wounds from the past.

I had to face up to the spiritual work I didn't want to do. I had proved to myself that I could achieve or even overachieve on all three of the other fronts (**Creation, Conditioning** and **Certainty**) but had neglected the fourth and probably most important, Connection, in a massive way.

When I looked inside of me, I felt angry. There were years of pent-up stress, frustration and losses that I was lugging around with me. I felt like the more success I was having in the external world, the more my inner child was rejecting it. The more I moved forward, the more little Timmy screamed and shouted, 'What about me?'

Waking up that morning, everything came to a halt. It was the end of the road. I needed to face my spiritual world that I had been ignoring for years.

My world came crashing down and I noticed how strongly I was self-sabotaging in areas of my life where I was going after achievement wholeheartedly. What a contradiction!

I needed to fundamentally shift my thinking and how I connected to my inner world on a daily basis so that I could progress, and change deeply ingrained habits so that I could receive the success and feel worthy of it, not angry and hostile towards it.

This meant getting extremely vulnerable and confronting issues from my past that I was carrying around with me. This weight was holding me back. The shame and the guilt, years of stress and burden, pinning me down. It was heavy.

Distracting is not coping

I had begun to rely on distraction again as an escape and I was drinking too much to be healthy as a way to quieten down my anxieties. I'd have one drink and find that the noise in my head would soften and I could feel my emotions start to numb and the sensation of relaxation come through. One drink opened the door to more, and I'd end up feeling frustrated and alone, destroying everything I'd fought hard to create. I was tearing down the walls of the castle I had taken so much pride in building.

To me, it was an escape. This may sound perverse, and it was, but the drinking was a way to put some self-imposed bumps in the road to achievement. If I was getting too close to success, having a few drinks would pull me off course, slow me down and give me other problems to deal with for a while. If life got too good, in came alcohol to ruin the party and distract me from where I wanted to get to and take me off course. Alcohol is a low energy drug that causes the body to have less energy. The self-destructive element for me comes from the fact that alcohol is a depressant and I know full well that if I drink it to try and quieten my feelings or emotions at times of stress, it makes me go off course. In that moment, I was using it to self-sabotage, knowing that with every drink I was slowing myself down, causing myself to be less creative and less caring about the outcome of certain projects or initiatives.

It becomes an addictive pattern because of the way it creeps into your mind and the justifications for drinking become more random. For example, when things went well, I justified having a drink as celebrating my current achievements rather than going after the really big goals. Hence, it would cause me to go off track and meant I put dealing with my fears and anxieties on hold for a little while longer. Again, it was a reliance on something external to provide relief or distraction and take me off course. The fact is destructive consumption of alcohol takes me further away from the best version of myself, and it's not a productive habit to engage in on a regular basis as that is what I value and desire to achieve. Wanting to be my best self but drinking too much is like wanting to lose weight and eating too many Mars bars, it's not going to work.

Alcohol also makes it more likely that I'll engage in risky behaviour, like crossing the street without looking or just doing stupid things that I have no place doing, having ridiculous conversations and generally wasting more time than I care to admit. Being a dad now, this is not the example I want to set for my son. I am the Co-CEO of a family and have a major responsibility to show him how to overcome challenges and achieve big goals whilst avoiding the pitfalls along the way.

It's also easy to integrate these habits into your life, especially if you are performing in the outside world. If I was anxious or needed to make a decision and was deliberating about it for too much, I'd use alcohol to loosen up a little. As Tony Robbins notes, there are 6 human needs, one of which is certainty. Like any drug that you put into your body, alcohol gave me the certainty that I could relax for a moment or find a kind of temporary relief or false security that would remove the stress for a night. It was like an old friend patting me on the back saying, 'It's alright old boy, you gave it a good shot, here you can take a load off.'

Except that's exactly the last thing I wanted or needed to do.

I realised after that rock bottom night that *this was it*. I needed to find a deeper connection to rid myself of these destructive habits that had been running riot in my life for so many years and showed up at different points to slow me down.

Even when I achieved success, my lack of self-love and obsession with self-loathing would continue to rage if it was not handled. It was not the example that I wanted to set and a pattern I desperately needed to change.

On the inside, I pretty much hated myself. It reminded me of those early years in my twenties, growing up when I disliked myself so much that I got pleasure from self-loathing. In response to this self-dismissal and lack of self-love and care, I chased instant gratification through various means, through something as simple sugar and as complicated as the high of sex.

When I first met Sandra, we went on a hike together and we stopped off on the way at a little café on a hill overlooking the Manly and Freshwater beaches. I decided to pick up some refreshments. I walked out of the café moments later, with no less than four different drinks in my hand, not one, not two but four! I had a chocolate milkshake, a can of sprite, a sparkling water and a vitamin water all for good measure.

This was my inner child acting out and rebelling saying, 'I am an adult now and I can have whatever I want.' It was my way of rebellion, my way of getting a hit of fun and a sugar high. I didn't need 4 drinks obviously, but my brain was hardwired to look for ways to express my inner child and chose liberation in any form that it could manifest.

We joke about this story, but it is a simple reminder of how my inner child is acting out in my life. It reminded me that my mates also called me 'Two drinks Timmy' because whenever we'd go to an exotic place like Thailand and the drinks prices were cheaper, I'd load up on them, downing chocolate milkshakes and feeling that sugar rush. It's a lack mentality playing out in adult form. *I can buy these drinks, so I will, even though I could just have one at once and it's not like they're not going anywhere. I'll still have them all now, thanks.*

When I looked deeper into my habits the same went for Haribo sweets. If there was a time when I felt depressed, low or out of energy, I would go find myself a bag of Haribo from the corner shop to chow down on and make myself feel alive through the pleasure of a pure sugar high.

What I discovered was the range of strategies I had in place for dealing with stress and emotion was incredible. Resorting to drinking too much was obvious, I drank as a method of switching off the stress, but it was astounding to then discover all of the other ways of coping that had weaved themselves into my daily life.

I feel that many of these habits were created simply to avoid or numb pain. To not have to deal with emotions. Especially around my dealing with overwhelm. For me to admit that I was drowning or not coping was like admitting that I wasn't able to achieve my goal. I linked this admission with failure, which wasn't something I was willing to do.

It's only now, after hitting rock bottom, do I realise the importance that massively successful people place on doing the spiritual work every day and consistently finding the connection that I have been writing about. They don't just read about them and think, 'Oh yeah, that's interesting, I might do that, one day,' they practise these habits to live a better life and accept their emotions. They give themselves the time that is needed every single day, to get closer to the Universe. To stay in that connection.

What's freaky is that at the time Sandra and I had stumbled across the same audiobook at the time. It was by Gabrielle Bernstein called *The Universe Has Your Back*.[2] To us, this was a sign that we were meant to be together.

I had chosen her, and she had chosen me. Deep down, I knew that one of the reasons I had been drawn to Sandra from the first moment I met her was that she wasn't going to accept my inadequate ways of dealing with life through reliance on external methods. She would force me to acknowledge and closely examine the areas in my life that had become unmanageable.

---

[2] Bernstein, G. (2016). *The Universe Has Your Back: Transform Fear to Faith*. Hay House Inc.

When we realised that we had both been listening to the same audiobook, Sandra randomly selected a YouTube video of Gabrielle for us to watch.

As we sat there, and Lewis Howes, the entrepreneur and pro-athlete began interviewing Gabby about her views on life and her journey through recovery. Not only did I feel less alone, I also felt like I was exactly where I was meant to be, we both did.

Then Lewis went on the reveal he had written a book called *The Masks That Men Wear* and we both couldn't believe it. This was meant to be. For me, knowing that other people had gone through similar issues of masking pain, dealing with burnout and come out the other side was a miracle. It gave me hope that this cycle could end if I put in the work.

This is where I realised that in order to fully be the lion, we must have a spiritual side as well. A connection to a higher power, to the Universe, to God. This is the side that I had neglected, as I had been so focused on the external world. I placed my value on external rewards like achievements, completing tasks, always aiming to perform at a high standard, etc. I was only good enough if people told me I was and I thrived on recognition, rather than my own sense of self-worth.

What I needed now was to believe this, with or without other people. To know inside that I was worthy of great success. To allow myself to have it without feeling guilty.

Sandra's help

It was also incredibly strange that at the same time I hit rock bottom, my Sandra had been asking the Universe to help her develop material for her latest *You Powered by You* course which she had designed to help you live your best life, yet she was struggling to find the content and come up with the exercises.

Then right slap bang, there I was going, *here I am honey. I needed her help and badly*. It's a phenomenal course and I recommend that you try it.

Over the next weekend, she sat down with me and went through my daily schedule, completely rewriting it in the process, including what my new week would look like and incorporating new habits and healthy ways to channel stress into empowering and uplifting beliefs and actions that nourished my connection.

At that point, my daily life was going at 100mph. I never scheduled any time to myself in a day. Maybe you can relate to that? I mean, there are a million and one things to do and so much opportunity to harvest. I was too busy in external action mode. Creating and making it happen.

Sandra crafted me a daily schedule that included morning meditation and affirmations. It reengineered my habitual processes, even down to taking 30 minutes to drink a drink, anything to slow me down so that I could get present, not rushing around to get that sugar fix or instant relaxing relief. She addressed each and every way that I manifested instant gratification to distract and feel good.

Over the next 24 hours she would then ask me to take an inventory of what I was telling myself. I was to keep a journal of my thoughts, the stories that I had told myself.

The results were horrifying.

- I am depressed
- I can't do this anymore
- I am a failure
- I am vulnerable
- My head hurts, when will it stop?
- I am not good enough
- I can't
- I'm not worthy

My inner story was at odds with my outer world. I was searching for joy in all the wrong places and punishing myself for the feelings inside. It was as if I was trying to create the world of how I felt inside. Literally saying you can't have a good life. It can't be happy. This was a profound and shocking revelation for me, in fact, it depressed me more, which actually made me feel even more overwhelmed.

How could I have been carrying around this for so long? Surely, I would have known? Why did I not stop and think? Is this normal? Is this good for my soul? In fact, when do I even connect with my soul?

It seems odd that a guy writing about how to achieve great things and overcome challenges wouldn't have this figured out. I needed to put in the work to change the internal dialogue I was having with myself.

If Sandra or any of my friends spoke to themselves in this way, I'd be the first to set them straight and tell them how absolutely freakin' awesome they were. And yet there I was, literally berating, belittling and abusing myself to the point of rejection. I was disgusted with myself.

It was shocking and scary at the same time. I was scared that I couldn't do the spiritual work. I knew I needed to do it, but the thought of confronting such enormous issues was incredibly scary to me. It was real. For the first time, I understood and heard that I didn't love myself, and that needed to change.

Gabby tells us that we are to own our journey. That's what has got us to this point, and in hearing this, part of me started to feel this truth.

I was drawn to reread *The Alchemist* and wasn't sure why, but a vision of the book came into my head, so I did.

Taking my spirituality seriously

I then signed up to Gabby's *Spirit Junkie Mastermind* course because I knew that if I got myself together, I could be of great service to others. I knew this journey of spiritual recovery would involve me stepping into the unknown and doing things that felt strange and uncomfortable. I would need to trust the Universe, trust Sandra and trust myself that this was all happening for a reason, and I was exactly where I needed to be, doing the work. For the rest of this part of the book, I want to share those spiritual practices and lessons that have really helped me.

1. **Quiet**. Find a quiet place to sit in silence each day and connect to your inner wisdom and listen to your inner dialogue. Is it positive, negative, or pumped? This is how you get a read on how you're doing internally. It can be difficult to find time to connect in your day, with the tide of messages, calls and emails making constant demands on your attention, but trust me, if you prioritise this time to surrender, it will help you deal with all of life's demands with more diligence and with more grace.

2. **Breathe**. Next, focus only on your breathing. Take deep, long breaths, in through your nose and out through your mouth. If you find your mind wandering – thinking about the laundry you need to do or the email at work that you need to send – bring it back to the steady rhythm of your breath. This technique helps to quiet the mind. It takes practise though, don't expect to be all Dali Lama in your first sitting over the course of the next few weeks. Try to do this for at least 5 minutes a day but building up to 20 minutes when you feel comfortable.

Breathing is also really important, I know this from my boxing classes. In order to keep up with the intensity of the boxing drills, your breathing needs to match the speed of your punches. This is so that your body has enough oxygen in the blood to keep your mind functioning and your muscles moving. My tendency, however, is to hold my breath, especially when I am concentrating, so my trainer pointed this out to me and told me that if I breathe through the punches I could perform at an even better pace. It felt like I was being supported. What I noticed was that I would hold my breath in other situations as well, like when I was deep in thought, or speaking fast. Regulating my breathing and breathing deeply gives a new lease of life to movement, cognitive ability and concentration.

Surrender is the same. Take long deep breaths in every time you are facing difficulty or having stressful thoughts, as part of your daily practice of surrender. The more you can integrate breathing deeply and letting go, through prayer and meditation, the better your life will become and the more easily things will happen for you. In the next chapter, I want to dive into the topic of surrender in more detail and explain the process that one of the world's best miracle workers uses.

CHAPTER 31

SPIRITUAL HERO: GABRIELLE BERNSTEIN: THE POWER OF SURRENDER

"The simple intention to surrender control
is all you need to experience miracles."

Gabrielle Bernstein

Meet Gabrielle

GABRIELLE BERNSTEIN IS a *New York Times* bestselling author of six books. including *The Universe Has Your Back[3],* which I will refer to frequently. She is also a motivational speaker and life coach. In her own words, Gabby says, "I've been on a spiritual path most of my life. It all started with me sitting by my mother's side, meditating in ashrams in upstate New York. I turned to spirituality on and off throughout my teens and early twenties. I was a dabbler until my darkest hour. It was spirituality that saved me in October 2005, when I hit bottom and got sober."

Gabby is famous for her journey to become a Spirit Junkie and for finding her alignment to her true purpose, which is being a source of love and inspiration to the world. Her mission is "to help you crack open to a spiritual relationship of your own understanding so that you can live in alignment with your true purpose, too!"

I was drawn to Gabby because I could really resonate with her story – "dabbling" with spirituality and only prioritising true

---

[3] Bernstein, G. (2016). *The Universe Has Your Back: Transform Fear to Faith.* Hay House Inc

connection after hitting bottom. Now Gabby is world renowned, she was featured on Oprah's *SuperSoul Sessions* in 2017, who calls her a "new thought leader" and included her in the *SuperSoul 100*, which is defined as "a group of 100 trailblazers whose vision and life's work are bringing a higher level of consciousness to the world."[4]

In this chapter, I will share Gabby's powerful 5 steps for Surrender and how her philosophies and teachings have helped me when I thought I was going to blow a big opportunity. I truly admire Gabby; she's courageously vulnerable, real and her mentorship has helped me through countless times of struggle.

Gabrielle's philosophy

Gabrielle Bernstein says, *"What I believe in is spiritually aligned action, taking action from a place of prayer, taking action from a place of meditative state, taking action from a place of allowing."*

For me this was something that I had I needed in my life, big time! And I needed to force myself to do it, to make time to meditate and connect. When I first started down this path and had the realisation, my brain fought this type of action. I am heavily biased to what I consider as *doing* and *creating*, not stopping and pausing, so I have to remind myself daily that this is what I must do! I still have to do this today, but it's more automatic than before, and I have trained myself to prioritise allowing and connection.

When you dig into Gabrielle's message, she believes that fear blocks us from love, and a power greater than you can only guide you to the next step when you surrender and stop relying on your own strength. When you open up to receive people, contacts, opportunities into your life, you allow resources to flow towards you. However, when you try to do all the heavy lifting yourself, and control the process, you invite fear back in because you are relying only on you.

---

[4] https://gabbybernstein.com/meet-gabby/

As I have described in the last few pages, making something happen is far more effective when it is not your only choice. Taking action, like choosing to double up my workload and resit all of my A-Levels, or pushing for the higher-level maths exam and finding someone to tutor me can only get you so far. What is far more effective is surrendering your path to God, to your higher power and to the Universe. That way you can take aligned action from a place of spiritual abundance and grace. This is because from this place, truth flows, and it's important if you want to become the most that you can be and live your best life that you surrender to your inner wisdom on a daily basis rather than trying to force the outcomes that you think you want to see.

Now you might be thinking, "I don't need this, I'm a hustler, I am an action-taking mean machine. I take ownership of where I want to go, I set the course and I get there damn it." What I would like to impress upon you is that I have been there, thinking what you are thinking, and trust me, the outcomes are so much better when you connect. The practice of daily surrender will enable you to take on bigger goals, the goals you really fear, and break through them. Below, we'll explore Gabrielle's 5 steps to surrender. This is important because when you come from a place of allowing, you connect, as you are empowered to make loving choices through which incredible things can happen. The Universe can only engage God's plans for us when you get grounded and aligned and stop forcing your plans. Gabby channelled these 5 steps at a time in her life when she'd been trying to "consciously conceive" a baby for over a year. She tells the story of how she was running around cancelling her speaking gigs, even trying to push back the launch date of her book and, in her words, "consciously control" rather than "consciously conceive" a baby. Gabby was trying to have a baby on her timeline rather than the plan that God had in store for her. Gabby channelled the 5 steps through her intuition, inner guidance and wisdom that came to her in a "divine spiritual encounter" when she asked the Universe for help. The voice said to her "your plans are in the way of God's plan, it's time to surrender". I won't go into the full details here, but I have summarised the steps below and urge you to take a look at the *SuperSoul Session* online.

Gabrielle's 5 steps for surrender[5]

The theme of surrender is a beautiful one. Take note of these 5 steps and go through them each time that you feel you're trying to force the outcome on the journey of making it happen.

Making it happen is the sum of the whole and it's a process, and part of this process is to surrender the plans to the Universe and stop getting caught up in our need to control everything. It's actually in these moments of surrender that we are able to progress and act from a higher plain of wisdom.

Step 1 Take your hands off the wheel through prayer

"The secret to prayer is to forget what you think you need. When we begin to stop praying for what we think we need but instead pray for what is the highest good for all, that's when we get lit up, that's when invisible doors begin to open for us, that's when we align with the truth and the magnitude of the presence of our authentic power."

Step 2 Focus on what's thriving in your life.

"Instead of focusing on goals and the outcomes you want, redirect your focus on what you do have." For example, your wellbeing, your relationships, your business, your commitment to learning.

Step 3 Recognise that obstacles are detours in the right direction.

Rumi says – '*The wound is the place where the light enters you.*' For example, divorce is an opportunity to start loving yourself some more, or a diagnosis of an opportunity to get closer to God. Gabby gives the example of hitting another bottom in her life, so she could have another awakening. In that wound, she was

---

[5] Blog 'Gabby': My SuperSoul Session Talk (2018) www.gabbybernstein. com/new-blog-super-soul-sessions-talk-5-steps-spiritual-surrender/#close-modal

awakened, and the journey of developing her spiritual condition in a way that it needed to be.

Step 4 Ask the Universe for a sign

When we ask we will receive. Ask for a sign that you are going in the right direction, you're on the right path.

Step 5 When you think you've surrendered, surrender more.

Gabby's favourite quote from *A Course In Miracles* is, 'Those who are certain of the outcome can afford to wait and wait without anxiety.' How wonderful is that! If we listen to our inner wisdom, taking action that is guided from a place of certainty, and truly engage with the divine synchronicity that is all around us the stars will align in greater magnitude than we could have ever thought possible.

(The above steps were taken from Gabby's website, I recommend that you go check out her blog post to get the full magnificence of her *SuperSoul* talk.)

What I learned from Gabrielle

Flexibility doesn't only apply to the gym

I want to leave you with a personal story that will blow your mind and leave you with no doubt about the power of surrender in your life.

To do this, I need to talk about a time that I faced a monumental challenge, not on the surface but in my mind. It was the afternoon of a challenging day full of meetings, calls, sales proposals and leads. At about 1.30pm, I had a final round interview scheduled for 3pm on the other side of town but my heart just wasn't in it.

To me, everything I had done that week had sucked, I was not in a good place mentally and the thought of dominating in the interview was freaking me out. The pressure was starting to weigh in on me from all angles – financial, reputational, relationship and the expectations I placed on myself. I needed this interview to go well. In my mind, this was the only outcome that I would tolerate, but I had nothing left in the tank. It felt like I was mentally spent and about to fail at the final hurdle, cutting me off from the role of my dreams.

I had worked so hard to produce this opportunity, meticulously preparing and making it through each round with strategic focus, calibrated questions and panache. I wasn't willing to let my mental state dictate the outcome. In essence, once again, the Universe was showing me I had to 'BE THE LION' and put the lessons of this book into practice.

It was abundantly clear to me, while going through this experience of pain, anxiety and mental anguish, that the principles contained within this book prepare us for the big game. When my mind wouldn't stay still, frantically darting between potential outcomes and disastrous scenarios, it felt like the hardest thing ever just to take a moment to think clearly and use the techniques to regain control over my mind.

It clearly stood out to me that this book and the success habits outlined in it need to be used not only when life is hunky dory and everything is going swimmingly, but also when we are faced with the nemesis of our fears and the anxiety of seeing our dreams slip away before our eyes. When we are moments from failure, from giving up and from accepting defeat – when we believe we cannot do it – this is when these principles are most vital.

I had physical pain in my throat, and it felt like my heart was going to burst. Sharp bursts of pain would interrupt my already bleak vision of the world. My throat began to tighten up and it felt like the walls were caving in.

The pressure, for whatever reason, also seemed insurmountable in my head. I couldn't navigate my way through the city to save my life. My thoughts were clogged due to the stress of wanting to perform and present my 'best self' and I didn't feel like myself anymore.

And then, like a lightning bolt, it hit me. I got a text from Sandra, which said, 'BE THE LION.' As I read it aloud it was like an awakening. I remembered that my path would be to surrender. I had to let go of all the negative talk in my mind, connect with my belief that I could do this and get myself ready.

First, I needed to surrender my mind. I used Gabby Bernstein's four fingers and thumb technique to remind myself that Peace starts with me. Every time my mind went back to the dark place, I would place my thumb on my first finger and repeat "PEACE". Then I moved to the next finger and said "STARTS", and then the next "WITH" and the little finger "ME" until I'd completed the affirmation. I repeated this process every time I had a stressful thought bubble. At times, I was in a state of constant repetition of this mantra, affirming to the world that *Peace starts with me* and bringing my mind down from its dizzy state to guide it back to the present moment.

Next, I focused on becoming more agile and flexible, as my body felt so rigid and tense, like a steel bar. I reminded myself that I needed to loosen up. So even though I didn't feel like it, I pushed out a beaming smile on my face. I didn't want to, every muscle in my face seemed to resist wanting to make this smile.

For a few minutes, forcing this smile made me feel sadder inside. It really got me feeling like a loser. I mean, come on, who does this? It was the exact opposite of what I wanted to do and what I felt like, but I persisted anyway. Then once I came to, I was further jolted back into the land of the living.

I had 55 minutes before the interview and was about 3 blocks away. I suddenly realised I was super hungry, so I went around the corner to a little restaurant. I followed my instinct and ordered a tenderloin steak, even though we certainly couldn't afford it. This steak was just what I needed. I realised I hadn't had a decent steak in months. It was the best damn steak I had tasted and as I chowed down on the juicy succulent bites of fat-free cow, I got a sense that I might be able to do this. I wasn't out of the woods just yet but I then remembered the Tony Robbins rulebook, and just as before any big pitch or presentation, I got my blood flowing by doing circular movements with my arms.

So there I was, sat in a restaurant 35 minutes before a big final interview, smiling my ass off, eating an entire steak and doing big circular gestures with my arms. I looked like a freak. It gave the waitresses something to laugh at, but I DIDN'T CARE. I was making headway and that's all that mattered.

With every few seconds of smiling and motion the fog lifted further and I began to feel more like myself. Clarity started to come to my field of vision and with this new-found state of presence, I began to pray deeply. I was praying to God to help me let go of the outcome and just to enjoy the process. As I got up from the table to pay, I caused a slight scene with my arms flailing and grinning, but I felt more human.

Next, as I marched off to the meeting, I went to my go-to appreciation memory – the thing that I appreciate in my life – Levi. I remembered his little face and fun spirit, it filled my body with warmth and love and I was further removed from the place of darkness. Focusing on what I appreciated took the focus away from myself and on to something bigger. I was transcending the present feeling inside and replacing it with something greater.

Sandra had as always been my rock throughout this process and the night before was giving me the pep talk of my life. It had worked all throughout the day. God knows how I would have felt if I hadn't had her by my side.

The opportunity was here in front of me, to BE THE LION. Ironically, this was the thing I needed to learn, and the Universe was giving me another situation in which to learn it in.

By the time I reached the meeting I had 15 minutes to spare. As I was walking to the meeting point, I spotted the interviewers in a booth. For the next 15 minutes, while I went through every one of these steps again, every time my mind would try to drag me to a place of pain or remind me of how much this needed to go right, I would respond by surrendering further. I had to let go of what I wanted the outcome to be and focus on knowing that by letting go, I was allowing.

> "Have a mind that is open to everything
> and attached to nothing."
>
> Tilopa

By the time the interviewer came to greet me, I wouldn't say I was in my peak flow or had reached my best state ever, but I was a million miles from where I had been 60 minutes earlier. I had got myself from a place of utter darkness to a place of high performance. I was switched on and articulate, ready to deliver my best self without feeling too needy.

The interview went as well as it could have, but like most of the stories in this book, the real win wasn't getting the job or not, but who I had to become in the process. The real win here was understanding that these techniques are to be practised and exercised when I least want to. This experienced showed me the need to be flexible, rather than operating from a place of fixed consciousness that was drowning out my chances of having a state of higher performance, and moving instead to a growth mindset that is agile and able to deal with anything that life throws up.

Because life isn't going to be a straight line, it's a journey, and much like in the gym, not being flexible will hold you back from picking up the heaviest weights. It will restrict you, it may even cost you an injury, but ultimately it will cause you to be weaker than your full potential. Similarly, life requires you to be flexible, supple and to be able to bend rather than restrict, adapt rather than force, mould rather than resist.

Life is all about what you put into it. For me to succeed in this case, I was required to put out what I wanted to receive. I needed to surrender the outcome and smile when I felt like scowling, move when I felt tighter than a metal bar, and appreciate what I had to be grateful for, over and over again, until it became my reality. Surrender thoroughly, do the 5 steps and pray when you next face difficulty and I promise you'll make it.

CHAPTER 32

FAITH

"To accomplish great things, we must only act, but also
dream; not only plan, but also believe."

Anatole France

The power of faith

FAITH IS LITERALLY the most awesome thing you can have. It's the starting point of all success and from this faith builds the expansion of thoughts, ideas, progress and growth. I love faith. It is a crucial part of being the lion because it binds all of the 4Cs together and illuminates the potential pathway ahead for success, without it we fail to go into the unknown. A lion must have faith in its ability to hunt, to fend off predators, to seize opportunity and know that it an integral part of the ecosystem.

> 'Faith is the head chemist of the mind. When faith is
> blended with the vibration of thought, the subconscious
> mind instantly picks up the vibration, translates it
> into its spiritual equivalent, and transmits it to Infinite
> Intelligence, as in the case of prayer.'
>
> Napoleon Hill, Think And Grow Rich

If you think about it, an acorn houses an entire oak tree. The potential is stored within that tiny seed for something so great and with it the right nutrients, it will sprout life and grow into a glorious and humongous strong looking tree.

If you imagine your idea as the seed and your beliefs and faith in the actualisation of that idea as the nutrients that surround the seed, giving it life, then you can see how faith grows an idea from being dormant to alive.

What Napoleon is saying in the quote above is that faith and thoughts, when mixed together, are powerful. Through the repetition of thought committed to memory and repeated until the vibrations of sound have reached your subconscious mind, you will allow the very thing you want to flow back to you in the form of the idea. So, in this respect, you can build your own life by first controlling your mind and the things that you repeatedly ask of yourself and then secondly by acting on what comes back in the form of ideas.

The river

When I think about reaching my subconscious mind and how to do this, I think of life as a river that constantly flows along at a pace, and then I visualise myself jumping into this river. One of two things will happen if I don't have a clear desire or a goal – I get swept away rapidly down the river with no aim.

But if I jump in with a clear destination fixed in my mind, I am then able to swim or paddle across through the force of the flow with relative ease.

I can see where I am headed and visualise myself reaching my jumping off point. I then push up from the river and climb up on to a jetty. I have arrived at my next destination. It has happened. Faith and life are like an ever-flowing river and when you jump in, you dive into the stream of the subconscious mind.

I have experienced this stream in the form of ideas randomly popping up into my head about how to obtain or reach certain things. If I follow these ideas I can create and replicate in the physical world the feeling that I felt in the subconscious mind, which brings me into the presence of my chief aim.

This is the vibrations part. The idea is the how, the vibration is the faith, and the results are realised by combining both and acting on faith. Not in fear, but in a steadfast commitment to the vision.

Getting started with faith

An exercise in growing faith is to commit your thoughts to prayer. By having faith that something *will* happen and removing your need to control *how* and *when* it occurs, it will allow a vibrational energy to work within your life.

It is the faith part of this equation that you must have for this to translate into reality. Without faith, it will remain merely an idea that never gets acted upon and you will miss the guidance, signals and people that are sent your way to help.

Practise prayer, know that what you seek has already been taken care of and you already have whatever you need to achieve it within you. You are complete and by taking courageous action in combination with faith, it will be so. You are activating universal intelligence to go to work on your behalf.

Make it a habit to speak your thoughts and desires out loud. Be specific and have trust that it is already on its way to you. The more you can let go of control, the greater it will flow to you in abundance.

Have you ever met someone who gives off a vibe that everything in the world is just right. This is a person with faith who trusts that they have both the capability and connectedness to bring whatever they desire into being. Aim to be more like that person.

CHAPTER 33

MY STORY: MANIFESTATION

"If it's gone make peace with it. If it hasn't
happened yet make peace with it. You don't need to
live in worry or stress about the past or the future.
Just relax and watch what happens."

Idil Ahmed

RIGHT, NOW YOU'VE got the 411 on spiritual surrender and faith, it's time to crank this mother up a notch. Let's talk manifestation. If you are ready to live a life of awesomeness then you're going to want to listen up and listen up good.

Manifestation is an important part of putting the Connection C to best use, particularly the way it leverages the work we did in the self-belief **Certainty** section. It should help you to increase the amount of certainty you have in your life and reduce the stress and burden by focusing on things that you can control. It brings together two pillars of being the lion, **Certainty** and **Connection**, which are further supported by taking courageous Creative Action and **Conditioning** the Mind and Body for success.

The power of manifestation

I love manifesting. To me, this is more than visualisation, it's about having the clarity of mind to know what you want to create, in your heart of hearts, in your mind, and then going after it with all of the hunger and strategies discussed in the **Creation** section of this book.

So, what is manifestation? Let's ask the expert...

'The ability to create, attract, and turn a consciously intended vision into a reality, it's consciously intending what you want to experience, it's not just random'.

Idil Ahmed

Wow! Consciously intending what you want to experience sounds like a pretty amazing thing to be dealing with. It comes back to understanding that perception and having a clear intention and energy are all important factors in any given day.

Idil Ahmed, is manifestation expert, motivational blogger, spiritual speaker and deeply inquisitive soul, learned from an early age to be curious about how the world works.

She is the author of the book *Manifest Now* (which I highly recommend you get to raise your frequency and guide you through the mental, physical and spiritual aspects of manifesting). Idil credits her dad as her main inspiration. While she was growing up, he made sure to instil in her a deep understanding that anything is possible.

Through this steadfast belief, Idil developed a curiosity for life and, at around the age of 11, began asking truly life-changing questions.

It was in the midst of this quest to understand that Idil continued to be inspired by what she found and focused her attention on what was causing life to happen. She began journaling every day, deepening her understanding of herself and her thoughts.

When she started sharing her message with her friends, she began to help them and changing their lives, and this led her to write on Twitter, which naturally spread to Instagram, and then it exploded. She published her first book in 2013 and hasn't looked back since.

Idil's philosophy is to connect with her audience through a process that she terms 'multi-dimensionality'. In this process her message is expanded and then owned and shared by others who can feel the message for themselves. It comes from a place of universal understanding and how she helps other people.

"Energy is a state of being, it's not something that you obtain, it's something that you are, you have that all the time and the way you can access more of it is the more you start to focus within yourself."

Idil Ahmed

This goes back to the work on raising your energy we did in the Conditioning section and links to Tony Robbin's daily routine of looking within to find gratitude. When you give your energy externally, you are searching outside to get stimulation when actually you already have the energy within you. You just need to change what you focus on and look within.

As you'll see right across the board, in the habits that top performers embody, there are patterns of behaviour that emerge and themes that appear consistently about how to manifest and create what you want to experience in your life.

When asked how we raise the energy vibration to attract what we really want in our lives, Idil answered, it has to do with 'eliminating the limiting thoughts like "it's not possible for me" or "I can't do something", people get stuck in the past. When they're thinking about the past, or someone who did them wrong, their energy is low. So, the way to increase your energy is to start to have more positive thoughts, and that comes back to understanding that you are new each moment'.

This means we have a choice in how we respond, what we chose to manifest in our own lives and the vibration we want to bring to the situation or experience. We are *response able* as Tony would say.

But how do we really turn a consciously intended vision into reality?

Idil states first that we must focus on the following questions:

1. What do I want to create?

2. What do I want to experience?

If you had access to everything your heart wants, what would that be?

The key is not to worry about the *how*, but to get crystal clear on the *what* it is that you want to manifest in your life. To do this there must be a clear intention so that you can define where you want to get from to where you want to go.

Getting started with manifestation

Idil offers some core principles in her own words in the book *Manifest Now*[6] and on *The Think Grow Podcast*[7] which I have paraphrased below. These are steps to implement immediately to help us cultivate Manifestation in our own lives.

1. **Setting clear intention on what it is you want** – Have that vision, it doesn't matter how scary it is, get very clear, it doesn't matter if no one understands.

2. **Believing in it** – You're in a state right now at this moment where you have designed your current experiences from past thoughts, so if you're going to enter something new, there are things you to have to change. So you need to believe in it because your walking into it, going into it, it's happening for you. While there are doubts coming up, removing that doubt is part of overcoming a habit. It's not a matter of, OK I'm scared of the vision, it's the fact that the doubt wants you to stay the same and do what you've always been doing.

3. **Feel and visualise it to be true for you** – It's not something you think is going to happen for you in the future, it's true for you in this moment. This is also where the action comes in, because when you say, 'I am going to change today and this is the new vision that I have,' you cannot do what you were doing yesterday. Action is very important because every time I have a thought it is like guidance, and this is the next step I am going to take. The visualising helps you stay motivated and keep that vision so clear that you step into it. You have to be active in your change. There is that timeline where things are happening

[6] Ahmed, I. (2018) Manifest Now. Idil Ahmed.

[7] The Think Grow Podcast. Episode 18. Keys To Manifesting Your Vision With Idil Ahmed. (2018). http://thinkgrowprosper.com/blog/idil-ahmed

for you, but you just have to keep going on and on, and take the necessary action.

4. **Trusting the process by using positive affirmations and positive thoughts** – This is where you keep yourself going. For Idil, affirmations are the power of words. You have to add strong emotion with your words. 'Today is going to be GREAT DAY!' If you're speaking, why not speak power into your life. Affirmations are words that you speak constantly which agree and align with the vision you have.

Manifestation and interviews

I myself experienced manifestation. I knew what I wanted, I set a clear intention and boy did I believe in it, but in order to act with integrity with myself (integrity is a word that gets thrown around a lot but to me it means to act in tune with your truth) when applying for my dream job, I had to push myself to move into spaces that made me very uncomfortable. To move to the next level, I had to do something that totally freaked me out, but was completely worth it. I was acting with integrity with my best self and that was all that mattered. Round after round, the interviews were going great. Each time I would perform a little better and articulate my vision and purpose in deeper and more captivating ways.

It felt sensational; however, I knew if I was fully going to go for it, secure the role, blow all other candidates out of the water and leave the employer with only one clear option, I needed to make an impact in the form of trusting my intuition and letting my creative instinct flow.

The thing that made me feel so uncomfortable was that I wanted to showcase my initiative in order to stand out from the crowd, by putting in the extra work, following up with the recruiters after each round, and creating a step-by-step infographic of how my career history had led me to find this company, and how the company values intrinsically matched my own. The extra work wasn't the issue, it was the infographic that got me. For some reason, it struck fear into my bones to press send. It seemed like a risk that could be construed as being over the top and even slightly obsessive. I worried that the senior leadership on the interview panel might think it was cheesy or desperate, instead of coming from the place I intended, which was dedicated and aligned.

Let's not forget that this was going to the Senior Vice President, based on her personal preferences. If she felt it was a waste of time or a silly last-ditch attempt to persuade, then my dreams of getting the job would be over, and all my hard work and hours of interview preparation would be left for dust.

I finally reasoned that the risk was worth it. I needed to be myself, so I decided I'd send in the infographic and if it caused me to be taken out of the running, then so be it. What mattered was the process and being authentically aligned to myself, the company and who this job could enable me to become.

I had to trust that by putting it on the table, it would be well received, understood and I would be greeted with open arms at the other end and welcomed into the business, rather than scupper my chances of success or damage the positive momentum I had built up face to face during the rounds of interviews.

At its core, I had to hand it over to God. I had to accept that what was meant to be, would be. I prayed a lot during this time before each interview round. It might not seem like a big deal, sending in a creative piece of work that highlights your attributes, but stepping outside of the box can be difficult for all people at various stages, and it usually occurs when we perceive it to matter the most.

Whilst walking to the interview, I prayed that I would be able to shine, that the words would flow and I would be able to articulate my answers in a well-formed manner. I wanted to enjoy the interview and find areas of connection with the panel and communicate well, using best practises, as this would encourage great answers to form in my mind. Above all, I prayed that I would be able to execute what I needed to at that exact time.

And it happened, each time I went in for an interview the next door would open time and time again. The interviews went phenomenally well. The feeling of connection with the interviewing panel was solid, passionate and authentic. I was truly happy with how it went down at each stage. When purpose meets opportunity, passion and action, then magic occurs, especially when you trust it. You become unstoppable, unflappable and connected.

After the final interview, a thought popped into my head to send in a final letter to the interviewers, summing up three reasons why the role aligned deeply with my purpose and I felt that together we would excel and create huge value.

But doing this scared me. All the interviews had gone so smoothly I didn't want to rock the boat by doing something potentially 'out there', but my inner guidance told me that I needed to do more, that I couldn't leave any stone unturned and that I had to go all in.

And the way I was being instructed to do this was by sending in this letter that shared my thoughts with the leadership team.

In essence, I had to BE THE LION again and go for it.

I had to believe that my way of doing things would bring me to my goal and by taking aligned action in this specific way, I could create the reality that I wanted. I was manifesting.

As the path unfolded before me with the next idea and action I needed to take, I got to the end of the process. This was it. "Give me 24 hours," the recruiter had said. For 2 days, I waited and painstakingly tried to take my mind off the inevitable call to inform me of my fate. On the morning of the second day, I got an email from the recruiter. The call was set for 3pm that afternoon.

By this point, I was doing both morning and lunchtime sessions at the gym, going for long drawn out protracted walks. The time could not go fast enough. I just wanted to know and get started with my new team and begin my new job on my mission. I wanted to start delivering. This was it, it was happening!

As I waited patiently for 3pm to come around, I was channelling my inner calm and centeredness. The phone rang, it was the recruiter, my heart was pounding.

After a minute or so of small talk, I was trying to access his mood, his tone – did he sound happy or like someone who was about to deliver bad news? I couldn't tell. My heart was racing and my nerves were shot.

Dear ███████████

Thank you for the opportunity to participate in this process, it has been an absolute joy to meet each of you and I very much appreciate making the connection, as well as the thoughts, insights and experiences you each shared.

Below I just wanted to summarise three areas in which I feel I could excel in this role at ███████ and why it aligns so deeply.

I've held a number of roles in my career, some for large organisations like AOL, Verizon and WPP and others in startups beginning their new adventure expanding into new markets or regions.

What I have found is that the most successful individuals who thrive no matter what the company size, hurdles and obstacles, are those whose purpose aligns with that of the company vision and culture at a fundamental level.

These folk become ambassadors and have an affinity for the brand, they are innovative, connecting the dots between opportunity and random meeting and when there is a deep alignment there is passion and there is trust.

Coaching
Leaders can often make the mistake of thinking that things need to be their way to achieve a certain goal, and while process and accountability is vital, it is important for leaders to understand the motivators behind the team member.

What matters to them? What are their goals and aspirations? And how do these feed into the larger company culture and vision for the future?

When linking motivators to company aspirations it lifts the standards of the whole team as a community rather than forcing a predetermined outlook on to an individual.

My style as a leader is to lead by example, that doesn't mean I will jump in a fix every fire at a moment's notice, I want each person to learn, to become the best version of themselves and therefore it's important for them to be helped through and coached what to do in a specific situation. When to communicate certain things, how to tackle mistakes, learn from them and navigate red flags. The important part is collaborating with a team to help them learn through the experience, raising their own self-belief and capability in the process.

Purpose
My passion is working with teams to create high performance and achieve outstanding results. It's not so much about achieving the goal, it's who the team collectively becomes in the process and how they then go on to flourish, living and breathing the company culture. In addition to this it's the psychological safety that's created, and the increase in the quality and cadence of the communication that's produced as a result. The beauty and impact of this is that the standards of the team collective are raised and as such the ability to produce results is enhanced.

My forte is aligned in this way as it has come in the form of 'opening closed doors' and coaching others previously on how to adopt this mindset and apply action in areas of sales.

For example, whether this has been hosting live cold calls with a team watching in to gather insights on the process of how to qualify a lead, to uncovering key information or reaching decision makers.

In other examples, I have conducted targeted one on one coaching specifically designed to improve results in a certain area of development, measured overtime or led strategy away days with teams who need to work more together closely to improve communication, trust and performance.

Contribution
It is now my goal to work for an organisation that I believe in fully, that I am proud to work for and one where I can contribute to going after big goals. It's my aspiration to work with ambitious individuals who are pushing themselves and others to go after a collective mission. ██████ excels all of these areas in droves

I very much enjoy working in collaborative teams where the bar is raised, where we strive for high performance and take an explorative approach to understanding the drivers of business in a changing landscape.

I am ready to commit and go all in, to help a leadership team by providing a voice on strategy, efficiencies, and opportunities and to do so to the best of my ability.

Proactivity, culture and action are competitive advantages that I would very much love the opportunity to contribute to and I fully believe that ██████ is not only producing results in these aspects of business but raising the bar.

In summary, the opportunity to utilise both my MBA Leadership coaching experience and Sales Leadership experience in an environment where we are producing ambitious results would thrill me no end.

Best Regards,

Tim Castle

My post-interview letter

And then I heard the words, "There was nothing wrong with any of the interviews, you made a huge impact but unfortunately..." *Was this really, happening? This was supposed to be the moment I was going to get my dream job.* "Unfortunately, there has been a restructure internally, it happened at the final hour later last night and the role doesn't exist anymore."

#gutted!

To my utter disappointment, this time it was not to be. This time. Then something strange happened. I felt an unusual sensation come over me, considering the circumstances. It was the feeling of being at peace. It was totally disappointing but that didn't matter.

What I learnt from manifestation and interviews

In the journey of pursuing my dream job, I had become who I needed to be. I had taken the risks I so badly wanted to take. I had proven myself with the best of them, I had gone all the way and presented myself to the best of my ability.

Overall, the process had all gone as well as I could have possibly hoped. I had delivered my best and I was completely satisfied with that because I had grown. I had pushed myself and developed a new resilience and presence within myself and this why I knew it didn't matter, because the growth was more valuable.

This, unlike the job, was not something that could be restructured. It was something that I would get to keep forever and build upon. It was the solid foundation of experience that could not be taken away from me.

I had also surrendered the outcome up to the Universe. Whatever was to happen – job or no job – well, that was what was meant to happen.

Now I had to focus my response on what this outcome meant to me, and on what meaning I applied to the situation.

Was it going to be a shitty outcome and a lot of wasted effort, or was it going to be a transformational outcome – my best example of a series of interviews and rapport building yet?

I chose the latter, and by doing so, it allowed me the freedom to let go of what might have been without beating myself up about the outcome and instead relish the incredible opportunity and experience that life had given me.

On top of this, I now knew the company's recruitment process, back to front. I had learned several key fundamental skills for interview success, how this company approached sales development and the importance they placed on coaching.

This was gold! I had the keys to the kingdom, the right contacts within the organisation, and when the next new role came up, guess who was going to be first in line....

A few words stood out from that final conversation with the recruiter when he told me I hadn't been selected for the role due to circumstances out of my control. He said, 'but you made a huge impact.' These words are powerful because we are able to make the biggest impact when we are operating from a place of abundance and joy. From this day on, I resolved never again to question the impact making. If I could creatively conceive how I could make an impact or add more value, boy, I was gonna do it.

I share the above thank you letter as a way of demonstrating the value of making an impact and standing out to the VPs of an organisation in the hope that it will encourage you to make your own impact by leveraging your strengths and unique abilities to manifest what it is that you want. If you have an inkling that it might make a difference, just go for it and don't look back.

The truth about success

Success is about who we become in the process. Without doing the work and taking the knocks, learning and reforming, we don't get true wealth. And by true wealth, I mean the fulfilment that comes from living closer to source energy. We each have a purpose within us.

I want you to think about a skill or passion that you could share with the world.

- What makes your fire come alive?
- What do friends regularly say you are amazing at?

After all, that is the highest form of success – sharing your gift with others, passing on what you have learned to others so they too can benefit.

Even better than this, you get to experience the learning and the gift twice over when you teach someone else.

As the legendary coach John Wooden[8] says, we should always be trying to do better and when we make it to the top, we should look

---

[8] The Tony Robbins Podcast. Episode 57 & 58 The Legendary John Wooden. What it means to build character, be a true leader and win the game of

around for ways to help others, and there are always ways you can do this.

When asked about failure, coach Wooden replied, 'Failure is knowing that you didn't do the things that you should have done.'

And the key part of his response is YOU. Next time you or someone else thinks you are a failure, ask yourself how hard you tried.

> 'To my way of thinking and my analysis, an individual is the only one who will truly know whether or not they're successful because they're the one that really knows whether they've made the effort to make the most of what they have under the conditions that existed for them and trying constantly to improve the conditions. Too much of the time we complain about what we don't have and as soon as we do that we're not going to make the most of the things that we do have.'
>
> John Wooden

---

life. (2016) https://www.tonyrobbins.com/podcasts/the-tools-of-titans-tim-ferriss/

CHAPTER 34

PERSEVERANCE

"It's not that I'm so smart, it's just that
I stay with problems longer."

Albert Einstein

Lions persevere

What is perseverance? To me, it is going after an objective that might take you months, years or even decades to obtain. It's a bit like writing this book. There are times when I've wanted to quit, to throw in the towel and just give up, but something kept calling me back to finish the job and push through. It's a deeper commitment that I couldn't let go. Perseverance is an important part of being the lion because when a lion has an unsuccessful hunt he can't just give up. In fact, statistics show that whilst the king of the jungle sits proudly at the top of the food chain, lions only have a hunting success rate of between 18%–30%[9], meaning that perseverance is intrinsic to their being.

Think about it another way, lions fail 70%–82% of the time but still come out on top because they keep on going.

Also, the chances of survival for male lions from cubs to adulthood is 1 in 8. At the age of 2, young males are kicked out of the pride and forced to go into the wilderness alone and fend for themselves. This is a rite of passage, and as you can imagine, most don't make it due to starvation, illness and being attacked or killed by adult

---

[9] https://africageographic.com/blog/africas-successful-hunters/

lions. It is only the strong, intelligent, fit males that survive to take charge of a pride[10]. There are many trials and tribulations that both male and female lions must face along the way and this quality of perseverance is a key trait that sees them thrive.

When I was writing my first book, *The Art of Negotiation,* I sat in the bathroom of my tiny studio in Manly Beach, Australia, while the rest of the household slept. This was because it was 4am and this was the only time I could find to get it done, I was building new perseverance muscle.

Why you need perseverance to achieve

I hadn't faced this challenge before and my goal was just to make it to the end. I wasn't bothered about a big book launch or finding a large-scale publisher, what mattered was making it to the end of the process.

I'm not sure if you've ever written a book but for those of you that have, or committed to any seriously large project, you might be able to relate to this. It's hard to explain. At times it makes you feel sick and at others, elated, one day you are on fire, words are flowing naturally and everything is going well, the next it feels like torture. So, to keep pushing takes perseverance.

My first book was an absolute grind. I didn't know what I had let myself in for but by sticking with the process and pushing through the times of pain and frustration in pursuit of the bigger goal, I got to the end after hundreds of hours. Things have been a bit different while writing this book. As it was my second book, I semi-knew what I was up against, so the process was less riddled with mines and more streamlined.

Purpose and perseverance

I wanted to help people really overcome challenges and make it happen in their own lives and this motivation transformed my mental ability to get up and keep going. Connecting to this deeper

---

[10] https://www.livescience.com/41572-male-lion-survival.html

purpose gave me the strength to write for hours and hours non-stop. Hours would pass, but they felt like minutes.

When external factors and circumstances were distracting me and trying to take me away from writing, I reconnected to my purpose. This required me to be super clear where I was focusing my time and energy. I also had to keep my growth mindset so that when I sat down to write, I could actually write!

Although I went through challenges while writing this, I also experienced phenomenal growth as a result. It was like I was living and breathing the BE THE LION process, and the Universe kept on prodding me to find new strategies if I didn't quite get the lesson. I have lived this book and my battles have been less about pushing through the book writing process and more about becoming more myself so that I could articulate my vision clearly and add value to you the reader.

It's easy in life to focus on the results and not see the hundreds of hours of blood, sweat and tears that have gone into training to produce that moment of success.

Examples of this can be found throughout the world. For instance, watching a basketball game. You focus is on what's happening up top, where the ball is, who's shooting for the basket, did it go in, did they score, rather than on the footwork and agility that allows the player to be able to dodge the defence, make a break for it and shoot a jump shot with power, grace and exactly the right motion to execute it.

There's perseverance in the hours and hours of drills, dedication and training that have gone into building the flexibility and muscle memory to deliver this exact shot and jump in a perfectly timed fashion. It's all the work done behind the scenes.

And it's like that in life, perseverance is required off the court, or off the stage or away from the track and the screaming fans. It's needed when we least feel like picking ourselves back up and trying again, and is a necessity for both progress and advancement.

Life will keep bringing you the same lessons until you figure out how to manoeuvre differently.

Perseverance is what keeps you driving forward to that bigger vision and will ultimately see you arrive at your desired destination, eventually.

The power of perseverance

However, not getting the dream job stung slightly more the next morning. In my quest to find something uplifting and mood changing in order to change my state, I stumbled across an audiobook entitled *Grit, The Power of Passion and Perseverance* which had miraculously found its way into my iBooks library. In it, the author Angela Duckworth writes this beautiful text[11] that begins with the words: '*the highly accomplished were paragons of perseverance…*' I recommend that you pick up a copy of this book even if it's just to read this paragraph that begins mid-way down on page 8. When I heard it, I got shivers down my spine and a sense that I was being guided to the words I needed to hear. I wrote to Angela to try and include it in the book. Sadly, the publishing company wanted a small fortune, so I had to decline. She granted me permission to use the following about how she defines Grit. It's magically powerful.

'*Grit is passion and perseverance for long-term goals.*
One way to think about grit is to consider what grit isn't.
Grit isn't talent. Grit isn't luck. Git isn't how intensely, for the moment, you want something.
Instead, grit is about having what some researchers call an "ultimate concern"-a goal you care about so much that it organizes and gives means to almost everything you do. And grit is holding steadfast to that goal. Even when you fall down. Even when you screw up. Even when progress toward that goal is halting or slow. Talent and luck matter to success. But talent and luck are no guarantee of grit. And in the very long run, I think grit may matter ay least as much, if not more.[12]'

---

[11] Duckworth, A. (2016). Page 8. Grit: The power of passion and perseverance. Scribner/Simon & Schuster.

[12] https://angeladuckworth.com/qa/

I never would have thought to put a section on perseverance in the part of the book about building spirituality and connection, but now I see how it is divinely connected to our inner self.

When you have perseverance, you are following your life's direction. You are able to swim through the current of the river and keep going, hungry for more. The chase is as thrilling as the destination. I realised this is what I had when it came to my pursuit of living my purpose and giving my gift to the world. And I had just taken one very giant step closer.

Getting started with perseverance

1. **Focus on the small wins.** The path to victory can take months and even years, depending on what it is you are trying to accomplish. That is why it is important to focus on the small wins as you pursue your goal. It can be daunting if you only focus on the accomplishment in its entirety. This perspective will aid your ability to manifest the stamina and perseverance when you feel like giving up and quitting on your dream. As they say, Rome wasn't built in a day, but it did start with the construction of the first wall. If, for example, your goal is to get a six pack or lose 10 kilos, it won't be possible in one sitting. Intensity isn't going to help, but it is possible to accomplish if you focus on doing 100 sit-ups a day or losing a few pounds each week and then raising the benchmark. Slowly, the 100 sit-ups lead to 200, 300, and so on, until you start to see the emergence of your abs. Doing 100 sit-ups *is* an important milestone on the journey and enables the rest of the transformation to follow.

2. **Compete against yourself, run your own race.** Set the benchmarks that are appropriate to you and then raise them each week. As the weeks march forward so too does your ability, and what you once considered to be impossible slowly comes into view. The mistake that most people make is to focus solely on what other people are

doing and to compare where they are to that benchmark of success. This comparative behaviour sometimes leaves your true capability on the table. At other times it may cause you to suffer an injury or make a bad decision because you were not fully prepared for the outcome. If you are training for an Ironman race, for instance, work backwards from the date, count the number of weeks between now and the race day, then set incremental goals, starting with where you are at right now, and then raise the bar each week. Celebrate each step of the journey. This goes for anything. Look at what it is you want to achieve, define what success looks like for you, so you'll know when you've reached it and then work through the steps of progression that you'll need to hit to reach your goal.

3. **Chaos happens to all of us. It's about how you pick yourself up and carry on that counts.** A frustrating combination of friction, adversity and tension is how we grow. It's not about avoiding chaos, it's about learning how to survive in the storm and becoming more. A lion is always looking for opportunities to outperform what it first thought was possible, and chaos and how you deal with it gives us a daily method of doing that. To really up your game, the next time you are under pressure with a tight deadline or a staff member calling in sick just moments before a big presentation, challenge yourself to rise to the occasion. Demand more of yourself and see your perseverance grow. We don't get fit, strong and healthy by not bothering. It comes through putting increased pressure on the mind and body. Over time this causes the muscles to tear and repair, and the brain to explore new ways of both approaching and solving problems. When you look at life from this mindset, you begin training for opportunities that haven't even occurred yet. This is when you have reached a new level, when you are prepared for whatever comes next, dying to take on that next challenge.

4. **Regularly find the time. The biggest excuse I hear people make is "I DON'T HAVE TIME".** This is completely nuts in a world where you can literally download an app that tells you how to optimise your time on a minute-by-minute basis so that you complete all of your intended habits and rituals. Apps like Fabulous give you a direct update on how you are currently spending your time across multiple fields, like meditation, exercise, breathing deeply, drinking enough water. This allows you to stay on track and accountable for the rituals you have defined as important. You've got one life, make sure you own it. Cut out the TV, the gossip, the indulgences on social media and get to work. You'll be surprised about how much time you can create if you get up at 5am and just start moving. For example, if you've only got 10 minutes, challenge yourself to send that proposal email to a new client explaining your services and offering to set up a meeting. Don't let the opportunity pass by telling yourself some excuse like, "I'll get to it later." As a lion, you need to get phenomenal at organising your day. This comes from understanding what you can get done in a matter of minutes rather than hours so that you are able to dedicate the appropriate amount of time to the important stuff like the habits in this book. When thinking about a task, don't automatically assume that it can't be done well quickly or you can't do it faster because it normally takes you an hour. For example, people often procrastinate about perfecting the best ever email to VIP clients when all the client normally wants is a well-articulated answer at speed. Deliberation and lack of decision making hold us back from the really big wins and this sometimes means we count ourselves out of the opportunity. The point is, we have far more time than society or other people would have us believe. If we buy into it, we're destined for a life of struggle and underachievement compared to what we're capable of, as well as a negative perspective of life itself. Next time you are faced with a decision or task to complete, try to challenge your assumptions around the

time you expect it to take. Go on, surprise yourself. I guarantee it will make you look differently at yourself in the mirror and say, "I got this, I am a badass."

In summary, the world we live in today is getting smarter, but it is also getting dumber. Technological advancements can be used to either aid our commitment to rituals that support our lion lifestyle, or they can be a deterrent. To encourage the perseverance of a lion in your own life, you must dedicate your time to the things that really matter. You need to start questioning the assumptions that you have made around practices and habits that you have adopted. By doing this and looking deeply at how you motivate yourself, what drives you and where your source of passion comes from, as well as challenging your current norm, you will be able to work smarter with more vigour and vitality. Consistency in your routines and sticking to them above all else, no matter what happens in your day, will see you gain monumental increments in success over time. I want this for you! I want you to witness and experience the wondrous benefits that come from setting up and structuring your daily life around the attainment of your goals. Share your perseverance stories using #bethelion #iamready.

CHAPTER 35

GRATITUDE & GIVING

"The more grateful I am, the more beauty I see."

Mary Davis

The power of gratitude

Thank you, God, for this day, thank you for this life, thank you for this opportunity. When we allow ourselves to feel grateful for all that we have we open ourselves up to all that the Universe has to offer. Gratitude is an important part of being a lion because this is what fuels the lion's powerful roar. What I mean by this is, if we are unaware of what we're grateful for, then we aren't connected to or passionate about the things that matter. Being grateful and showing gratitude to the world for what we have can sometimes be hard to muster, especially when we think we are up against it or life isn't going the way we predicted or would like. But gratitude is a number one, top-tier component that allows you to draw all the beautiful and wonderful experiences, opportunities and people that life has to offer towards you. It's a mindset shift that allows you to see and experience all the beauty in the world. This subtle shift in focus can make all the difference. I am not saying it's always easy to do, but if you can embrace gratitude it can make a colossal difference to the outcome and reshape how you approach and deal with problems.

My advice is to go big on gratitude, feel your passion, open your heart and let your love for the world flow. Miracles can happen when you least expect them and when you most need them.

Spiritual guru, Gabrielle Bernstein, says "*A Course in Miracles* teaches the presence of fear is a sure sign that you're relying on your own strength."[13] She continues to unpack the real power behind this message, which is, no matter what we are facing, no matter how difficult it may seem, the Universe will never give us anything we can't handle.

To surrender like this, we must let go of the idea that it is us, and us alone, that can solve our problems. Gabrielle insists that the Universe is always supporting what is our highest good.

We must learn to rely also on the Universe to help solve our problems and have faith that it always has our highest good in mind. In this respect, we need to strengthen our faith in our higher power and practise surrender.

> 'Thank you, Universe, for presenting me with this divine assignment for spiritual growth and healing. I am ready and willing to show up for this assignment with love. I welcome your support. Show me where to go, what to do and what to say. I trust I am being guided.'
>
> Gabrielle Bernstein, The Universe Has Your Back[14]

Just stop for a moment and think of all the wonderful and amazing things that we have in our lives right this second. We are so incredibly lucky to be alive at this time in the world's existence. It has never been more abundant. There has never been more opportunity to create and connect with others from all walks of life and to go big.

I want you to understand that gratitude is a door opener when you switch from focusing your attention to what you don't have to the abundance of the world that surrounds you. Even simple pleasures, such as the ability to go grab a cup of coffee with a friend, create a website and launch your business into the world in the space of only a few minutes and clicks. The level of abundance and opportunity that we come into contact with daily is astounding.

---

[13] https://gabbybernstein.com/fear-holds-us-headlock-get/

[14] Bernstein, G. (2016). *The Universe Has Your Back: Transform Fear to Faith*. Hay House Inc

We live in times of unprecedented growth, and something powerful starts to happen when you connect with the world in this way. There is a divine synchronicity that shows up which is now able to be witnessed because the lens through which we are viewing the world is one of love. When we look at the world through a lens of love, gratitude and abundance, we tune into the world's symphony of infinite possibility and, as a result, create more of those experiences.

We each have a gift to share with the world. We were put here for a reason. You may even be reading this knowing what it is you were put here to give, and doubt has previously been holding you back. Well, here it is, this is a sign. If you've made that connection, then now is the time to act on it.

Getting started with gratitude

If you want to get the most out of life and sing its song, then spend one day being grateful for everything that shows up and honour the privilege that you receive just by being alive in this exact moment in time. It's gratitude that will transform your world and open you up to receive what the Universe has in store for you.

The Universe is constantly sending you messages, however, the closed mind cannot receive them. The Universe is looking for abundant souls to support. Let it find you.

How to get started with gratitude:

1. Think of 3 things that you are truly grateful for, e.g. being alive at this specific time in history, your health, your family. This might sound simple and unimportant, but these are big miracles that we experience and take for granted daily. By bringing awareness to all of the goodness in your life you give it power. (I am obviously thankful for not falling off the edge of that cliff when I was 19 and now getting to experience being a husband, father and life liver). Commit to doing this practice each night just before you fall asleep.

2. Take time to walk in nature. Stroll through the forest just noticing its magnificence, strength, resourcefulness, abundance and resilience. For example, the tree does not complain when it is broken by high winds, it simply starts to rebuild one step at a time. Witness how nature handles adversity and gives thanks for being alive and think how you can apply these lessons of gratefulness in your own life.

3. Share with someone you trust the first 10 things that come into your head that you are grateful for. Call them up right now and just go for it. Don't overthink it, just do it. This will break the cycle and habitual pattern that you normally engage in and shock you into a new thought pattern.

The power of giving

I truly believe in the power of giving, as to give is to be alive and to give shifts your focus from one of lack to one of abundance. It's a thrivers way of living.

Giving doesn't have to be money, although that's what most people think of. It can relate to how you coach your friend through a practice interview, or listening to a colleague tell you about their upbringing so that they feel more connected to you and the company.

There is a power in giving; the world seems to smile and repay those who give in greater and greater abundance.

Getting started with giving

1. **Know when to give.** The next time you spot an opportunity to give and to make someone's day just a little bit brighter follow your intuition and act accordingly. By taking action in this spiritually aligned way, you are allowing yourself to be supported by the Universe. I do this by giving cash to strangers. This

could be when a taxi driver tells me about their life and how they are struggling to pay the bills or it could be in the form of leaving a large tip. I'm not saying I do this all the time or I'm walking around handing out money like I've got a giant ATM sign on my back, but on occasion, my intuition kicks in and tells me that I can make a difference. I might give them $50 or $100 dollars, but one thing's for sure, I know that I have opened their eyes to the kindness of the world a little. WARNING: Some people will take great offence, inappropriately so, to your giving. Be aware that just because you've decided to give, you don't then need to highlight it or talk about it. People get very offended and have strong opinions about this type of thing. So save yourself the trouble of explaining and keep it to yourself.

2. **Notice the ways you can give.** As you go about your day-to-day life keep a record of all the different ways that other people give. Try out some new ways of giving yourself, such as volunteering, teaching a sport or hobby for free, like boxing, personal training or painting, or maybe even proofread your neighbour's screenplay. You'll be surprised at the variety of ways there are to give when you start to open your eyes. Even the simple act of holding the lift or letting someone go in front of you in the queue is a form of giving. Lions give to restore the natural order within the world.

3. **Give anonymously.** Leave money, food or drink with a sleeping homeless person. Pay the person behind you in the ticket queue's train fare. Give without anyone else knowing it was you. As stated above, giving doesn't have to monetary, it could be asking a grumpy colleague if they're OK or getting them a cup of coffee, or smiling at a passer-by in the street. It all counts. The Universe is listening.

CHAPTER 36

MY STORY: 8 WEEKS THEN AND 8 WEEKS NOW

"If you want to be a lion, you must train with lions."

Carlson Gracie

Thinking I was invincible

THROUGHOUT MY TWENTIES, I was the ultimate self-destructor. I made no time for rest. I knew how to push myself beyond my limits in all areas, forcing my body to continue without rest, chasing the night, and never wanting the party to end. I was a thrill seeker. I wanted to be around fun, to be in the fun and to be the fun.

I remember going on holiday to Mykonos with a really good friend and wondering how I would survive the rest and relaxation element of the weekend break. Part of me was fearful as there would be no clubs, no bars, no partying, just pure rejuvenation. How was I going to handle this? Could I cope with a pause in the constant barrage of entertainment and fun that my life had become? As it turns out, I have since discovered that I am a complete master of R&R and I absolutely love the luxury of a spa. Some might say I have now become a spa connoisseur.

Attempting to relax, whilst taking in the sites.

A few days later, loving life, relaxed.

Well, it was a revelation. I couldn't believe that I had never allowed myself to stop and pause like this before. I was recharged. As a result, my ideas were stronger, my resolve replenished, and my determination and focus clearer than ever. It was a game-changer for me. Never before had I acknowledged that I could just stop the repetitive cycle and allow in space, with no agenda, no calls, no 'musts' and that it could enhance my experience of life. It was as if a new door had opened and I had given myself permission to walk in and discover the wonders of rejuvenation for the very first time. What I found was miraculous, and I have not looked back since.

In fact, I came back from that holiday and withdrew my notice (a few weeks prior, I had announced that I was going to go travelling and explore Asia and Australia). I actually regret not sticking to that plan, but the draw of a stable income and an ability to fund my new-found love of Grecian spa weekend getaways had me in its clutches, and I decided to stay on.

This was to my detriment. Deep down, I knew I needed to change because my lifestyle in London was becoming unmanageable. I often wonder what would have happened if I had stuck to my guns and taken the trip.

I had already booked my flights, even the accommodation for the first month in Thailand, but I reasoned that I didn't have the money and it was the safer option to stay employed. Funnily enough, around the time that I'd originally planned to take this trip, I came into more than enough funds to last me for the six months in Asia, and I kicked myself for not committing to my original plans.

Living 24/7 in London

Before the holiday, I had reached a low point. I was stuck in a cycle of distraction and doubt. The problem was, I couldn't help myself when you put me in a party environment like London. I had little discipline and the more I was offered, the more I took. I traded my values for experiences and told myself I was growing up. But these experiences didn't fulfil me, inside I was empty and craved real moments that I knew existed.

Working in media, almost everything was free. I had access to the best restaurants, drinks and parties were all laid on night after night. Between my job as a media manager and my active social life in London, it was rare that I ever had a night in.

Before going to Mykonos, I was out for 8 weeks in a row; every single night I had plans, whether that be a house party down in Brighton, clubbing in East London, or dinner with friends, I had plans. It's not that it wasn't fun, or I didn't enjoy it. There was a real sense of community among my friends, and I loved having a full life in that respect. However, the problem was this acceptance of everything spilt over into multiple commitments and wasn't filling me up inside, as I knew it wasn't a productive or healthy way for me to live. It was like I couldn't let an event go by without me saying yes, I just had to be there. Whether I was physically and emotionally exhausted or not, I craved the pleasure and fun of it all. My work life and my social life blended into one, which isn't a bad thing in itself, it's just that I had lost a sense of what my deeper purpose was, my connection to my inner self.

For example, the weekend prior to the Mykonos trip, I had been to Berlin, and the week before that I was in the South of France, and before that Ibiza. I was working during the week in London and attempting to manage all that that entailed as well. This compounded my party lifestyle and fed my need for constant entertainment. It also made things much harder as working usually involved long lunches entertaining clients at the most exclusive restaurants and members clubs followed by more grand events in the evening like a box at Wembley Stadium or a VIP table an awards ceremony. It sounds great doesn't. It was a rollercoaster and I was addicted to the spontaneity and adventure. I tell you this not to brag, but to demonstrate the level of the chase for significance through experience I was pursuing in my life.

Amid all of this excitement, fancy restaurants and bars, luxury holidays and adrenaline-pumping weekends away, I was missing out on a crucial part of my own well-being, growth and development. It took a huge toll on my body. These trips and my work weeks were packed to the brim and I took it to extreme most of the time, expecting my body to keep up.

In all honesty, back in those days, there wasn't much self-development occurring, and certainly nothing of a spiritual nature. It was as if I had pushed it down and drowned it out with the sound system of a nightclub, washed down with anything I could get my hands on.

I was in a spiral of denial, guilt and sabotage. Each time I went out I wanted it to be bigger and better. I wanted the nights to go on for longer and the stories to be wilder and more entertaining. It was a hoot; however, I felt empty inside and knew deep down that I wasn't fulfilling my purpose to its highest potential. This was all a distraction, a distraction from pain.

I was arrogant and immature. I didn't like myself much.

I am, however, proud of the journey I am on, as I know that it has brought me to be who I am today, which has changed the way I think, and I like who I'm becoming. I will always be a work in progress, a lifelong learner who is dedicated to adding value to others through sharing what I have learned.

My goals back then were led by short-term gratification and often gave me a headache, providing more frustration and disappointment than they were worth. I lost myself for a while, years in fact. I became whatever anyone else wanted me to be, whatever was easiest for them, rather than connecting with my inner source. I knew that I could do and make more with my life. I knew that this was not it. This was my experimentation and procrastination phase.

I kick myself for not taking action earlier I did try, it took guts and I got pretty far, and then I would give up again and the cycle would repeat itself, each time building up to the point when the bubble would burst and I'd need to rethink what I was doing with my time.

What I learned from Mykonos

Towards the end of my 27th year, this started to shift. Five months after I had originally planned to go on my one-way trip, I moved to Australia and took myself out of the scene that was creating so much toxicity in my life. This was a conscious move.

It took me two years to really acclimatise to the slower pace and limited options that Sydney provided for evening entertainment. This allowed me to gradually break the cycle and I gave up drinking for 18 months. Working in media that's a fairly difficult thing to accomplish!

Drinking has never given me anything of substance. It was an escape, which provided, at times, confidence, stamina, courage, and escape, but 9 times out of 10 it was to forget that life was happening around me and to fill the void of not having found a bigger purpose.

This was because I undervalued myself. I had a hatred for myself that meant I didn't value what I could bring to the world. Drinking is ultimately a depressant which, in turn, causes more anxiety, depression and worsens the situation in every imaginable way.

By detaching from this excessive clutch, I was able to focus on implementing the basics.

The Mykonos trip taught me some important lessons that I have tried hard not to forget (as I previously mentioned a few chapters ago, burnout can appear almost by surprise if we're not careful). The biggest insight I remember having from the trip was the value of finding and creating the time to disconnect from the world and invest in replenishing the mind, body and soul. I felt more at one with myself and it opened up a completely alien world to me, one I loved with a passion, where I could pause and relax without feeling guilty, anxious or craving a distraction. On this trip, I allowed myself to practice stillness for the first time and didn't respond to the need to be entertained or distracted. I allowed myself to shine through.

Before embarking on this trip, taking a moment's reprieve wasn't something I was well versed in. After Mykonos, I realised I needed to change the destructive habits that were causing me so much torment.

It was time for me to head in a new direction and build a life that allowed for time out, structure and habits. It was this realisation that enabled me I began my journey and move away from chasing the illusion of comfort that is found in excess, distraction and external validation that my life had become so intertwined with and dependant on.

I was determined to escape the idea of what I thought life needed to be like – to be fun – and go after my real deeper purpose. This didn't happen overnight and I am still a work in progress, but the realisation was profound.

To reiterate, as you'll have read a few chapters ago, burnout and not listening to the body's needs can appear, even when you have good intentions like working hard towards the pursuit of your life goals and to support your family. What I've found helpful here is the daily check-in with how you are going. This is part of self-love and it gives you the discernment to make the right decisions when you need to. If you can relate to what I am saying, I am here to tell you that there is a way out of your own destructive cycle. You can build strong habits that you can rely on to take you towards a life of fulfilment and you can start today!

Doing something more productive

I always knew I would complete an MBA in Business and was just waiting for the right place and time to do it. I don't quite remember how, but I came across the University of Sydney's MBA program, and from the moment I came into contact with the program, I knew it would literately change my life.

Learning allowed me to open up.

Surrounding myself with high performers made me raise my own standards. It offered me new perspectives, challenged my assumptions and gave me a network of friends in which I felt accepted and at home.

The MBA program at the University of Sydney Business School was the best formal learning experience at an institution that I have ever had the privilege to experience. The program has an emphasis on practical learning, so you are forced out of your seat to deal with situations as if you are the CEO of a business. You're forced to take responsibility and make decisions.

This gave me the challenge I had been looking for and I got involved in any way that I could. I promoted it to my work colleagues, completed any available extra lectures, attended breakfast guest speaker seminars, signed up to represent the University at competitions, completed a toastmasters' public speaking course, and coached the Leadership Practise and Development module for two subsequent MBA cohorts, which required over 200 hours of in-depth leadership training.

I was in my element, for once I had found my people!

The MBA program allowed me to value myself more; it gave me a sense of self-worth and pride in how I was choosing to spend my time. It also showed me what was possible when you put your mind to it and opened me up to find the love within myself.

At one stage, I opted to complete 3 MBA modules at once. Technically this made me a full-time student and as I was working full time in a leadership position for AOL at the same time, it pushed the boundaries of what I thought I was capable of mentally and physically.

On top of this, I did this only 3 weeks out from recovering from a 6.5-hour hernia repair operation (which was funnily enough performed by an MBA alumna) and Sandra was 7 months pregnant. The goal was to get as much done before the little one made an appearance into the world.

Taking on this challenge meant that I didn't have a single day off for 57 days in a row. I was working every morning and night to make this happen. I was at work during the day and then in class at the Business School at night, followed by a double dose of class 9am-5pm on both days of the weekend, for 8 weeks straight! That doesn't include all the time I spent doing the reading, assignments and group work. Often, I wouldn't get home until midnight after taking the last ferry back across the harbour to Manly, then I would rise at 6am to do it all again.

Staying on top this hectic schedule, required me to be ultra-focused about where I needed to be and what I needed to have done by when. To do this, I had numerous A3 sheets of paper drawn up for all of my commitments, detailing what assignments needed to be completed and by when. I am a visual person so having these reminder sheets placed in strategic and convenient places around the apartment helped me feel at ease and stay on track. As I was taking 3 modules, it meant that I was often doing back-to-back MBA classes or meeting up with different unit groups from each of my classes throughout the week and before work. There really was no days off!

The pressure grew

As I kicked off this mammoth feat, I felt calm and in control but then as the weeks ticked by and the commitments started to grow it began to get challenging to manage. At about week 4, competing projects between work, MBA studies, different group work and my personal life started to collide. Every day was a new battle, which started by taking each hour at a time. Sandra was amazing throughout and understood why I was putting myself under so much pressure to get it done before the birth of our son. She was my rock throughout and talked me down from pulling out of one of the modules on a number of occasions. When I didn't want to get up, when I was exhausted, she gave me a pep talk and pulled me through, giving me mental strength. By reminding me and tapping into my *why* (my purpose) she helped me to connect back into the bigger picture of why it was important for me to keep going.

After about week 5, fatigue started to set in and the thought of facing one class, in particular, was painful. I wanted to drop it right then and there, but Sandra's words helped me stay the course. She calmly explained to me that I had an excellent team around me and it was an opportunity for me to learn from some amazingly talented people in my group, and although I was tired and didn't feel like another 12-hour day inside when I could be on a sunny beach, it would all be worth it in the end. She was right. I had the opportunity to spend up to 12 hours a day with some phenomenal individuals that I am still impressed by today. This was worth its weight in gold. Here was where the lessons would be found, embedded and taught. I was pushing through my own boundaries.

I was way beyond where I would normally have given up, I was in unknown territory and beginning to like it.

With her pep talks and encouragement, I made it through to the end. I made some incredible friendships and had a whale of a time doing it. The key principle that helped me endure these 8 weeks with no days off was to focus on the present and take it one day at a time.

If I could just get through today and survive, then that's all that mattered right now. By breaking the feat down into short-term goals and persevering, I was able to reduce my state of overwhelm. I'm not saying that overwhelm didn't spike up regularly throughout the day, but by focusing on what I needed to do in the present, I was able to bring it under control and it made the process more manageable in this way.

At the end of it, I felt tougher. I was a stronger lion. It was like I had endured a marathon. I felt like anything that came after this point would never be as intense, whether it be a client pitch for work or starting a new business/ I had cracked through the ceiling of my own understanding of what I thought I was capable of.

The next time you're faced with a daunting challenge, I recommend pushing through and testing what you are really capable of.

Where previously, I used to push myself by going out to gigs, clubs and events night after night, relentlessly without reprieve, here I was pushing my learning, understanding, ability to apply concepts and theories and manage multiple projects, giving my best to each.

It's strange to think back that this was once my life in London, but caused by a hectic social life and destructive habits and now I was creating the same 8-week scenario for a very different outcome and for very different reasons.

This type of intense and gruelling commitment of pushing myself was completely and wholeheartedly aligned with my mission and purpose. It felt totally different to the excessiveness of the nights out and partying from my early twenties.

This time, it had meaning. I was developing the right connections, expanding and building friendships to last a lifetime and learning every single day. It was my kind of utopia, I was exhausted but stimulated, awake but growing, sleeping yet building. I was connected.

I have had the privilege to work alongside the most exceptional, hardworking, bright and creative individuals who have inspired me no end throughout in this MBA experience. It was the best learning experience I could have asked for.

What I learnt doing an MBA

What I loved about the MBA at the University of Sydney Business School was the course had been designed to focus on experiential learning, so you actually got to experience the leadership situation and make decisions as if you were in the environment itself. This was muscle building at its finest.

We called this practice, doing reps. It was here that I would learn an important lesson about reps. Reps are a magnificent tool because they allow us to grow through the experience and develop new habits so that when we are faced with the challenging conversation, decision or circumstance, you have the muscle to overcome it. You have been there before and have the tools at your disposal.

It's like rehearsing the experience so that you have the stamina and knowledge to put it into practice. This focus on practical learning literally transformed people over the course of an MBA weekend. You could enter on Friday night and emerge on Sunday evening even stronger, filled with vitality, ideas and ambition. New leaders were born in a weekend.

The MBA network and the amazing teachers have given me a platform to find value when I saw little and have helped me claw my way out of destructive patterns of behaviour that no longer served me.

Say what you want about MBAs, but this was a major course correction, or as Mastin Kipp says, divine synchronicity.

CHAPTER 37

STEP INTO THE UNKNOWN

"If you do what you've always done, then you'll
get what you've always gotten."

Tony Robbins

THIS CHAPTER IS short and sharp, much like the time it takes to make the decision to do something differently. In it, I will show how to change the way you look at things to push yourself into new and potentially uncomfortable yet rewarding situations and experiences. We'll also discuss how to spot the synchronicity that is at play in your life and how to harness its full power.

Step into a luxury hotel

I'm a luxury hotel fan, I adore them. To me, they represent a reflection of the symphony of life. If you walk into any 5-star hotel you are presented with growth and fulfilment in all forms.

From the level of care that the staff take to remember their regular and most important customers, to the craftsmanship of the ornate flower display, to the thought process of the architectural design, and the ambience that is so conscientiously and consistently maintained.

I will regularly spend time in hotels, not for work, but to raise my game, to raise my level of thinking. 5-star luxury hotels are a bold reminder that anything is possible, and yes, you might argue, of course, anything is possible, they have piles of money to splash around. To this, I say, it's not about the surface, it's about looking deeper. Each hotel, each concept started with an idea and was built up from there.

Each day that 5-star hotel is still fighting a battle for loyalty in a fiercely competitive marketplace and is on a mission to deliver more than they did yesterday, to provide more value to their customers to ensure they will keep coming back time and time again.

I recommend that you go sit in a luxury hotel and just notice what goes on around you, notice how you feel, notice the harmony that is maintained. Then look outside back to the streets and you'll see the hustle and bustle. Out there it is easy to give in to thoughts that life must be hard to be worthwhile, that it's supposed to be a struggle.

Step into the unknown

From now on, every time you are stepping into the unknown, I want you to imagine you are stepping into a luxury hotel, in which you will be greeted by an abundance of opportunity.

The unknown is very much like a luxury hotel, because without stepping forward and allowing yourself to be transported into another world, you stay outside in the street, fighting the same old battles, the same old routines and approach problems in the same old fashion.

Life is like this, you only ever a doorway away from another world. If you are outside passing by and you don't make the commitment to walk in, to change the patterns, to accept the new job, to push yourself to achieve more every day, to go the extra mile and seek out new levels of growth and possibility then the unknown stays somewhere distant and isolated.

Step into the fun

Embracing the unknown also comes down to having fun. I learned this lesson from a colleague who brought charisma to every meeting. The reason they were able to do this and have fun was because they were truly themselves with the world and through this oneness, they lost the hang-ups that can usually keep us from going for it and expressing our full selves.

That doesn't mean they didn't get nervous, feel embarrassed, or have fears; it meant that when they experienced these feelings, they were able to own them completely and reveal them to the world in an open and positive way. This meant that other people could also relax and feel comfortable because they knew they were getting the real version of this person and not someone who was trying to hide how they were feeling.

Essentially, the fun that was brought to life by this person, which helped them to open more doors, win more sales and overcome all manner of would-be obstacles than if they had chosen to stew and deliberate on them.

Overanalysis kills dreams. Overthinking is the same. By engaging with the fun that you have inside of you, and by stepping into the unknown, you will be unstoppable.

Synchronicity

Dr Wayne Dyer says it best, *'When you change the way you look at things, the things you look at change.'* To me, this is an incredibly powerful idea that sums up what it means to step into the unknown and change your circumstances through how you are being and interacting in that moment.

I can't tell you the number of times I have had this happen in my life when the right people, messages, truths, friends, money show up at exactly the right time and in the way they were intended. I'll give you an example. One day, I was struggling to find a path that led me to new and inspiring content. In a world where there is an unlimited amount, I was overwhelmed. In desperation, I turned to YouTube and up popped Wayne Dyer, a man I knew nothing about other than he was frequently referenced by Gabby Bernstein. I clicked play on the video and was instantly hooked.

Wayne's deeply authentic and certain voice drew me in, and I began listening to his words intently. I worked my way through two or three videos and there it was, a message. Wayne kept referencing this book, *Ask and it is Given* by Esther and Jerry Hicks. This rang a bell and when I got back to the office after a quick gym session, I Googled to find out Jen Sincero's recommended books, and low and behold there on the list was this book again, staring me in the face as if to say *go on read me, I dare you.*

That's not the strange part though. When I got home, I went into the office and began tidying some things, as I had a work conference call later and wanted to be prepared in an uncluttered and calming space. As I looked up at my bookcase, I saw it, plain as day. There was the book*, Ask and it is Given*, just sitting there on my bookshelf.

It's kinda freaky how these things happen, but it's the closest sensation I feel to alignment with universal power. That's 3 times in one day I have been prompted to read a book and then it shows up in my house, and out of the hundreds of books I have, it is placed facing me, just so I would recognise that it was connected. I had no recollection of even buying the book, no idea how or when it came into my house, but it had been with me for a while, sitting there waiting for me to discover it at the exact right moment.

You have to laugh with joy with the synchronicity sometimes. And this is my point about the unknown: when you operate in this alignment, you are not alone. There is a guiding force that will bring things into your life as you are meant to find them.

The pathway will become unblocked and the connections to the right people, technologies, and solutions will all be opened. What was once inconvincible will appear and be real and ideas will flow.

This aligned way of being in the unknown will allow everything you need to flow towards you. You can rest assured that you need not fear the unknown for it is already made. Just listen and connect. The deeper you can connect, the more your inner purpose will reveal itself. By connecting to our inner purpose, we are fulfilled.

I want to share one of Dr Wayne Dyers main principles with you today and that is 'Don't die with the music still in you.' What this profound truth brings forward is the fact we all have some music playing within us and it is our job to figure out what that is and start to dance on our mission.

Wayne says, 'There is an intelligence that is a part of everything and everyone and too many of us are too afraid to listen to that music and march to it.' What he's getting at is we all have a mission so don't wait to get started, begin today. I hope that you are inspired to take action on your journey into the unknown and remain open to the possibility that it can and will happen for you.

CHAPTER 38

TIME FOR A FINAL PEP TALK

"It always seems impossible, until it is done."

Nelson Mandela

You can do anything you put your mind to

Do you find yourself getting excited about ideas, but then not doing anything with them?

Do you have a burning desire to be, do or achieve something outstanding?

It's possible to know all the right next steps to take in theory, but if we don't actually take them or act on the drive to see it through to completion then we miss out big time! We miss out on being the fullest version of ourselves and expanding into what we were put on this Earth to create.

A possible reason that we pull back when we reach the edge of our comfort zone is ear, we are perhaps afraid of looking stupid, making a mistake or feel scared that it won't work.

To counter this doubtful mind, try focusing your thoughts on everyone you admire. They got where they are because they took the leap and pushed through into the unknown despite the fear. At one time or another in their lives, they made a decision to continue on and keep taking action, no matter how small, in spite of the fear.

Progress is made by taking small steps in the right direction, and if you keep taking them day after day, you will experience growth.

And from growth, you will create a passionate energy that ensures your flame to succeed will continue burning and be guided towards your life's mission. It's like a machine, once you get it firing, there will be no stopping you.

When we know what to do and have all the tools to make it happen, but don't take the action required, it just sucks. It's a letdown and all our negative feelings rush back and swoop all the glory.

If you have an idea, it's important to get into action mode as quickly as possible, so don't dwell in thought mode for too long.

Given time, doubts can creep in if the idea is far beyond our current comfort zone and we begin to talk ourselves out of it. The more we try to rationalise these thoughts the more we hold back. It then becomes incredibly difficult to take that first step, whereas we'd be down the road already if we had just got on with it.

Gabrielle Bernstein has an interesting take on how to get into action mode quickly. When Gabby really wants to go for something, she counts backwards from 5 in her head and then just does whatever it was that she wanted to do.

Counting backwards from 5 acts as a distraction in the brain and does not allow the doubt and fear to creep in.

The best time to make decisions is when you are in a state of high passionate energy, when you believe that anything is possible, and you are ready to take on the world, kick ass and start taking names. This is when life-changing decisions can be made. Once the decision is made go for it, start the wheels in motion and don't look back.

Steve's story

I will give you the example of my friend Steve. For years, Steve had been rejecting the idea of starting a personal training business. Then when he moved to Dubai, he found the market was crying out for personal trainers and ripe for the taking.

There was an abundance of stay-at-home moms and affluent, health-conscious individuals *ready* and *willing* to pay for his fitness services, so the market was wide open. Yet he couldn't quite see it.

Even when one of his best friends, who was living next door, was telling him to his face, "I need a personal trainer, I want to find a PT and pay for it," he still didn't quite get the calling. This was because he was blocking himself from receiving his new path.

Did I mention that Steve was job hunting at this stage? Every job interview he had been going for in the corporate health world was not the right fit – the hours were long and the vibe just wasn't right. In essence, the world was pushing him to recognise where he really needed to be.

He had told me in numerous texts that he just wanted to full-time work in the health and well-being industry for months, but couldn't find any suitable roles.

Then one night, he called, sounding upset and frustrated that he couldn't find the job of his dreams and we began a discussion about how to find his own clients. We discussed what he would need to do to make the PT business work and strategized how to close the gap between his 'thinking about it' and 'going for it'.

The key for Steve was to start off small, by working with his best friend next door and taking the opportunity that was being handed to him on a plate. He could practise on him and build up his confidence until he felt ready to take on more clients.

By labelling and reframing the story in his head, Steve could connect that the personal trainer path was actually supporting his ultimate dream of working in the health industry. Steve eventually saw that he would not only get more job flexibility by working as a PT, which he craved so that he could spend time on his other side businesses, but he would also get some excellent content for his blog. Steve would be at the forefront of the health industry on the ground, with real clients hearing what they had to say and the issues that came up. The personal training would allow him to experience a more diverse set of issues that his clients faced which would fuel more interesting content online for his readers.

This shift was about connection. Steve could see how all the pieces were coming together and if that perfect job did come up, he could look at doing both. But for now, this might be the perfect job and, in fact, could even lead to the creation of his perfect job. It was certainly going to expand it. Sometimes the opportunity we have been looking for can be right in front of us.

> The lesson is this: the Universe gives us signs to try and show us where we need to take action in our lives and if we connect with its language and see what it is trying to show us then we can rest assured that we are moving towards our life purpose.

When one door closes, instead of getting bummed out and sulking and playing the victim, we can grow by shifting the focus and looking for the meaning and the opportunity.

This new entrepreneurial business venture may well be the greatest thing that ever happens for Steve, he has taken control by not taking a corporate job where he will work for someone else for 60+ hours a week, fuelling their dreams and lining their pockets with dough. Instead, he has decided to take the plunge and move his own ideas forward.

This is where the magic of the Universe happens. It is where our dreams begin their first footsteps. Like the powerful quote in *The Alchemist*[15] – "And, when you want something, all the universe conspires in helping you to achieve it" – the shift occurs, and we begin walking down our universal path. Destiny awaits us.

Impossibility and awe

Move in the fields that excite you. When I speak of fields, I am referring to both the physical and the fields of energy. They will guide you along your way, for everything is connected, each part serves the next.

Think of the movement of millions of people around the world daily; to conceive of such an idea that this volume of people would be able to move at will on a daily basis would have seemed an impossibility to some in the past. An unfathomable thought and therefore not attempted.

---

[15] Coelho, P. (1995) The Alchemist. Harper Collins.

Think of the train station. Each day we pass through it, but do we stop to marvel at its wonder, about how it came to be. Each and everything started as a thought in a person's head; therefore, it started at the same point and began even before the person knew the thought was coming.

We are all connected, the grass, the rain, the air, the trees, we are all one and in one we serve.

There are different planes in this world, the physical, the emotional, the creative, the soul. And in each of these planes, we experience different expressions of the world revealing itself. The spark of love in a heart that is uncontrollably there with the presence of a thought or memory, the power of an earthquake or the force of a waterfall, the beauty of fashion and technology, and the words that leave us touched forever.

When moving towards your destiny, listen to the signs. Remember the quote from *The Alchemist*: "and when you want something, all the universe conspires to helping you achieve it" and "people are capable at any time in their lives of doing what they dreamed of". When we truly want something and go after it with all our hearts, the Universe will help us along the way. I make it a commitment to read *The Alchemist* at least once a year to keep myself humble to the wonder of the world.

Do you ever get that feeling that you have been here before?

Something that is so familiar or strange like, you have dreamed it, or you have actually been in that exact situation. Or like when you meet your soulmate, you know the full reasons why you are with them. You fit.

Love is an eternal bond that pervades the boundaries of time. Now I am going to suggest something really weird, what if time in its linear form wasn't real.

What if we were all places in different lives at once. Moving through, on the physical plane at one pace and the emotional plane at another and the soul's time at another.

What if the Universe was a place for us to figure out our destiny, our gift to share with the world and when we do we move to the next plane. Life in itself is growth and with growth comes ability and expansion.

What if the physical world is level one and when we learn to master the skills of the emotional world in the physical world, we progress to level 2 and we die in the physical world and move into the spiritual word. And here we are setting on a new quest to learn the next, and so on and so on.

If we then go back into the world when we die, and form the nutrients in the Earth, are we not then connected to the cycle of life and growth once more?

Step out of the created comfort zone and remove the blockers from your path, whether these are self-imposed or otherwise, and truly live in the moment that you are experiencing right now. Believe that all that can be thought is possible and exists. Feel into the situation where your heart is leading you to go. Seek the path of your greatest choice, expression and fulfilment.

The flow state

My gosh there's a lot out there on getting into your flow state or creating the flow state. What I believe this is really about is manifesting and getting closer to the experiences and things that your heart wants you to spend time doing. This is sharing your gift with the world through the creation of words, products, pictures, sounds, love, experience, tales, family, giving. Whatever makes you lose track of time without forcing it, is where your heart is.

Do not confuse Flow State with Peak State. Peak State is a different realm. Peak is about bringing your best self to the party and delivering with absolute certainty your mission, your change, your courage and your lion.

To try to force a flow state is about as sensible as trying to control love. Flow state is about noticing patterns in your natural desires, listening to your heart and watching when you enter this state.

- What are you doing when all of time seems to stand still?
- Where is your mindset when you are in this state?

- How can you get more of this in your life?
- What actions can you take?

I believe that flow state is a connection to God, a connection to the gifts that God gave each of us and tapping into it is like glimpsing that which we often cannot see.

Miracle baby

When I made my entrance into the world it was all systems go right from the beginning. I was pale blue, gasping for breath and had only moments to live. If it wasn't for the quick thinking and dedication of the doctors and the skill of an Indian surgeon, who attempted one of the most advanced surgical techniques of the time, my journey into this world would have been over before it had begun.

I was born with a diaphragmatic hernia, which doesn't sound like much, but as a baby developing in the womb it caused havoc to the development of my vital organs and more specifically my lungs. It meant there was a small hole in my diaphragm whereby my intestines could move up into my body causing my lung cavity to be squashed, which was stopping the growth of one of my baby lungs.

So there I was, seconds after appearing in the world, blue and fighting with every breath to stay alive for one more second, surviving on one lung with a severely reduced oxygen supply.

I can only imagine the trauma and stress that my parents must have felt, welcoming their first much-awaited baby into the world in the mid-1980s. Having gone through a similar medical panic with my own son, I know they were roaring like lions to do everything they could.

I was rushed to the Nottingham City Hospital to undergo a long surgery with a specialist paediatric surgeon named Miss Leela Kapila, the woman to whom I owe my life.

She performed intensive surgery on my small baby body and conducted a new type of skin grafting procedure which allowed the skin to regrow over the hole instead of forcing my stomach back together. I was later told that I was one of the first babies in the country to have this innovative form of surgery and only one of two babies who had survived the initial trials. I would wear the scars for a lifetime as the tubes inserted into my side to feed me were in for weeks and weeks and the surgery was highly invasive, not like the keyhole surgery you can get today.

For 6 weeks I remained in an incubator, as family and friends prayed for my second lung to grow. As the Universe would have it, once the intestines were out of the way, the prayers, and miracles occurred, and the second lung began to form and started to grow in size.

My parents called me a miracle baby and I was taught to believe in miracles from an early age. The love, support and prayers of everyone around me, from family and friends, to people all over the globe was insane. I even got a special visit from Torville and Dean, the British, European, Olympic and World Champion ice skaters, who came to see me in hospital. I didn't know it yet, of course, but the news had spread far and wide.

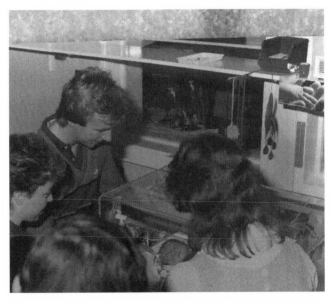

The miracle baby

Along with being a miracle, my mother always told me that I was a fighter, and I had been in that surgery, facing death head on. She cried at not being able to save me herself or be able to help me during the surgery. She said that I must have tried with all my strength to survive, to say, 'This is not my time, I am going to live.'

I have always felt I had a purpose, a reason for being here and I have felt compelled to write it in this book, *Be the Lion*. I was drawn to create it and tell the stories contained within.

When my mother died, 21 or so years later, I was heartbroken. I was angry at God and at the world for taking a good person, a person that, no matter what, always tried her best. I found it unmanageable to deal with the emotion. How could the world do this? We had some much more to share.

It is only in writing this book that I now understand that she is not gone, that the emotional connection lives on, that she is around me and I am still connected. This means that I have now made peace with God, it was not his fault, he was moving her to the next level. For anyone who knew her, I am sure they would agree, as much as we would all have liked her to stay, that she had other work to do.

CHAPTER 39

CONGRATULATIONS, YOU MADE IT

*"It is better to be a lion for a day,
than a sheep all your life"*

Elizabeth Kenny

I WANT TO give you a high five, a pat on the back and a great big, genuinely warm hug. In reading this book you've gone through a lot. You've probably questioned your purpose, possibly changed some of your habits and certainly entertained the idea that whatever the challenges are, you can overcome them. Whatever limiting beliefs you've held previously have now been discarded and new more inspiring and creative beliefs, that won't take no for an answer, are steadfastly in place.

I hope that this book will serve as a guide that you can dip back into when faced with an overwhelming sense that hurdles and challenges are on the way, or just as a reference point to apply a strategic approach to getting more out of yourself and living your life the way it was intended.

Growth takes commitment, it's a never-ending journey that requires us to push through our boundaries and find the light within ourselves to move into new realms of the unknown and chart a new course.

By taking action in areas that we have not before, and by following those random niggling ideas that pop ever so discretely into our heads and refuse to disappear, we create the expansion of our own lives that we know, deep down, we're capable of reaching.

It is action and our commitment to taking action, repeatedly, that sets us free. It is the instant calling that resides inside of you that, once followed, the Universe supports with ideas and openings where there were none before.

Remember to listen to your intuition, to trust your instinct, and to develop in each of the 4Cs of **Creation, Conditioning, Certainty** and **Connection** and you will get to your bliss and beyond.

It's been real. I hope one day that we will meet and discuss your journey to be the lion.

Peace and Love,
Tim

BONUS CHAPTER: THE MAKE IT HAPPEN MACHINE

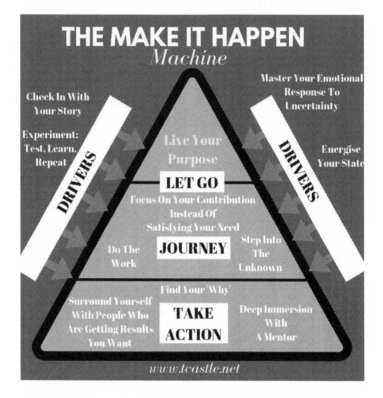

THE MAKE IT HAPPEN
Machine

Check In With Your Story

Experiment: Test, Learn, Repeat

DRIVERS

Master Your Emotional Response To Uncertainty

Energise Your State

DRIVERS

Live Your Purpose

LET GO

Focus On Your Contribution Instead Of Satisfying Your Need

Do The Work

JOURNEY

Step Into The Unknown

Find Your 'Why'

Surround Yourself With People Who Are Getting Results You Want

TAKE ACTION

Deep Immersion With A Mentor

www.tcastle.net

WELCOME TO THE ultimate Make It Happen Machine. This bad boy will take you from action all the way to purpose and back again. Imagine the triangle as a continuous feedback loop that is always listening for inner guidance and signs, and is in connection with the flow of the world.

This is my interpretation of making it happen and is the way that it shows up for me. As you digest it, you'll see that many of the topics we have focused on already appear as core dimensions, from experimental strategies, such as Test, Learn, Repeat, to Deep Immersion With A Mentor (thanks Mastin).

Below is a blank version of the Make It Happen Machine for you to complete. The purpose is to recognise and solidify the lessons that have resonated with you so far in the book. Stick it on your wall, keep it on your desk, put it somewhere visible so that you can visualise it daily.

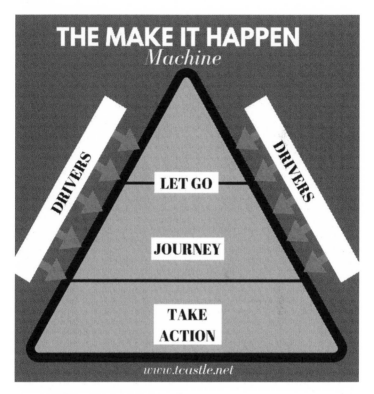

For example, yours could include…

- Eliminate the unnecessary
- Focus only on the top priorities, ignore the rest, discipline is required
- No overthinking
- Act on the opportunity, in spite of your fears

Below is a selection of books across each of the 4Cs that I recommend your read to deepen your understanding of each of these pillars of the Be The Lion philosophy. I found all of these books to be so valuable in my journey and constantly refer back to them for new insights, guidance and inspiration.

RECOMMENDED READING

Creation (Action)

The Third Door – Alex Banayan

The 4-Hour Work Week – Tim Ferriss

Zero to One – Peter Theil

Losing My Virginity – Richard Branson

Finding My Virginity – Richard Branson

Conditioning (Mind & Body)

The Richest Man In Babylon – George S. Clason

Think and Grow Rich – Napoleon Hill

Manifest Now – Idil Ahmed

Tools of Titans – Tim Ferriss

Can't Hurt Me – David Goggins

Certainty (Self-Belief Strategies)

You are a Badass at Making Money – Jen Sincero

The Law of Divine Compensation – Marianne Williamson

You are a Badass: How To Stop Doubting Your Greatness And Start Living An Awesome Life – Jen Sincero

Sell It Like Serhant – Ryan Serhant

Option B – Sheryl Sandberg and Adam Grant

The Four Agreements – Don Miguel Ruiz

Connection (Spiritual)

The Universe Has Your Back – Gabrielle Bernstein

The Alchemist – Paulo Coelho

Daily Love – Mastin Kipp

Grit – Angela Duckworth

Spirit Junkie – Gabrielle Bernstein

Ask And It Is Given – Ester and Jerry Hicks

A New Earth – Eckhart Tolle

RECOMMENDED PODCASTS

RECOMMENDED LINKS

Tony Robbins' Energy Tricks
https://www.businessinsider.sg/tony-robbins-energy-tricks-2015-10/

Jen Sincero on Money
http://time.com/money/4742356/jen-sincero-mind-tricks-badass-making-money/

Gallup StrengthsFinder
https://www.gallupstrengthscenter.com/home/en-us/strengthsfinder

Marc Benioff on Taking Time Out
https://www.cnbc.com/2018/12/30/salesforce-marc-benioff-talks-tech-ethics-time-magazine-and-vacation.html

Gabrielle Bernstein's Spiritual Surrender
https://gabbybernstein.com/new-blog-super-soul-sessions-talk-5-steps-spiritual-surrender/#close-modal

Gabrielle Bernstein on Knowing the Universe Has Your Back
https://gabbybernstein.com/know-universe-back/#close-modal

RECOMMENDED COURSES

Spirit Junkie Masterclass – Gabrielle Bernstein
https://spiritjunkies.com/digital/index.html

Date With Destiny – Tony Robbins
https://www.tonyrobbins.com/events/date-with-destiny/

REFERENCES

Ahmed, I. (2018). *Manifest Now.*

Bernstein, G. (2016). *The Universe Has Your Back: Transform Fear to Faith.* Hay House Inc

Bernstein, G. (2012) *Spirit Junkie. A Radical Road To Self-Love And Miracles.* Harmony.

Coelho, P. (1995) *The Alchemist.* Harper Collins.

Duckworth, A. (2016). Page 8. Grit: *The Power of Passion and Perseverance.* New York, NY, US: Scribner/Simon & Schuster.

Graham, S. (2006). *Diversity: Leaders Not Labels. A New Plan For The 21st Century.*

Serhant, R. (2018) *Sell it like Serhant. How to Sell More, Earn More, and Become the Ultimate Sales Machine.* Hachette Books.

Sincero, J. (2013). *You Are a Badass: How To Stop Doubting Your Greatness And Live An Awesome Life.*

Sincero, J. (2016). *You Are a Badass at Making Money: Master the Mindset of Wealth.* Viking

The Tony Robbins Podcast. (2016). 'Talking With Titans.' Episode 54. Tim Ferriss.

The Tony Robbins Podcast. (2016). 'The Legendary John Wooden. What it means to build character, be a true leader and win the game of life.' Episode 57 & 58.

The Think Grow Podcast. (2018). Episode 18. 'Keys To Manifesting Your Vision With Idil Ahmed.'

ACKNOWLEDGEMENTS

*B*E THE LION is the amalgamation of life experience, adventure, the goodwill of people and the loving nature of those around me who've shared the beauty of their souls. Without so many people this guide to overcoming challenges would not have come together in the way that it has.

This book started out as a handbook for kicking goals and making it happen. However, once I had really got to grips with the deeper concepts that I was exploring, I realised the emphasis wasn't so much on forcing things to happen, but aligning oneself for success.

In writing this book, I uncovered the powerful combination of four core tenants (the 4Cs Framework) that, if practised in a balanced and consistent way, will work in complimentary unison in order to promote fulfilled living, which ultimately leads to overcoming challenges and making it happen.

I discovered more fully than ever that it was about developing a connection to a higher power rather than merely hoping for change. It was about deciding to raise your energy and attitude to meet the hurdles you face so that you can cultivate momentum in any given situation and open new doors that you never imagined were possible. I also found that it was about having faith, trusting the path that the Universe has laid out towards your vision and believing it will come into form. Time and time again, as the signs, the intuition and the trust grew stronger, the path unfolded in larger and more profound ways; perhaps not how I had first thought it would, but as I went on, it synchronistically felt how it was supposed to be for me to either recognise the lesson or move on to the next level. In a word, I became aligned to the life that I aspired to live.

I began this journey thinking that I had the answers already but like so many things in life, it wasn't until I gave myself fully to the process of discovery that I realised I needed the lessons, habits and tools more than ever before. As you will have read, I managed to burn out even towards the end of the book writing process, as I had forgotten that all important piece of the puzzle yet again.

The glue that holds it all together, the connection to myself and my maker. The final section of the book was written with this in mind and although it was incredibly difficult to write, relive and understand, I know it is a truthful and necessary element to make your daily practice.

I give this gift to you in the hope that it might inspire you to change in whatever capacity supports your own greatest good and provide you with hope that, if you are struggling or up against it, there is a way forward, a path for you to take, a structure to channel your ambitions, and this will see your talents come alive in a way that you've never imagined.

At its core, this book is about possibility, fulfilment and the combination of self-work that needs to be done, both externally and internally, to really overcome challenges and make it happen.

Thank you to my beautiful wife Sandra, I am quite convinced you are an angel. You inspire me to be better, give me hope in times of darkness and encourage me to go after my really big goals. This is more than I could have wished for. You gave me the time and space I needed to write this book, believed in my passions and kept me looking inward. The fact that this book focuses mainly on stories from the past five years, between the ages of 27-32, and that we have been together during that period of transformation does not escape me. You have helped save me from myself and opened my eyes to a new world, a new way of living, and given me both the support and encouragement to take big leaps into the unknown. I love you and admire the woman that you are.

To Levi, you are my champion. I love being a father to you and watching you take on the world in every way you know how. Your energy, humour and cheeky smile will see you go far my son, you can do absolutely anything in this world. I have dedicated this book to you because I love you. These are my lessons and I am sharing them to give you a head start. I will always be there for you with open arms, proud and ready to take on the world with you.

As I have mentioned before, I felt like *Be The Lion* wrote itself, as if I was being guided. The words poured out of me over the course of nine months and I was left with something I hoped would hold value for others.

However (and this is a big one), if it wasn't for Leila Green and her team of mavericks at I_AM Self-Publishing, what you have just read wouldn't have been anywhere near the book it is today. I am in absolute amazement at your ability to take a mountain of content and shape, structure and edit it into a book, as well as prod me into looking at areas that needed my attention over the past year. Once again, you have worked your magic to fashion this raw tale into the expertly presented manifesto you see before you today, one that truly captures the very essence of the Be The Lion philosophy. Your ability to tame even the wildest submissions into their best selves is phenomenal and I know that I have tested those boundaries. You are truly an artist and I thank you and the rest of the team (Ali, Eilish and Tim) from the very bottom of my heart for all your late nights, deeply considered thoughts, dedication and commitment to excellence in the realm of publishing.

Thank you to my family, including my dad for showing me the way of the world from an early age by teaching me how to build using my own hands, how to navigate mountains, forests and various terrains using my body and how to put my mind to work. You helped develop a confidence, which has helped me to trust my instincts.

Thank you to my mum for instilling in me the belief that anything is possible, as well as your enthusiasm for life. There is not a day that goes by when I am not reminded about you in some way, and although it gets easier as time heals the pain, our bond still grows, and I know you are watching over us. Thank you for expanding my love of adventure and pushing me to go after it. You are in my heart always. Every. Single. Day.

To Eileen, thank you for taking care of my dad these last few years, for your stories that have kept us so entertained and for being an excellent grandmother to the new kids on the block. It is wonderful to see and lovely to know that you are there.

To the rest of my wonderful family and friends, you know who you are! The world would not be the same without you and I thank you for being so special and making the effort. I learn so much from you all and feel so lucky to be surrounded by such incredible people.

A massive thank you to all the inspirational leaders, self-help coaches, mentors, investors and entrepreneurs for showing me that life can be lived big and teaching me the lessons, including how to structure my daily routine for success, and the importance of not taking "no" for an answer and pursuing my vision with persistence. Collectively, you have taught me the 4Cs. Through your bold example, you deeply inspire others to go for it, fuel their fire to make it happen, and give them faith to believe it is possible.

I would like to give a special mention the following mentors as you have either contributed through direct contact or had a major impact in some way.

Alex Banayan

Angela Duckworth

Carrie Green

Gary John Bishop

Gabrielle Bernstein

Idil Ahmed

Jack Ma

Jen Sincero

Mastin Kipp

Marianne Williamson

Napoleon Hill

Peter Thiel

Ray Dalio

Richard Branson

Richard Branson's PAs on Necker Island (Hayley and Amy)

Ryan Holiday

Ryan Serhant

Sheryl Sandberg

Tony Robbins

Tim Ferriss

Lastly, thank you to God for giving me strength on a daily basis, for keeping me on track and revealing this adventure that we call life in abundance.

Believe it is possible.

ABOUT THE AUTHOR

TIM CASTLE IS an author, success coach, speaker, and travel photography aficionado. His mission is to encourage others to go after their own really big goals, to inspire change, whether that be ditching destructive habits or realigning your lifestyle and getting the most out of your fullest potential.

He developed the 4Cs Framework as a tool to overcoming big challenges and making it happen. In conjunction with this, he also founded the Be The Lion community which was officially started in 2019 with the goal of bringing people together to share in their journeys and to show support for more purpose-centred living.

His motto for life is 'believe it is possible' and this is evident in the tapestry of events that has seen him overcome all manner of obstacles. Tim lives by this philosophy day in, day out, and has achieved a number of accolades, including multiple moves to new continents, completing extreme expeditions, an MBA and leading sales in APAC for a number of innovative technology companies.

He currently lives in Singapore with his wife and baby son and is loving every minute of it.

10% of the profits from this book will go towards helping destitute children in Asia.

www.timjscastle.com

 @TimJSCastle

 @TimJSCastle

 @TimJSCastle

And remember…

> "A gem cannot be polished without friction, nor a man perfected without trails."

Seneca

And

> "I was never afraid to fail.
>
> Which meant I was never afraid to try.
>
> I was never afraid to look silly.
>
> Which meant I was never threatened by a new idea."

Jerry Weintraub

ALSO BY THE AUTHOR

Anyone can learn to become a good negotiator. Let me show you how. I became a professional negotiator at the age of 23, and within just 12 months, I was single-handedly negotiating $1,000,000 deals. Being a negotiator has been such an empowering experience, and I've been able to transfer my professional skills into my personal life. Whether it's buying a home, budgeting for a wedding, or even buying a car, we all need to negotiate.

In this book, I'll share insider tips, as well as teach you how to master the fundamentals, set clear objectives, overcome obstacles (i.e. turn 'no' into 'yes') and build long-term relationships, whether you are negotiating for yourself, or on behalf of your business. I will also give you practical advice and run through real-world scenarios to ensure you have the confidence to tackle your next negotiation head on. Ready to see what you can achieve?

Available now on Amazon

ON THE PRECIPICE
THE ART OF DECISION

TIM CASTLE

Making good decisions quickly is what marks out truly great leaders from the rest of us. Decision-making is one of the most sought-after skills today, but one that most of us have never been taught.

Aged 19, I went off-piste snowboarding, way before I had the skills or experience to do so, and very quickly found myself hurtling towards the edge of a cliff face on sheet ice. Within minutes, I was literally hanging onto a boulder for dear life, with my legs dangling over the precipice.

Every single decision I made over the next few hours was life or death. There were no easy choices. Each right decision could be undone by a wrong one, and I was very aware of how close I was to death the whole time: the cold, the wind, the fading light, the fact that I had snuck off so no one knew where I was, the fact I had no food or water on me.

That day, my brain worked overtime to keep me alive. What I learned has enabled me to approach decisions in all areas of my life with ease.

In addition to sharing my story with you, I will also explore 6 of the best decision-making models, as well as teach you how to maintain the mindset of a master decision-maker. **After reading this book, you'll find making good decisions quick and easy and will no longer waste time stressing over them or avoid stepping up to making them.**

Made in the USA
Middletown, DE
15 March 2022

62703340R00276